ON STRIKE

Major Strikes in Canadian History

1 On Strike: Six Key Labour Struggles in Canada 1919-1949

ON STRIKE

Six Key Labour Struggles in Canada 1919-1949

Edited by Irving Abella

James Lorimer & Company
Publishers
Toronto 1975

Published with the assistance of the Social Science Research Council, using funds provided by the Canada Council.

ISBN 0-88862-057-8 (paper)
0-88862-058-6 (cloth)

Cover design by Lynn Campbell

James Lorimer & Company, Publishers
Egerton Ryerson Memorial Building
35 Britain Street
Toronto 229
Canada

Printed and bound in Canada

For J.J.

My thanks to the following who made this book possible: the contributors; my colleagues at Glendon College, Norman Penner and Joseph Starobin for their helpful and timely advice; Tony Silberman who did some of the typing; and especially to Susan Kent and Jim Lorimer for their invaluable comments and criticisms which made this a better book.

I.M.A.

Contents

Introduction

"A conspiracy of silence." In this telling phrase, Professor Stuart Jamieson, in his study of labour unrest in Canada,* explains why the literature on labour violence and industrial conflict in Canada is almost non-existent. And indeed, aside from his own work, Jamieson is absolutely right. For some reason Canadian academics seem to have shied away from writing about the violent aspects of our history, as if violence and strife were surely part of the American past, but definitely not of our own. The subjects they chose as worthy of study tended to reinforce the great theme of Canadian history—the eventful but peaceful evolution of a Canadian nation based on a spirit of order and compromise. Thus, most of our historians have concentrated on political studies and biographies. Very few—indeed, almost no one—chose to write about our labour movement.

For this reason Canadians are appallingly ignorant of their labour past. They probably know less about their trade-union movement than any other people in the Western world, and likely know more about the labour history of the United States and Great Britain than they do of their own. For many Canadians, names that have become the rallying cries of other labour movements—the Wobblies, the Tolpuddle Martyrs, the Molly Maguires, the Haymarket and John L. Lewis—are far more familiar than the OBU, the Workers' Unity League, the Provincial Workmen's Association, the Globe Strike, Murdochville and Paddy Draper, all key names in the history of the Canadian labour movement. Quite clearly, Canadian academics and labour leaders have done a miserable job of educating their audience.

One of the major objectives of this book, therefore, is to break through this insidious "conspiracy of silence," to introduce a large

---

***Times of Trouble: Labour Unrest and Industrial Conflict in Canada, 1900-66,* Privy Council Task Force on Labour Relations, study no. 22 (Ottawa, 1968).

number of Canadians to aspects of our history that have been shamefully ignored by historians and to bring alive some of the forgotten, yet significant and colourful events of our labour past. Obviously, this is too great a task for one book; years of neglect cannot be overcome so easily. What one book cannot do, however, several might. It is our intention, therefore, to make this the first of a series of books on the important strikes in Canadian history. Clearly, it was impossible to include in this one volume all the significant industrial conflicts of our past. Nor was it possible to include the bloody labour battles which seem a hallmark of the labour history of British Columbia and the Atlantic provinces. In subsequent volumes of this series, however, these omissions will undoubtedly be rectified.

The period covered in this book was perhaps the most important in the history of the trade-union movement in Canada. The thirty years between 1919 and 1949 were a time of torment and travail for Canadian labour, a time in which it was beset by crisis after crisis, catastrophe upon catastrophe. It was subject to ruinous attacks not only from business and government, from where it most expected them, but also from within the ranks of its own membership. There were times during those thirty years when the very survival of an organized labour movement in Canada seemed in the balance. Yet it emerged in the 1950s, triumphant and successful, its mettle tested, its survival insured, for the first time a powerful political and economic force strong enough to challenge industry and government.

Labour's trauma started at Winnipeg in 1919. Until then its horizons seemed unclouded and propitious. Union organization had expanded rapidly during the war and, with peace, labour's prospects seemed limitless. With the suppression of the Winnipeg General Strike, however, the rapid demise of organized labour in Canada began. For Canadian unions, the 1920s were an unmitigated disaster. Organization was at a standstill; membership declined drastically, and union leadership was divided. Though this was a period of great economic development, the craft-obsessed, frightened unions of the Trades and Labour Congress were paralyzed. They simply could not cope with the economic challenges of the decade and especially with the rise of a mass-production industrial work force.

This decline was exacerbated by the Depression. Union leaders seemed in a constant state of shock; workers wanted jobs, not unions. They got neither. As a reaction to the hidebound TLC leadership, new radical unions sprang up under the leadership of the Communist-dominated Workers' Unity League. But wherever they appeared, both government and industry combined to combat them. The strikes at Estevan and Stratford were symbolic of the frustrations of the workers during the Depression and the lengths to which the state would go to crush these new, militant labour organizations.

In 1935, when the economic situation improved and unions began picking themselves off the floor, a new disaster struck. A bloody internecine battle broke out within the labour movement itself between the aging, conservative TLC leadership and the young radicals of the CIO, who were demanding industrial organization. The CIO victory in Oshawa in 1937 marked the beginning of industrial unionism in Canada. The reactionary TLC would no longer dominate the Canadian labour movement, and hundreds of thousands of previously unorganized industrial workers could now become part of organized labour in Canada.

During the war years 1939 to 1945, labour prospered. Both strikes and union membership skyrocketed, and labour made great breakthroughs in the areas of recognition, job security and working conditions. But with peace, management again flexed its muscles and attempted to limit labour's wartime achievements. In particular, it was determined to undermine labour's key accomplishment—union security. Equally determined not to give up its hard-fought gains, labour girded itself for the inevitable confrontation.

The battleground was Windsor, Ontario; the combatants, the management and workers of the Ford plant. The struggle was bitter and lengthy, but the triumph of the union was complete. This settlement put securely into the economic fabric of peacetime the gains and recognition that unions had achieved during the war. Moreover, the Ford victory served as a stimulus for other Canadian workers. 1946 was a record year for strikes in Canada, as union after union attempted to emulate the success of the Ford workers. Most succeeded. Organized labour in Canada had finally reached the secure legal status it had fought for so desperately since 1919. The way was now clear for it to become the economic and political power it is in present-day Canada.

Though the Second World War obviously had a great impact on labour in English-speaking Canada, its impact on Quebec was even more profound. It accelerated an urbanization and industrialization that was already changing the face of the province. In the twenties and thirties, the Quebec labour movement had been Church-dominated, conservative and seemingly intent only on maintaining close ties with both management and the provincial governments. It did little for the French-Canadian workingman. But after the war a new generation of labour leaders took control of the Canadian and Catholic Confederation of Unions. They were concerned more with working conditions than with the catechism, and they were supported by a growing number of young clerics who were dragging a reluctant Church with them into the twentieth century.

The Asbestos strike was the culmination of these changes. It was the "first shot of the Quiet Revolution" and a decisive event both for the history of the province and for its labour movement. In effect, it marked the birth of the modern trade-union movement in Quebec.

In their way, therefore, all of these strikes mark notable turning points in our history. Some are watersheds for the Canadian labour movement; others are more significant for their political impact, but all are of major importance. Yet, except for the Winnipeg General Strike—and, for those who read French, the Asbestos strike—no full-scale comprehensive examination of any of them has ever been published.* In Canadian history books, if they are mentioned at all, these strikes are passed off in a sentence or two. Even in studies of our labour movement, most receive only a superficial description. This book, we hope, will serve as an antidote to that. Each of the essays is written by a specialist and is the result of years of intensive research. The articles are all based on careful and exhaustive examination of primary sources never before consulted. In several cases, the articles will be the first published results of their efforts.

For the most part the contributors to this anthology are well-known scholars with many publications to their credit. David Bercuson of the University of Calgary is an expert on Western Canadian labour and has written several articles on union conditions in Winnipeg before the strike. Stanley Hanson of the University of Saskatchewan is that university's archivist and has just completed a massive study of the Estevan strike. Desmond Morton, a historian at the University of Toronto, is a recognized authority on civil-military relationships in Canada and is now deeply involved in a study of the Canadian left. Fraser Isbester of McMaster University has been a student of the Quebec labour movement for many years and is now writing the authorized history of the federal Department of Labour. Perhaps as a change of pace, the final contributor, David Moulton, is a recent university graduate who spent two years researching the Ford strike, and is now a union activist, deep within the bowels of a meat-packing plant.

Though clearly the political ideologies of the various authors are disparate, nonetheless several common themes pervade these essays. Perhaps the most obvious common denominator of the book is the role of the state. In the years before 1919, governments, though by no

*The 1956 study of the Asbestos strike has finally been translated and is now available in English. See Pierre Elliott Trudeau, ed., *The Asbestos Strike* (Toronto: James Lewis & Samuel, 1974).

means friendly to organized labour, were not overtly hostile either. In most labour disputes, they were only benignly pro-management. But with the Winnipeg strike, the attitude of the state changed drastically. It came to see itself as an ally of business, able and willing to use its full powers to crush any labour organization that proved too threatening to the interests of capital.

In each of the strikes discussed in this book, the heavy hand of government—in the guise of the Royal Canadian Mounted Police in Winnipeg and Estevan, the Conservative premier of Ontario in Stratford and the Liberal premier of Ontario in Oshawa, the municipal and provincial police in Windsor and the Union Nationale premier of Quebec in Asbestos—grinds down upon labour. In each of these conflicts, the state comes down forcefully and aggressively on the side of capital. Labour was left to fend for itself against both business and government. Workers were to be crushed and unions destroyed whenever they posed a serious threat to industry. And to support business, the full resources of the state were always available. The army, police, legislation—all were at the disposal of industry in its efforts to keep labour weak and divided. Appropriately, this is a major theme, as well, of the history of the Canadian labour movement during those years.

A corollary theme of this collection is the prevalence of violence in industrial disputes. To the amazement of many Canadians, Professor Jamieson's study concluded that labour-management conflicts in Canada are far more likely to lead to violence than those in Europe. Not surprisingly, in each of the strikes studied in this book, violence, or the threat of violence, is a key factor. And usually, the violence is the direct result of the intervention of the state at the behest of industry to crush a strike.

The essays also present a particularly poignant description of working-class conditions in the post-World War I and Depression eras. At the same time, they bring home the immense obstacles faced by the union movement in its attempts to organize the unorganized. Taken together, these essays provide a biting indictment of government policy in this period. They will also remind Canadians of a scarcely recognizable labour movement—a movement that was weak, yet at the same time radical, militant and idealistic, and whose members lived in constant fear of losing not only their jobs but perhaps even their lives.

IRVING M. ABELLA

Glendon College, York University
Toronto
March 1974

1 The Winnipeg General Strike

by David Bercuson

General strikes are cataclysmic events; they are, by their nature, unlikely to be created in a day. The first moments of a general strike take place against a background of many years of bitter relationships, class polarization, frustrated ambitions and real or imagined oppression. The Winnipeg General Strike of May and June 1919 fits snugly into this well-established pattern because its taproots may be found growing into the very bedrock of Winnipeg's development as a booming modern industrial centre. The attitudes and conditions that created the general strike were an integral part of the Winnipeg scene almost from its beginnings, although they were compounded by the effects of the Great War. Winnipeg was ripe for a general strike in the spring of 1919 because the division of the city into two separate and increasingly hostile camps had started so long before and had reached a point of no return.

Winnipeg was destined to be a boom town, the new Chicago of North America. The analogy was to be used many times to describe the future of the city, particularly after civic leaders had succeeded in capturing the Canadian Pacific Railway route from the town of Selkirk in the early 1880s. Over the course of the next forty years, Winnipeg endured several periods of boom and bust, liberally watered by speculation dollars. This atmosphere of expected prosperity but realized chaos acted on the serious-minded men who had come to Manitoba to make their fortunes, and prompted them to assume leadership of the community, not only in business matters but in politics as well. They believed in the great future of their city but became convinced that it could only be realized if certain conditions prevailed: a rational and efficient city administration, a beneficent climate in which business could grow and prosper and the absence of any factor which could, if allowed to develop unchecked, disrupt the peace and prosperity of the business community. Unions fell within this last category.

Business in Winnipeg was anti-union from the beginning, but this was no different from the situation in other cities. What did make Winnipeg different was both the extent to which the business community ran the city—assuring the political powerlessness of the working class—and certain economic factors that affected Winnipeg to a greater extent than other cities. Winnipeg had the potential to become a great manufacturing and marketing centre, especially after all three Canadian transcontinental railroads established their repair shops, marshalling yards and roundhouses in and around the city, but it was distant from its sources of supply and its industrial markets. As long as the business community was content to allow Winnipeg to remain a trans-shipment point and distribution centre for the thousands of new prairie farmers who began to flood the plains after 1895, Winnipeg was not at any disadvantage. When they raised their sights to larger markets, however, they felt the pressures of higher transportation costs. When they began to think in terms of manufacturing for a national and even international market, they had to consider the price of bringing the raw materials in and shipping the finished goods out. To balance these higher costs they would try to keep other costs as low as possible, and this invariably affected wages.

There was yet another factor behind the long history of intransigent anti-unionism that developed early in Winnipeg's history: the myth of the self-made man.[1] Many of Winnipeg's political and industrial leaders were men of poor or humble origins who had made their way west to find their fortunes. They believed that they were destined to lead, having demonstrated their superior abilities by their rise through the social strata. Social Darwinism was a strong religion, diligently and consistently worshipped by many of the *nouveaux riches,* who were not yet confident or secure in their new-found wealth and station. These individualists scorned those whom they considered weaker than themselves—the men who were forced to resort to combination and organization to protect their jobs and living standards. Here workers and their unions stood indicted.

Trade unions did not play a passive role in this situation. Unions began to develop early in Winnipeg and grew quickly in the years prior to World War I. These organizations were led by strong-willed, tough-minded men, many of whom were immigrants from the industrial heartland of the British Isles and who had received their training in hard-knock schools such as Birmingham, Leeds, the Clydeside or the black mines of Wales.[2] They were fervent believers in the necessity of trade-union organization and many were followers of one socialist school or another, self-educated in the intricacies of Marxian analysis and rhetoric. These men were never timid in their assertion of labour's rights and challenged the power and prerogatives of management at every opportunity. Each victory confirmed them in their belief that theirs was the correct path; each defeat convinced them that society itself would have to be changed before the worker would ever receive his due.

Patterns of political and social separation developed early and were aggravated by physical separation. As new immigrants began to pour into Winnipeg they tended to settle in certain districts, usually together, seeking the security that new arrivals in a strange land crave. For the most part they gravitated to the area immediately north of the CPR mainline—the "north end."[3] This became Winnipeg's version of "the wrong side of the tracks," which it was in fact, clearly marked off from the new areas being opened up by Winnipeg's wealthier citizens. The rich and the aspiring to be rich settled along the river banks to the south, in locales such as River Heights and Wellington Crescent,[4] where they built magnificent mansions with long, broad driveways, well-manicured lawns and large stables or garages. The "south end" became as strongly symbolic in its own right of a bastion of privilege as the "north end" was of the home of the worker and the immigrant.

The results were almost predictable—Winnipeg was wracked by bitter strikes from the turn of the century, many involving the use of strikebreakers, court injunctions and even the armed militia on one occasion.[5] In most instances the issues were the same, the demand of workers that their unions be recognized and collective agreements entered into, and the absolute refusal of employers to allow unions in their plants or stores. The class polarization inherent in the city was heightened by these strikes because in most cases the very existence of the unions was at stake and courts and governments invariably sided with the employers. During the last boom period before World War I, some of the bitterness was dissipated as men with skills were able to wrench higher wages and better working conditions from their employers, but it never disappeared entirely because the basic attitudes creating it remained unchanged. By 1919, in addition to those attitudes, there was a history of bitterness, hatred and mistrust, and a martyrology to support it.

In August 1914 Canada entered the first large-scale war of her history ill-prepared for the hardships and trials that would test the national mettle in the next four years and three months. The effort involved in raising and equipping an army of over half a million men would have been monumental enough, but it was compounded by Canada's role as a breadbasket and arsenal for the allies. Within a short time the national economy began to suffer from manpower shortages, rapid cost-of-living increases, imbalances in supply and production and the machinations of unscrupulous men who tried to reap large and undeserved profits from munitions and war-supply contracts. Given these conditions, it is not surprising that labour-management relations began to break down on a national scale after 1917 and that this deterioration greatly affected areas such as Winnipeg, where conditions were already ripe for industrial strife.

Inflation was, without doubt, the single most important factor causing industrial strife in the war and immediate postwar period. Though few reliable statistics are available to give an exact measurement of the increasing cost of living during the war, it is safe to estimate, on the basis of what data was collected by the federal Department of Labour and published monthly in *Labour Gazette,* that it increased from fifty to seventy-five per cent between 1914 and 1918-19.[6] Increased demands for all manner of manufactured and semi-manufactured commodities, as well as foodstuffs and raw materials, drove prices skyward. This was coupled with shortages of skilled manpower and, consequently, higher wages in certain industries, which furthered the inflationary trend. The net result was that tens of thousands of Canadians who were not in any position to earn substantial wage increases saw their already low standards of living further decline. The only worker groups able to stay ahead of the rising cost of living, and then only barely, were those in great demand for war industries and munitions production—machinists, tool and die makers, shipyard workers. The majority of workers in Winnipeg, however, did not fit into this category.

One group of workers in the city that was able to keep ahead of the rising cost of living was, at the same time, the most radical—the railway machinists. The machinists were in great demand throughout the war both in the maintenance and repair of railway equipment and in the manufacture of shells. They were irked, however, by a constant failure to organize their colleagues in the other machine shops and considered that the long hours of work and low wage scales in those shops posed a dangerous example for other metal workers in the city. They were frustrated also by the knowledge that their unions were strong enough to face Canada's powerful transcontinental railways across the bargaining table, but were still thwarted locally by the owners of three small contract shops which together employed fewer than five hundred men.[7]

In early 1917 the government of Prime Minister Robert Borden decided that conscription should be instituted to meet Canada's moral commitments to total support of the allied war effort. Labour leaders in western Canada were almost unanimous in their intense and unwavering opposition to this measure and led the forces inside the Trades and Labour Congress of Canada advocating a national general strike against compulsory military service.[8] In the end, they could not garner adequate support and the idea of a strike was shelved, but the bitter anti-government feelings created by the campaign prompted many union men to decide that the government, rather than employers, was their greatest enemy. This, in turn, strengthened the influence of those labour leaders who were affiliated to one or another of the many socialist parties flourishing in the West at that time and resulted in a general shift to the left throughout the Prairies. The two main centres of this radical shift were Vancouver and Winnipeg.

War created labour shortages in hundreds of industries. Tens of thousands of skilled Canadians volunteered their services to the armed forces at the same time as the new war industries were exerting greater demands for manpower. Conditions for trade-union growth were better than they had been in many years and labour leaders were not slow to take advantage of them. In 1917 and 1918, vast organizing drives were launched throughout the country in almost every conceivable industry, and many new workers were brought into the fold. Even areas hitherto considered sacrosanct were entered: policemen, firemen, civic employees and provincial government employees, among others, became union members.[9] This growth process was bound to create industrial tensions as a byproduct.

In the days before the closed or union shop, automatic checkoff, labour-relations boards and certification votes, union organizing could be a hazardous business. In fact, union membership itself was sometimes hardly any safer. Unions were forced to battle tremendous odds, often including the forces of government and the judiciary, to sign members and thus had to demonstrate to prospective adherents the great advantages of affiliation. This could only be done by winning significant improvements in wage rates and working conditions, by demonstrating that the union was respected by employers and governments and by assuring prospective members that the union could protect them against arbitrary and unjust actions of management. This meant, in turn, that as the organizing campaign wore on, union leaders demanded more and were unwilling to settle for less—a situation creating militancy. When these unions confronted employers who were determined that workers and unions should not benefit from the labour situation created by the war, an irresistible force had met its immovable object.

Winnipeg was the scene of several such meetings in 1917. Three times in the year employers defeated strikes by applying for and receiving *ex parte* injunctions against picketing. In each case packinghouse workers, store clerks and contract-shop employees were unable to continue their respective strikes and suffered defeat.[10] The effect upon industrial relations in the city was traumatic; workers were forced to realize that very little had changed since the original use of injunctions in the city in 1906. All their organizing could come to naught if employers still had the ability to defeat recognition strikes by getting anti-picketing court orders and then bringing in scab labour. Labour leaders were forced to conclude that unions would have to band together and pool their resources if they hoped to force intransigent employers to the bargaining table. The formation of the Metal Trades Council in the spring of the following year was at least one result of the 1917 experiences.

In April 1918, three unions of civic employees struck for a new and higher wage schedule after having been offered a war bonus by city authorities. Almost immediately the straight dollars-and-cents issue was obscured by the question, posed by the *Free Press* and echoed by business leaders, of whether civic employees should have any right to strike. The atmosphere became further charged when sister unions rushed to the defence of the strikers and began to discuss the possibility of a sympathetic walkout of all civic workers. Even city firemen were in a fighting mood and issued an ultimatum threatening to strike unless their own pay demands were quickly met.

The city council reacted by appointing a committee of six, including the mayor and two Labour aldermen, to negotiate with the striking unions. The two sides settled down to serious bargaining and within a few days hammered out the rudiments of a settlement. On Monday, May 13, they presented the terms of the agreement to a full meeting of city council but were stunned when the council, led by Alderman F.O. Fowler, amended their proposal and added a proviso that all civic employees undertake to pledge that they would not strike at all in future but would have their grievances settled by arbitration. In effect this "Fowler Amendment," named after its sponsor, put the city council on record as opposing any right to strike for civic employees.

The new measure did not come out of the clear blue sky. It was clearly an accurate reflection of a new mood of toughness in business and city government circles and was strongly supported by the *Free Press* and the Winnipeg Board of Trade. It was a naked challenge to the Winnipeg Trades and Labour Council and was accepted as such. At this point, after the successful organizing drives and the frustrating strikes of 1917, labour was not about to turn from a fight on so fundamental an issue. The effects of the amendment were immediate and electrifying.

On Tuesday morning, May 14, city firemen walked off their jobs. Within the next ten days ten other unions joined the strike as the city government, supported by volunteer help supplied by the Board of Trade, attempted to continue the operation of civic services. By Friday, May 24, thirteen trades, totalling about seven thousand workers in government and industry, had met Fowler's challenge. Fire, water, light and power, public transportation, telephone service and railway maintenance were directly and drastically affected and there was every sign that the movement would continue to grow.

At this point the city government had become virtually paralyzed by indecision and passed responsibility for negotiations to a new, private body, formed for the purpose of helping to maintain essential services and bring about a settlement with the unions—the Citizens' Committee of One Hundred. On May 19 the first meeting between this group and the strikers took place and negotiations continued for the next few days. The two parties eventually succeeded in working out an agreement on almost all major points and were helped to the final solution by the intervention of Senator Gideon Robertson, newly appointed to the upper House and, at the time, special assistant to the federal minister of Labour, who travelled to Winnipeg at the behest of Prime Minister Robert Borden. The agreement was essentially the same one that had been presented to the city council on May 13 but this time it was accepted by that council, largely because of Robertson's prodding. On Friday evening, May 24, the settlement was agreed to and the strike was over. The workers' victory was almost complete.[11]

The 1918 general strike strengthened the hand of the radicals in the city and pushed the labour movement further left. Labour leaders concluded that the combined power of the unions acting together was irresistible and was responsible for the crushing defeat inflicted upon the city government. Almost every commentator underlined the plain fact that the original striking unions would surely have been defeated if they had not been supported by the rest of the city's labour movement.[12] When this was contrasted, publicly and privately, with the events of the previous year, the lesson appeared to be obvious—individual unions could not face tough employers supported by governments and/or the courts, but a combination of unions could and had defeated an enemy just as powerful. From this point on labour men began to think of the general strike as a necessary adjunct to individual strikes, to be used when those individual strikes failed or showed signs of failure.

One concrete result of the metal workers' defeat in 1917 had been the creation of the Metal Trades Council. The reasoning was simple—since individual unions had no chance of defeating the contract-shop employers or forcing them to the bargaining table, perhaps a combination of unions could. A Metal Trades Council would bargain for all those workers in the plant and would, if necessary, have the authority to call all those workers out on strike. This was not industrial unionism, although many of the supporters of the Metal Trades Council clearly believed in industrial unionism as opposed to craft organization; it was, rather, modelled on the type of bargaining conducted by railway-shop craft workers in the United States and metal workers in other Canadian cities, such as the Vancouver and Victoria shipyard workers.

In July of 1918 the Metal Trades Council struck the contract shops after failing to receive recognition following a long and apparently fruitless mediation procedure involving the federal government and a royal commission. The Winnipeg Trades and Labour Council threatened a general strike to support the contract-shop employees but did not act. By the end of September the strike had petered out and the workers had suffered yet another defeat. R.B. Russell bluntly attributed the failure to the fact that the rest of the city's workers did not back the Metal Trades Council adequately in its fight.[13]

The lesson of 1918 was now clearer than ever. Not only was it increasingly difficult for individual unions to win fights against intransigent employers; it was growing harder for combinations of unions in a single industry—such as the Metal Trades Council—to achieve victory. The civic workers, on the other hand, had achieved one of the most clear-cut victories in many years and only because they were promptly and adequately supported by workers in *every* industry. Where the workers had not been radical enough they had lost; where they had been, they had won. This finalized the trend towards the use of general strikes in industrial disputes and made the general strike in the spring of 1919 necessary in the eyes of many labour leaders in the city, radical or otherwise. The experiences of 1918 convinced them that a general strike was just like any other kind of strike, only larger, and that it enabled labour to bring its full power to bear in circumstances where that power was necessary. The Trades and Labour Council capped this process in December 1918 when it passed a motion giving itself the power to call out every union member in the city if a motion for a general strike was approved by a simple majority of all Winnipeg's union members.[14]

By the end of the war, labour leaders in the city were ready to reach for new objectives and were prepared to utilize new tactics in the effort. At the same time, the arrival of peace released the pent-up hope of many thousands of Canadians that the great sacrifices of the war would not have been in vain and that a new, more just, more equitable society would be fashioned out of the ruins of war. Men and women all over the country had worked ceaselessly to assure the victory while sixty thousand men, approximately one out of every ten Canadians in uniform, would never return. When it became increasingly apparent that there would be precious little forward movement and that the government's reconstruction efforts would, for the most part, be confined to dismantling the regulatory and managerial agencies established during the war, those who sought change grew more vociferous in their opposition to the status quo. By the end of 1918 the winds of change were already sweeping the rest of the world. Revolutions in Russia and Germany appeared to confirm that those who called for rapid social change were not isolated but, on the contrary, were the heralds of a great, globe-spanning move towards true reconstruction.

Western Canadian workers had always felt that their situation was somewhat different from that of their fellow labourers in central Canada and in the populous regions of the United States. They were numerically weaker, were, for the most part, engaged in extractive, resource industries, and were physically isolated from each other in small population centres scattered over the Prairies, in the British Columbia interior and on the Pacific Coast. These conditions, combined with the ideological leadership provided by former American progressives and British socialists who moved to Canada during the periods of great immigration, prompted western workers to call for trade-union participation in politics, organization of the tens of thousands of unorganized workers in extractive and mass industries all over the country and establishment of industrial unions which would group workers together on an industrial rather than a craft basis.[15] All these ambitions were in direct conflict with the ideological foundations of North American trade unionism, which was guided in thought and action by the principles of the founder of the American Federation of Labor, Samuel Gompers.

Gompers and his supporters believed that trade unions should not enter directly into politics, but should throw their support to the candidates or parties that favoured pro-labour principles. In addition, Gompers firmly believed in the necessity of keeping the labour movement relatively small and confined to the highly skilled, who had the best chance of wringing concessions from employers. Thus the principles of the AFL and its Canadian affiliate, the Trades and Labour Congress of Canada, contrasted sharply with the ideas held by western Canadian labour leaders, ideas which they believed had to be acted upon if the labour movement in the West was to survive.

These traditional points of contention had caused sharp disagreements in the TLC before the war—the numerically inferior West was almost always defeated. But three major inter-union squabbles during the war widened the gap between East and West and laid the groundwork for a western assault on the eastern bastions at the 1918 TLC convention. In the fight against conscription, westerners had been much more vociferous in their opposition and many believed they were being sold out by the congress's predominantly eastern leadership. This crisis in 1917 opened the first breach. The negotiations between Canada's railway-shop craft workers and the major Canadian railroads in 1918 made it almost permanent.

By the summer of 1918 negotiation procedures for railway-shop craft workers in Canada had been radically altered. The unions had joined in a loose bargaining federation known as Division 4 while management was combined into the Canadian Railway War Board. These two bodies met for the first time in late April 1918 to work out one contract to cover over fifty thousand railway workers. The unions demanded substantial wage increases, pointing to the greatly increased cost of living as justification, and threatened to pull every railway maintenance worker in Canada off the job if their demands were not met. Since this would eventually paralyze all national transportation, the government took a hand in the bargaining and prompted the railway managers to offer wage parity with American shop craft workers.

The move created a split in union ranks. Eastern labour leaders, heavily supported by the leadership of the AFL and the head offices of the shop craft unions in the United States, pressed for acceptance. They had no intention of forcing or risking a nation-wide rail strike against the opposition of the employers and the government, which was threatening to draft all railway maintenance workers and work them at military pay rates should they walk out. Western union leaders were disgusted at this attitude and, when they realized they could not prevail, called their negotiators home.[16] There was both anger and consternation directed not only at the government, but against the leadership of the international unions and their central Canadian supporters.

The third East-West split took place during Canada's first national postal strike in August. Once again eastern union leaders were prepared to order their men to accept compromise arrangements while westerners dissented. This time, however, the westerners continued their strike after the eastern postal employees returned to work; they were not only able to wrench more concessions from the government, but also secured pay for the time they had been on strike.[17] Another Canadian union had split geographically because the westerners were more daring and perhaps more radical than the easterners.

Thus the stage was set for the September 1918 convention of the

TLC in Quebec City. Westerners were sorely outnumbered but went ahead to present several resolutions demanding a reorganization of the TLC as an industrial congress, and the removal of civil liberties restrictions imposed during the war—the release of political prisoners and the ending of government-imposed censorship. Each time they were defeated both on the floor of the convention and in committee rooms; when they appealed committee rulings they were defeated again. Recorded votes were called and they were defeated yet again; the eastern establishment controlled the steamroller and the westerners were flattened. To add insult to injury, the president of the TLC, James Watters, a westerner, was defeated in his bid for re-election by Tom Moore, a conservative and a friend and admirer of Samuel Gompers, in one of the very few contested presidential elections yet held by the congress. The West's defeat was total.[18]

The TLC convention was absolute proof that wars and industrial strife might come and go but things would never change for westerners within the congress. If their demands were to be satisfied, extraordinary measures would have to be taken. With this in mind several western delegates met in caucus at Quebec City and decided to hold a meeting of all western representatives prior to the next TLC convention to plan strategy and decide on a unified program. This was the objective of the man responsible for calling the meeting, Dave Rees, a United Mine Workers official from British Columbia and a TLC vice-president, but it was not shared by all.

The Socialist Party of Canada was a small, closely knit organization that proclaimed itself to be the only ideologically pure guardian of Marxist theory in Canada. Its members were dedicated, hard-working, and had met rather exacting standards before they were admitted to membership. The party was the most uncompromising of a plethora of socialist parties that had grown up in the West since before the turn of the century and it frequently ran candidates against other left-wing and labour political groups. Ordinarily it might not have achieved any significant influence in labour affairs but for the radical temper of the postwar period and the adherence of some of the best-known trade unionists in western Canada, including R.B. Russell, R.J. Johns, Victor Midgley and W.A. Pritchard.

SPC members were determined to seize the opportunity that now presented itself to build a new labour centre in Canada. Ostensibly they were interested in fulfilling the desires of western workers for industrial unionism and more intensified political action. These men had no intention of allowing the conference of western labour representatives to move in the direction Rees wished it to go, but prepared, instead, to begin a secessionist movement from the TLC and the

AFL. They pressed for and were successful in securing a meeting not directly prior to the 1919 TLC convention, but in the very early spring in Calgary.

The Western Labour Conference opened in the foothills city on March 16, 1919. Rees reiterated his desire to forge a united policy for presentation to the next TLC convention, but at this point there was little possibility of the meeting following his suggestions. The British Columbia Federation of Labour, meeting the previous three days in the same city, had just opted for a program of unmitigated radicalism. Over some objections from moderate delegates, the federation had supported the idea of a new secessionist movement, attacked the federal government for allowing censorship and imprisonment of political dissenters to continue and sent greetings to the Bolshevik government in Moscow.

From the very beginning of the western conference, then, the moderates were outmanoeuvred. The meeting declared itself in favour of a nation-wide vote of all TLC-affiliated unionists on the question of secession and adherence to a new organization to be laid out along "industrial" lines. The policy committee, headed by Winnipeger R.J. Johns, suggested that the new body be called the One Big Union and that a five-man committee be elected to popularize the OBU, raise funds and organize the referendum. These men were subsequently chosen, along with provincial executives to act in conjunction with the new Central Committee.

The referendum decided upon was not to be a simple poll of all union members in Canada, since the ballots were to be divided between those from east of Port Arthur and those from the West. In addition, the question was to be decided by a majority vote of those organizations considered to be vital trades—transportation, metal trades, mining, etc. Locals of other trades were also to be polled with those members not voting to be counted in the affirmative. A second vote was to be taken in conjunction with the referendum to determine if Canadian workers favoured a nation-wide general strike on June 1 to institute the thirty-hour week.[19]

The Western Labour Conference did not actually launch the One Big Union; it was a declaration of intent to do so. But it reflected the mood of militancy that had been growing in the West for some time. Resolutions sending greetings to the new Soviet government in Russia, demanding Allied withdrawal from the Soviet Union and an end to government restrictions on civil liberties were only the outward manifestations of the new radicalism. The significant part of the three-day meeting was the delegates' decision to take secessionist action.

The One Big Union did not officially come into existence until the first week of June, when its founding convention was held in Calgary. By that time the Winnipeg strike was already over two weeks old and not a single member of the Winnipeg Trades and Labour Council was able to attend.[20] Nevertheless, the announced intention to found a radical Marxist labour union, industrial or syndicalist in nature and sympathetic to the aims and aspirations of the Bolsheviks, provided the enemies of the strike with a focal point for their deepest fears. Governments and employers asserted that the OBU was behind the strike, that the strike was a test of OBU tactics and that its defeat would prove to be a knockout blow against the One Big Union. In fact there was no connection between the events in Winnipeg and the One Big Union except that the Calgary convention formed part of the backdrop and contributed to the atmosphere in which events immediately leading to the strike took place.

The general strike was touched off by disputes in the metal and building trades that surfaced in April and May. The inability of the unions in these two industries to win concessions from management—higher wages in the case of the building trades, union recognition in the metal trades—prompted them to turn to the Trades and Labour Council for help. A sufficient number of workers believed the issues to be important enough to the welfare of all organized labour to enable the supporters of radical action to push a general strike vote through the Trades Council.

The Winnipeg Building Trades Council, uniting all the city's construction unions in one organization, had taken on a new task in the spring of 1919—henceforth it would negotiate working agreements to cover all of its constituent trades directly with the employers' organization, the Winnipeg Builders' Exchange. This arrangement was welcomed by all since it meant that both sides would be unable to take advantage of disunity in their opponents, while the employers were particularly pleased since they would only have to negotiate one agreement to cover the entire industry. The discussions were difficult, because the unions were determined to win large wage increases to make up for the small gains they had made during the war. The employers, however, would not agree to anything better than half the amounts sought by the unions. They knew this was not sufficient and conceded the fairness of the unions' demands, but claimed it was all they could pay to avoid bankruptcy. Half a loaf was better than none, they pointed out, and a strike would only mean that no wages at all would go into their workers' pockets.

The workers' claim to large increases was buttressed by statistics showing they had been left behind in the race to keep wages ahead of the rising cost of living. This had increased by approximately seventy-five per cent since 1913, although the average wage in the building trades had only risen by about thirteen per cent. The employers, however, were actually in a real bind because the depression of 1913 had killed Winnipeg's construction boom while the war served to keep it dead. War priorities kept building at an all-time low and the builders were hard pressed to keep out of debt. Though many expected construction to pick up in the summer of 1919, these hopes had not yet been realized and the employers were no better off than they had been in the previous five years. These conditions created an impasse in the negotiations and prompted the Building Trades Council to call a strike for Thursday morning, May 1, 1919.[21]

While the crisis in the building trades was mounting, another impasse was developing in the city's metal trades. The Metal Trades Council, an amalgam of various metal craft unions whose members worked in the city's independent contract shops, automobile repair establishments and so on, had been formed in the spring of 1918 to increase the power of the individual unions in their attempt to gain recognition from the owners and managers of the contract shops. These unions had been trying to win recognition since 1906 and had fought and lost three bitter strikes in 1906, 1917 and July 1918, which saw the use of *ex parte* injunctions, damage suits and professional strikebreaking agencies. In April 1919, the Metal Trades Council prepared to do battle once again and sent letters to the contract-shop owners asking for a higher wage schedule and the forty-four-hour work week. It did not ask for recognition, since all parties realized that the acceptance or negotiation of the Metal Trades Council's demands would have amounted to *de facto* recognition. The contract-shop owners had successfully resisted the unions in the past, and again studiously ignored the letters from the Metal Trades Council.

One of the contract shops, Vulcan Iron Works, was owned and managed by E.G. and L.R. Barrett, brothers who had been in the forefront of opposition to union recognition for over thirteen years. In the third week of April they sent letters to each of their employees setting out their position on the question of union recognition; they claimed that although they would meet individual workers or a committee of workers they would not, under any circumstances, negotiate with the Metal Trades Council. They were running "an absolutely open shop" and would never bargain with any group or organization which contained members or representatives from other shops or factories. This letter was the only reply of any sort from the largest three of the contract shops; only three of the smaller establishments in the city signified their willingness to negotiate with the union.[22]

On the last night of April, metal-trade union members crowded into a room in the Labour Temple on James Street to hear the news that the council's approach to the contract shops had been spurned and that the executive was left with little choice but to turn matters over to the membership for some sort of decision. The meeting then voted overwhelmingly to begin a strike the next morning at eleven but was persuaded by the executive to postpone action for another twenty-four hours. The extra day of grace brought no response from the "Big Three" and on Friday, May 2, at eleven A.M., Winnipeg's third metal-trades strike in three years closed the factories down. The issues were familiar ones to this troubled industry: union recognition, a shorter work week and wage parity with metal workers in the city's railway repair and maintenance shops.

At this point many union members in Winnipeg were ripe to respond to a call of support for the two striking trades since several other unions were involved in disputes of their own. In the last week of April a strike of telephone operators was narrowly averted when the provincial government met demands for a pay increase scant days before the deadline ran out. At the same time, the policemen's union was also involved in negotiations and had a great deal of trouble squeezing higher wages out of the civic administration. The men had voted overwhelmingly to strike but received a new contract with higher wages in the last days of April. The street-railway employees had begun negotiations with their employer on April 21; after reaching an impasse, they had voted 900 to 79 in favour of strike action. They held off, however, until receiving the report of a conciliation commission appointed under the federal Industrial Disputes Investigation Act.[23]

Thus, when the metal-trades delegates entered the Labour Temple for the regular weekly Trades Council meeting of May 6, there was already widespread labour unrest in the city. Two trades were on strike, one was threatening to strike and two had just concluded bitter and protracted negotiations which had almost broken down. Metal-trades delegates were instructed by their locals to bring the matter of their own strike before the council and to ask for the council's support. They intended to tell the meeting that a defeat would now jeopardize the gains of the entire union movement and would set labour back many years.

The meeting hall in the temple was crowded to capacity as the Metal and Building Trades Councils reported on the lack of progress in their struggles. Delegate James Lovett told the meeting that union recognition had never before been an issue in the construction strike but that the Builders' Exchange was threatening to withdraw its recognition of the Building Trades Council unless the employers' offer was accepted. Lovett added the charge that the bankers were behind the current impasse since they would not allow the builders to increase wages to the levels sought by the workers. Lovett asked the Trades Council to help the construction trades because the Building Trades Council's strike had not been sanctioned by international union headquarters and the members were not receiving strike pay.

As the meeting progressed someone handed a note to Secretary Ernie Robertson informing him that a worker of German origin, who had been visiting metal-trades shops at the instruction of his local, had been arrested. A number of delegates immediately volunteered to go to the police station and returned shortly with the worker in tow. His impromptu speech, charging government support for the employers, was a sensation. It was nothing, however, to the one delivered by R.B. Russell, secretary and acknowledged leader of the Metal Trades Council. The fiery Scot was the centre of attention as he reviewed the dispute thus far and charged the Barretts with responsibility for the stiffening employer opposition. Winnipeg, he warned, must stand firm for the sake of labour everywhere. This strike was made necessary by the defeat of 1918, he claimed, and there must be no more defeats.

Finally Harry Veitch, former Trades Council president, told the delegates of the great progress that had been made in previous weeks in organizing non-union workers in the city, and claimed that a general strike would tie Winnipeg up completely. This was the final argument. The meeting voted to take a poll of every union member in the city and to make a final decision by May 13.[24] In accordance with action taken by the council the previous December, a simple majority of all union members in the city would suffice to instruct council delegates to call the walkout.

The next few days were feverish with activity as Robinson arranged the printing and distribution of eighteen thousand ballots. In a few cases, such as that of the letter carriers, the vote was taken by an open show of hands but in most instances ballots were simply filled out at work and returned to Robinson. Ballot boxes were rarely used and votes were added up as they came into the Labour Temple. The Typographical Union was the only organization affiliated with the Trades Council that refused to participate in the voting and it was bitterly attacked by other unions who charged that the typos were afraid to lose their funeral expenses and old-age homes.

On Tuesday evening, May 13, excited delegates gathered in the Labour Temple to hear further reports on the course of the building and metal-trades strikes and to receive the results of the general strike ballot. Lovett told the meeting that the Builders Exchange had carried out their threat and were now refusing to deal with the Building Trades Council. Delegates were also told that Premier Norris had met with the contract-shop employers and the Metal Trades Council earlier in the day in an attempt to work out a compromise. The Big Three told him they might form an employers' association in the future and would, at this point, consider union recognition, but discussions with the unions at the moment were definitely out. Undaunted, Norris appointed Russell and Trades Council solicitor T.J. Murray to an *ad hoc* conciliation committee. The union men ridiculed independent arbitration at this point, however, since their precondition for any settlement, union recognition, was not even being considered by management.

Robinson then read the results of the vote to the meeting. Union members in Winnipeg had demonstrated solid support for a general strike—over eleven thousand endorsed the idea while a mere five hundred were opposed. The council thus set Thursday, May 15, as the day and eleven A.M. the hour in which the general strike was to begin. In addition, Lovett, A. Scoble of the street railwaymen's union, Veitch, Russell and W. Logan of the machinists' union were appointed to act as the nucleus of the Strike Committee, which eventually consisted of three delegates from each of the unions represented on the council, to act on behalf of the strikers in all future negotiations.[25]

Several abortive attempts were made to avoid the strike in the seventy-two hours preceding the Thursday morning deadline. Both the premier and Mayor Gray tried unsuccessfully to bring the two sides together. In almost all cases it was apparent that the building-trades workers and their employers were not far removed from an agreement, but the relative lack of disharmony here was overshadowed by the total absence of any spirit of compromise in the metal trades. The unions continued to demand recognition for the Metal Trades Council while the Big Three refused to recognize unions in any form.

On Wednesday night, May 14, Gray, Norris and the provincial attorney-general made an eleventh hour attempt to stop the strike. Gray telephoned James Winning, president of the Trades Council, and asked him if there was a chance of abandoning the strike should the ironmasters be persuaded to adopt a more reasonable approach. Winning, a moderate, was probably somewhat dazed by the rapidly developing events of the previous two weeks, but he was astute enough to realize that the movement towards a general strike had generated a momentum of its own. "It might help," he answered, "but it is too late to discuss that now."[26] The stage was set for the walkout to begin.

At precisely eleven o'clock the next morning, Winnipeg ceased to work. The strike was complete and overwhelming in its proportions as over twenty-two thousand workers answered the call within the first twenty-four hours. Ninety-four of ninety-six unions participated to a man. Firemen left their stations, telephones were shut down, the city's electrical workers left turbines and transmission equipment unattended; telegraphers and others responsible for keeping a modern city in touch with the world refused to work. At the waterworks a skeleton staff remained behind at the request of the Trades Council to provide a meagre thirty pounds pressure, sufficient for single-storey dwellings. Commercial establishments of every sort, from moving-picture houses to restaurants, were closed.[27]

The general strike was called in a moment of intense and hopeful enthusiasm amidst the certainty that labour would win this fight even more decisively than the strike of 1918. The duration of the strike and its completeness is only explained, however, by the fact that this was the culmination of over twenty years of struggle for the city's unions. This was to be the final battle in which nothing would be held in reserve. Years of despair and frustration fuelled the intense hostility of workers towards the employers and governments who had foiled their ambitions for so long. In this battle labour would win or lose all—the unions knew it, and so did the employers. This was a challenge to traditional ideas and methods that labour's opponents could not ignore and to which they responded in tough and decisive fashion.

From the first days of the walkout the strikers faced the powerful opposition of employers, governments and the Citizens' Committee of One Thousand. The last-named organization was loosely patterned after the Committee of One Hundred which had taken so active a role in the 1918 strike. Though it purportedly voiced the interests of the city's "neutral" citizens, it was strongly anti-strike, supported the employers, labelled the union leaders Bolsheviks and provided thousands of volunteers to run the services and equipment the strikers had abandoned. Citizens' Committee representatives sat in on secret government policy conferences and advised the contract-shop owners throughout the six-week period of the strike.

The new Citizens' Committee was an amalgamation of the old committee and individual members of organizations such as the Board of Trade, the Manufacturers' Association and the Winnipeg bar. Of several names that appeared most frequently, for example, H.B. Lyall was an official of Manitoba Bridge and a member of the Board of Trade. A.L. Crossin was a broker with Oldfield, Kirby and Gardner, a firm dealing in insurance and loans, and also a member of the Board of Trade. A.K. Godfrey, chairman of the Citizens' Committee of One Thousand, was the 1917-18 president of the Board of Trade and an executive of the Canadian Elevator Company. J.E. Botterell was a senior partner in the grain- and stock-brokerage firm of Baird & Botterell and also a member of the Board of Trade. Isaac Pitblado, KC, was a senior partner in the law firm of Pitblado, Hoskin & Co., which handled the personal business of the Hon. Arthur Meighen, federal minister of the Interior.[28]

Direct anti-strike involvement by the Citizens' Committee added an element not present in the 1918 sympathetic walkout, but it was not as serious as the intervention by the federal and provincial governments. When the political leaders of the country and the province opted to intervene on the side of the employers, the strikers were faced with the choice of having the massive political, legal and military power of those governments levelled against them, or ending the strike. Though this was not immediately apparent, it became more evident as the strike dragged on that the governments were playing an active and interested role in events.

Within a week of the outbreak of the new strike, Gideon Robertson and Arthur Meighen were on their way to Winnipeg. Even before they reached the city they met with several members of the Citizens' Committee and heard biased accounts of what was going on in Winnipeg. Robertson, as a former labour man and an ardent supporter of the conservative craft-union status quo in the AFL and TLC, launched an immediate and all-out verbal assault against the OBU as soon as he arrived in the city, charging that the strike was a One Big Union affair aimed at revolution and the destruction of the international craft-union movement. Robertson and Meighen also decided to take post-office matters into hand and get the men back to work as quickly as possible. Robertson fixed a deadline for all post-office employees to return to work, under threat of dismissal if they did not show up. When the deadline passed, the vast majority of postal workers in the city were fired and replaced with volunteers.[29]

The ultimatum soon became the accepted method of dealing with government employees at every level. Robertson used it with great effect to end a one-day strike of railway mail clerks while the provincial government utilized it in an effort to force its telephone employees back to their jobs. Even the city got into the act and issued ultimatums to its firemen, clerks and waterworks employees. In most cases, employees did not heed their deadlines and lost their jobs.

Meighen and Robertson represented the government in body and in spirit. Their anti-strike views accurately reflected the beliefs and attitudes of the cabinet to which they belonged. From lesser luminaries such as C.C. Ballantyne, minister of Fisheries, up to Prime Minister Borden himself, the government was uniform in its condemnation of the strike, its assertion that the strike was revolutionary in origin and intent, and its firm resolve that the workers could not be allowed to win. Though they tried hard to convince some of the more hysterical voices, such as the New York *Times,* that Winnipeg was not in the midst of a revolution and that legitimate government authority still prevailed, they spoke in the House of Commons and to the newspapers of threats to constituted authority and of the strikers' desire to smash the traditional order of labour-management relations. Meighen revealed the innermost fears of the government when he attacked the general strike in the House in early June. If unions were going to be allowed to combine into larger unions, he asked, where was the logical end to the process going to be? Eventually there would be only one union capable of calling one tremendous strike which would bring anarchy to the country. This, he warned, could not and would not be allowed to happen.[30]

While talk of revolution surged and ebbed around their heads, the strike leaders bent every effort to keep the streets peaceful and to convince their followers to keep out of trouble. In most cases they even refused to grant permission for peaceful picketing. Though incidents involving strikebreakers did occur on occasion, they were usually initiated spontaneously by hotheads. The strike leaders had asked the police to remain at work and asked their followers to do nothing because they feared that the least provocation would bring the armed forces into the streets of Winnipeg, assuring defeat of the general strike.

What the strike leaders failed to realize was that the type of campaign they had embarked upon was different from any they had known before and was bound to present great difficulties which could not be easily resolved. An entire city had been paralyzed, but no one had taken the time to think about the ramifications of this beforehand. Workers too had families, let alone those people who sided neither with strikers or employers, and they also had to be fed and heated, their garbage collected and their milk, bread and ice delivered. The maintenance of essential services was of the utmost importance and was one of the most difficult problems wrestled with by the strikers.

On May 16 the intense and hostile public reaction to the termination of bread and milk deliveries forced the Strike Committee to begin to think about and attempt to find a solution to the problem of staples distribution. The strikers approached a sub-committee of the city council, a meeting also attended by A.J. Andrews, W.J. Botterell, representing the Committee of One Thousand, and J.W. Carruthers, owner of the Crescent Creamery Company. Carruthers suggested that the problem of staples distribution could be solved if special cards were issued to delivery wagons notifying the public that the men delivering bread and milk were not scabs. This was accepted by the meeting and approved by the Strike Committee, which soon issued cards reading "Permitted by authority of Strike Committee" to bakeries, dairies and other establishments.[31]

A degree of normalcy returned as businesses deemed essential to the well-being of the city reopened under the protection of the permits. The arrangement, however, made certain people uneasy. Mayor Gray was moved to point out that people should not think the necessities of life were now being supplied by an authority other than the legitimate elected government of the city. This did not stop the mounting criticism of those who charged that the administration of Winnipeg had now passed to the hands of the strikers. The strikers, for their part, claimed that they had no intention of assuming government authority and had merely issued the cards to protect their own men.

Pressure began to mount for the removal of the cards only a few days after their use had begun. Gray and Premier Norris told the strikers they objected to the cards, even though they knew why they had been issued in the first place. On Monday, May 20, Gray told the strikers that the permit cards would have to be removed before any effort could be made to solve the root causes of the walkout. The following day the mayor brought the issue before city council and demanded the removal of the permits since they had outlived their usefulness. Many people all over the country, he asserted, were under the false impression that their use signified the erosion of constitutional authority in Winnipeg. The result was a heated debate between the mayor's supporters and the Labour aldermen who claimed that the cards were absolutely necessary for the continuation of essential services. A.J. Andrews explained that, even though he too knew and understood why the permit cards had been decided upon, he believed that the city's necessities were being supplied by permission of the strikers and this was an erosion of constituted authority, whether intended as such or not. When the debate cooled, the council voted seven to four to have the cards taken down. The following day the Strike Committee complied.[32]

The permit episode cast a heavy shadow over the Strike Committee. Though the permits were not decided upon unilaterally and in fact were approved by two representatives of the Citizens' Committee and a subcommittee of city council, their wording created the impression that the strikers alone were responsible for the maintenance of essential services in the city. This naturally lead to a belief in some minds that the government of Winnipeg had passed to the Labour Temple, which now had the power to operate or shut down these facilities. From there it was but a small step to the assumption that the Labour Temple was now the "James Street Soviet." This cry reinforced the opinions and spurred the activities of those who claimed the strike was nothing but a revolutionary plot in the first place. Foremost among this group was the federal government.

The Borden administration led a coalition of forces which opposed the strike and could accept only two solutions—a total and complete collapse of the strike, or a compromise settlement that would leave little doubt that the strikers were accepting terms dictated by management. If the latter could not be accomplished, the former was necessary because in no way could the general strike be allowed to succeed or even to have the appearance of success. Agents of the federal government, in the persons of Robertson and Meighen, Brigadier-General H.D.B. Ketchen, officer commanding the Manitoba military district, Commissioner A.B. Perry of the RNWMP and A.J. Andrews, worked long and hard to see that the government's purpose was accomplished. The federal government was thus deeply involved in each of the five major steps which led to the disintegration of the strike in the last week of June.

At the request of the Strike Committee, the members of the city police force had remained at their posts on May 15, but anti-strike forces, convinced that the police were either under the control of or were sympathetic to the strikers, found the situation intolerable. Anti-strike members of city council tried to rectify this by presenting the members of the force with an ultimatum: they were asked to sign a pledge dissociating themselves from the Trades and Labour Council and promising not to participate in any future sympathetic strikes. The police were nearly unanimous in their rejection of the ultimatum and the city council was left in the difficult position of having to ignore its own ultimatum or doing what the strikers had not dared to do—leave the city devoid of police protection.

The solution was provided by General Ketchen, who suggested the employment of an alternative force of "special police" to supplement or replace the regular constables. Supported by Ketchen and the Citizens' Committee, the city began to recruit special police, mostly from amongst anti-strike veterans and students, and paid them six dollars per day, a higher wage than that earned by the regular police. When a force of close to two thousand had been successfully recruited, the council repeated its earlier demands that members of the force sign the pledges. When they refused as they had on the first occasion, 240 of them, almost the entire force, were fired.[33] From June 10 the city was in the hands of a large group of men who were, with few exceptions and without pretence, hostile to the strike and the strikers. The fact that they were also inept was demonstrated on several occasions when fights and disturbances broke out due to the inability of these untrained men to conduct themselves properly.

The first afternoon of their service, a group of mounted specials rode down Main Street to a point near the junction with Portage where a crowd had gathered to hear a man speaking from a parked car. The specials, armed with clubs, attempted to disperse this group and rode up on the sidewalk. As they began to walk their horses slowly into the crowd, swinging their batons to force the group to scatter, one of their number was thrown from his horse and badly beaten. Sergeant Major F.G. Coppins, VC, was riding his horse slowly along the sidewalk when someone cupped his hands under Coppins's stirrup and heaved upward, unseating him. As this happened several men grabbed Coppins, helped pull him off the horse and began to beat him. Coppins, already injured, jumped to his feet swinging his club and had to be rescued from the crowd by other specials. He was subsequently taken to Tuxedo Military Hospital suffering from severe bruises.[34]

Ketchen was instrumental in setting up the force of special police, but he did not intend to rely solely on them should he have to use force to maintain order or put down the strike. From the very beginning of the walkout he directed the buildup of a large military force in the Winnipeg area and, with the help of his superiors in Ottawa, the Mounted Police and the Citizens' Committee, did it without bringing a single regular soldier to the city. By co-ordinating his activities with the Mounties and initiating a training program using newly recruited citizen volunteers for the militia, Ketchen was able to build a large force in a relatively short time. To direct this group he called on former officers residing in the city, and to transport the militia he arranged for the use of trucks supplied by the Citizens' Committee to augment those already on hand. From outside the city a secret shipment of machine guns was forwarded by Ottawa, marked "regimental baggage" and included in the freight of the 27th Battalion, travelling to Winnipeg to demobilize. In addition he had an armoured car available which was regularly stationed in the city.

weapons

By Tuesday, June 17, Ketchen had a formidable group of Mounties, militia and civilian auxiliary volunteers at his disposal. At Fort Osborne Barracks an armoured car equipped with three machine guns and manned by three officers, two drivers and six riflemen was kept in readiness. The Citizens' Committee had completed the organization of an auxiliary motor-transport service and placed it under Ketchen's command. The Mounties, in addition to a reinforced complement of officers and men, had been issued four machine guns mounted on motor trucks and could put sixty men on horses into the streets in a matter of minutes. Two mobile militia groups had been placed in readiness, one stationed at Fort Osborne Barracks, the other at Minto

Barracks. Each consisted of a troop of the Fort Garry Horse, one motor machine-gun section with two guns apiece, infantry escorts in motor trucks and one company of motorized infantry. The total force immediately available in an emergency numbered eight hundred and Ketchen had worked out special arrangements to call the rest of the militia into action at a moment's notice.[35] If necessary, the government had all the armed force it might require ready and available.

In the last few days of May a committee representing six railway running-trades unions approached the unions and the contract-shops employers with an offer to mediate the dispute. The offer was accepted and the committee got down to work inviting proposals from both sides. The Metal Trades Council and the contract-shop owners stuck close to their original positions, but the mediation committee saw nothing extraordinary about the unions' desire to gain recognition for a Metal Trades Council. They thus worked out what they believed was a compromise solution, which included recognition of the Metal Trades Council, and offered it to both sides. The unions accepted the settlement, the employers rejected it and the committee prepared to announce that its efforts had failed.[36]

At this point Senator Robertson arrived in the city once again. There were, at that point, ominous rumblings from the railway yards to the effect that train crews, including locomotive engineers, firemen and carmen, would join the general strike, paralyzing East-West rail transportation at its most vital point in the national communications network. Robertson could not let this happen and determined to find some immediate solution to the strike. The best opportunity appeared to be to use the offices of the mediation committee and to put pressure on the mediators to accept a solution, short of recognition of the Metal Trades Council, that they could bless. This task was relatively simple because Robertson was of the same ilk as the mediators, probably knew them all personally, and played on their fears of the rising power of the One Big Union.

On Sunday evening, June 16, Robertson finally succeeded in forcing the contract-shop employers to offer to recognize individual craft unions in their plants—there was no thought or mention of the recognition of the Metal Trades Council—and had the offer published in the newspapers the next morning.[37] He believed that this offer, containing part of the recognition the unions had sought for many years, might confuse the strikers and weaken their resolve to continue—the strike was already over four weeks old—and give the moderates on the Strike Committee a platform from which to advocate the end of the general strike. To insure that the radical hold on the Strike Committee was weakened at this crucial point, he ordered the arrest of Russell,

Johns and the other radicals on Monday night.[38]

In the early hours of June 18, six Anglo-Saxon strike leaders along with a token handful of "enemy aliens" were arrested under authority of a new Immigration Act amendment which had been passed through Parliament in less than one hour on June 6.[39] They were taken straight to Stony Mountain penitentiary and placed in cells while the government decided their fate. Meighen wanted them deported immediately, while A.J. Andrews believed this would alienate the public and therefore argued for their release on bail. By early Friday, June 20, it was decided to release the men if they promised to take no further part in the strike.[40] By then deportation had become completely unnecessary since the moderates had taken Robertson's bait and were preparing to negotiate an end to the strike on the basis of the offer of June 16.

At this point control of events slipped from the Strike Committee's hands. Since the last days of May, several thousand veterans who supported the aims and tactics of the strikers had grown increasingly vocal and militant in their demonstrations of solidarity. On the final day of May, and for some days after, they had paraded in large numbers in the downtown streets of Winnipeg, to the city hall and legislative buildings and in front of Citizens' Committee headquarters. On days when they did not take to the streets they held boisterous meetings in Victoria Park, listening to speeches and reports from their leaders and members of the Strike Committee. To counter this new element, anti-strike veterans organized parades of their own; on one occasion the two groups narrowly missed each other while marching near the legislature. To avoid the possibility of a massive and violent confrontation the mayor issued a ban against parades and twice repeated the order during the course of the strike.[41] On June 20, however, the pro-strike veterans held a mass meeting in a park across from city hall and declared their intention to demonstrate the next day because of the arrests of the strike leaders and the resumption of streetcar service.

At 10:30 the next morning, a hurried meeting convened in Robertson's suite in the Royal Alexandra Hotel. Three veterans' delegates had come to present their terms for cancellation of the planned parade to Robertson, Gray, Andrews and Commissioner A.B. Perry of the Mounted Police. The returned men planned to march from city hall to the Royal Alexandra, where they hoped to be addressed by Senator Robertson, return down Main Street and take possession of the Industrial Bureau, headquarters of the Citizens' Committee. Government and city officials could avert the demonstration, the veterans claimed, if the streetcars were removed from the streets, the strike settled within the next four hours and Robertson agreed to speak to the men in the

Industrial Bureau. Gray retorted that it would be impossible to bring about a negotiated end to the strike within the time limit indicated and he had no intention of sending the streetcars back to their barns. They would, however, try to fulfil the third of the conditions and, at that point, Andrews left immediately for the bureau to line up meeting space for the afternoon. By the time he was able to report back to the hotel, events had already passed him by.

The meeting continued after Andrews's hurried departure as Gray tried to dissuade the veterans from precipitating a crisis by going ahead with a demonstration that would violate three proclamations. He would stop the demonstration peacefully if possible, he declared, but would resort to "other measures" if they insisted on forcing his hand. While the mayor and the veterans continued to argue, crowds were already gathering in Main Street, across from the city hall, in anticipation of the parade's 2:30 starting time. At fifteen minutes to two Acting Police Chief Newton telephoned the mayor to inform him of the crowds. Gray hurriedly left the hotel and rushed through back streets to city hall where Newton told him he thought the situation was already out of hand and that his force of special police could not restore order. Gray suggested that the RNWMP be called in, Newton concurred and the mayor drove to Mounted Police headquarters to ask Commissioner Perry to send his men out to patrol the streets. Perry complied and dispatched fifty-four men on horses and thirty-six in trucks.

the parade is out of hand

By 2:30 the gathering crowds were filling the east side of Main Street between William and Rupert. A streetcar moving slowly north along Main was surrounded by several hundred people who tried unsuccessfully to stop it. When it forced its way through, they turned their attention to a southbound car, pulled its trolley off the wires and began to smash its windows. The crowd, now almost completely out of control, rocked the car back and forth, trying to tip it on its side, but when the task proved too great they broke the rest of the windows, slashed the seats and set the interior ablaze. While the attack on the streetcar was in progress, the Mounted Police arrived on the scene.

They swung north along Main from Portage Avenue, half in khaki coats and half in the traditional scarlet, batons in hand. Twice they charged north through the crowd and both times they met with flying stones and bottles. After the second charge one Mountie's horse tripped over a piece of streetcar fender lying in the street, threw its rider to the ground and began to drag him wildly, his foot caught in the stirrup. Within moments several men separated themselves from the mob, grabbed the officer and began to beat him. When the rest of the force caught sight of their comrade they wheeled north once again, this time with revolvers cocked in their hands. Mayor Gray, watching anxiously from a parapet in front of city hall, decided to take further action and formally read the Riot Act. The time was now 2:35 and the crowd was given thirty minutes to get off the streets or be arrested. As Gray turned to go inside the building, he heard gunfire in the street below.[42]

The officer commanding the Mounted Police detachment, Inspector Mead, had concluded after the second charge that his men could not handle the large and excited crowd without extraordinary measures and ordered them to fire a volley into the throng. The command was given only moments after the Riot Act had been read and shooting continued intermittently for several minutes afterwards. One man was killed instantly and many others were wounded. It was claimed afterwards by Mayor Gray, the Manitoba *Free Press* and the Mounties that the order to fire was only given after the Mounties themselves had been shot at by unknown assailants in the crowd. They had certainly come under vigorous attack from bricks, stones and bottles, but the only shots fired that day came from police revolvers. Newspaper casualty lists published in following days listed all serious wounds suffered in the riot, including those of the RNWMP officers, not one of whom had been hit by a bullet.[43] Mayor Gray told reporters that he had not heard shots until shortly after he read the Riot Act and "presumed" they came from the crowd but, in fact, this was almost the exact moment when Mead was ordering his men to shoot. Mead himself, in early reports of the day's events, explained that he had ordered his men to use their sidearms only after he realized how hard pressed they were; he made no mention at all of being fired upon.

Panic swept the crowd as the bullets spattered and ricocheted against the streets and walls and people fell where they stood. Hundreds trying to escape police bullets swept down back alleys and ran up the streets where they met cordons of special police, armed with clubs and revolvers, thrown across Main Street and other streets and alleys in the vicinity of city hall. Now vicious fights broke out and many were arrested as Mounties and specials started to clear the downtown area. Meanwhile, Gray had driven to Fort Osborne Barracks when he heard the gunfire and asked General Ketchen to turn out the militia. The general complied, dispatched an emergency force and within minutes a mixed group of cavalry and the motor machine-gun section began to move into the downtown area in the auxiliary transport so obligingly provided by the Citizens' Committee.

By this time most of the crowd was trying in every way possible to escape the scene. Over eighty who were not successful were caught in the dragnet and arrested. The special police and the militia, aided by the Mounties, threw up cordons to block access to Portage and Main from Garry in the south to the CPR station in the north and remained on duty until midnight. Soon all was quiet; the day known to history as Bloody Saturday was over.[44]

The events of June 21 climaxed the Winnipeg strike. The dénouement came four days later when the Strike Committee called off the walkout effective Thursday morning, June 26. The strikers had failed to achieve any of their objectives, and after six weeks of effort, the futility of the strike had become painfully clear. All that the strikers were able to gain was an agreement on the part of the provincial government to appoint a royal commission to conduct an impartial investigation into the causes of the dispute.[45]

In embarking on the course taken in the spring of 1919, the workers of Winnipeg were travelling a path few North American wage earners had trod before. There had been other attempted general strikes, the most complete in Seattle, Washington, in February 1919 involving sixty thousand workers, but they were either of short duration (Seattle's strike lasted four days) or incomplete. There were thus almost no campaign histories that could have been consulted and no previous successes or failures to guide the Winnipeg strikers. Therein lies the source of their failure to examine fully the consequences of what they were planning and to prepare themselves and their city for the days and weeks to come. This, more than anything else, assured the defeat of the strike and the resultant grave weakening of the city's labour movement.

Workers in Winnipeg and western Canada had spoken increasingly of general strikes since mid-1917, but rarely gave any consideration as to what a general strike would involve. They talked and wrote about general strikes either as political weapons to oppose conscription or as the ultimate manifestation of industrial conflict, this being especially true following the 1918 Winnipeg civic workers' victory. There was, however, never any thought given as to which essential services should be maintained, if any, and how this might be done. Workers were quite blind to the fact that they were going to be forced to assume some responsibility for the maintenance of society in the event they were to launch an open-ended general strike. This held true whether or not they were planning to create a revolutionary situation, since they could never separate themselves and their families from the rest of society.

Trapped into a situation in which they appeared to be assuming government authority, the Winnipeg strikers were not equipped or prepared to cope with the political and military implications of this new situation. By launching a general strike the workers had embarked on a radical course, but they were not radical enough to escape the consequences of their action. Once the unions had decided to shut down the entire city and keep it shut until they won, they ran directly into the power of three levels of government. And when the federal government decided to involve itself in countering a revolution that never existed, the workers were lost: their only choice was between unacceptable compromise, complete defeat or direct, perhaps armed, resistance.

The Winnipeg General Strike was not a revolution and was never planned to be one. It did, however, raise basic questions concerning the nature and composition of "constituted authority" as well as what qualifies as a *bona fide* challenge to that authority. There can be no doubt that the strikers intended to enhance their own position at the expense of the normal political and economic power of capital. In using as blunt an instrument as a general strike, however, they also ran the risk of challenging the *de facto* power of at least one level of government. General strikes are intended to bring the normal functions and activities of society to a standstill and they therefore transfer to the workers part of the option of what will continue to operate and what will not—this is inevitable if anarchy is to be avoided. To this degree the existing order *is* undermined, whether by accident or design and whether on a purely local level or a more national one.

The rapid increase of labour's power in Winnipeg was a shock to the cosy arrangements and alliances that had existed between capital and government for at least four decades. This threat to the status quo was compounded by the belief in some quarters that the workers were embarked on a campaign to supplant the municipal and even the provincial and national governments. The charge was not true, but it did reflect the unions' rapid rise to new positions of power. The leaders of the strike urged their followers to hold to a non-violent course so they could avoid open confrontation with the government and its police and military forces. They did not realize that this confrontation actually began at eleven A.M. the morning of May 15. Many years of mostly unsuccessful industrial struggles and the victorious sympathetic strike of 1918 had convinced them that a general strike would enable them to bring their full power to bear in an industrial dispute. This was a basic flaw in their thinking, however, because a general strike was not and could not be just another larger strike. By its very nature it is a political weapon and must, to a certain degree, challenge areas of authority of legally constituted governments. The strikers were, therefore, caught in a dilemma of their own making and the result was a crushing defeat.

In a very real sense the Winnipeg General Strike marked the end of an era in Winnipeg and western Canada. The Winnipeg strikers had manned the battle lines for their western brothers and their loss seriously undermined the strength of all western labour. The defeat of the strike assured the weakening of those unions and labour leaders who had championed its use and who had called it. The strike was, therefore, a key event in the climactic happenings of a postwar era of turmoil. Much of the vitality of a labour movement grown powerful and energetic during four years of war was sapped in the grinding and hopeless struggle of the six-week confrontation at Winnipeg.

Notes

1. See, for example, Testimony of T.R. Deacon, Evidence Presented to the Royal Commission on Industrial Relations, Winnipeg, 10 & 12 May 1919, Department of Labour Library, Ottawa.

2. D.C. Masters, *The Winnipeg General Strike* (Toronto: University of Toronto Press, 1950), pp. 8-10.

3. *Ibid.*, p. 7

4. *Ibid.*

5. D.J. Bercuson, "Labour in Winnipeg: The Great War and the General Strike" (Ph. D. dissertation, University of Toronto, 1971), pp. 17-37.

6. See Canada Department of Labour, *Eighth Annual Report on Wholesale Prices in Canada, 1917,* and monthly tables in *Labour Gazette* for 1918 and 1919.

7. Bercuson, "Labour in Winnipeg," pp. 101-102, 105.

8. Martin Robin, "Registration, Conscription and Independent Labour Politics, 1916-1917," *Canadian Historical Review* 47 (June 1966): 101-118.

9. Bercuson, "Labour in Winnipeg," pp. 189-190.

10. *Ibid.*, pp.175-178.

11. *Ibid.*, pp. 200-217.

12. T.J. Murray to Rigg, 28 May 1919, Rigg/Rees Papers, Public Archives of Manitoba; Manitoba *Free Press,* 25 May 1918.

13. *Western Labor News,* 4 October 1918.

14. *Ibid.*, 13 December 1918.

15. See P. Phillips, "The National Policy and the Development of the Western Canadian Labour Movement," in *Prairie Perspectives 2,* ed. A. Rasporich and H. Klassen (Toronto: Holt, Rinehart and Winston, 1973), pp. 41-61.

16. Bercuson, "Labour in Winnipeg," p. 134.

17. *Ibid.*, pp. 227-228.

18. Trades and Labour Congress of Canada, *Proceedings of the 34th Annual Convention* (Ottawa, 1918), pp. 32-33, 128-131.

19. Masters, *The Winnipeg General Strike,* p. 38.

20. *Western Labor News,* 16 June 1919.
21. *Ibid.,* 2 May 1919.
22. Bercuson, "Labour in Winnipeg," p. 289.
23. *Ibid.,* p. 291.
24. *Western Labor News,* 9 May 1919.
25. *Ibid.,* 16 May 1919.
26. *Ibid.,* 4 June 1919; Winnipeg *Citizen,* 20 May 1919.
27. *Western Labor News,* 17 May 1919.
28. Bercuson, "Labour in Winnipeg," pp. 312-314.
29. *Ibid.,* pp. 330-331.
30. Canada House of Commons, *Debates* (2 June 1919), pp. 3035-3043.
31. *Western Labor News,* 17 May 1919.
32. *Ibid.,* 22 May 1919.
33. Winnipeg *Citizen,* 10 June 1919.
34. Manitoba *Free Press,* 11 June 1919.
35. Ketchen to Ottawa, 17 June 1919, Department of National Defence Papers, File 5678, Public Archives of Canada (PAC).
36. *Western Labor News,* 12 June 1919.
37. Manitoba *Free Press,* 16 June 1919.
38. Robertson to Borden, 17 June 1919, Borden Papers, PAC.
39. Masters, *The Winnipeg General Strike,* pp. 103-104.
40. *Western Labor News,* 20 June 1919.
41. Manitoba *Free Press,* 23 June 1919.
42. *Ibid.*
43. *Ibid.*
44. *Ibid.; Western Labor News,* 23 June 1919.
45. *Enlightener (Western Labor News),* 25 June 1919.

2 Estevan 1931

by S.D. Hanson

At the stroke of midnight on September 7, 1931, the miners of the Souris coal field in southeastern Saskatchewan walked off the job to reinforce their demands for increased wages and improved working conditions. The wildcat strike lasted a month, involved a total time lost of 5500 working days and affected twenty-two coal operators and six hundred miners, two hundred of whom were employed at the time.[1] Before the operators and officials of the fledgling local of the Mine Workers' Union of Canada (MWUC) could be brought to the bargaining table, some three to four hundred striking miners and their families clashed with police on the streets of Estevan, Saskatchewan, in a bloody riot culminating in three deaths, a number of injuries and the arrest of many of the participants.

The origins of the infamous Estevan strike and the tragic events of "Black Tuesday," September 29, 1931, may be traced to the nature of the Saskatchewan coal industry itself during the early decades of the century. Coal mining in Saskatchewan has always been highly seasonal. At the time of the strike, approximately seventy-five per cent of the lignite mined in the Souris field was produced for the domestic market; as a result, little demand for coal existed during the late spring, summer and early fall. This, of course, meant that mining was not profitable during about six months of the year. J.R. Brodie, vice-president of Bienfait Mines, asserted at an investigation into the dispute that the mines would be better off financially if it were possible to close them down completely between April 1 and September 1.[2]

Because manpower requirements varied substantially during the course of a year, the position of the miners was also affected. Major layoffs preceded the months the mines were essentially idle. In the twenties, many seasonally employed men were able to supplement their earnings by obtaining work on farms in the spring and summer months. With the coming of drought and depression, however, the situation changed. As John Robinson, an employee at Bienfait Mines, pointed out, there was "no work on the farm" owing to the depressed condition of the agricultural industry.[3] Consequently, commencing in 1929, a greater number of miners were left without means of support when the mines curtailed operations during the slack period. Among other things, the resultant labour surplus created a growing feeling of independence on the part of management and increasing insecurity among the workers—the mine operators could pick and choose their men, while the miners were faced with layoffs or dismissals.

In addition to the seasonal nature of the industry, the coal producers of the Souris field in the late 1920s and early 1930s found themselves faced with an even more complex problem—a reduction in realization from the sale of lignite. This decrease during 1931 varied from twenty-five to seventy-five cents per ton on domestic as well as industrial coal. In that year the average cost of producing and marketing Saskatchewan lignite was $1.61 per ton, while the average realization was only $1.67, leaving the Bienfait-Estevan mines an average net profit of only six cents per ton.[4]

Although this downward trend in prices was owing in part to intense competition from American and Alberta coal, rivalry among Souris producers themselves also plagued the Saskatchewan industry. There had always been a certain amount of competition among operators of the larger producing deep-seam mines in the field, but with the advent in 1930 of Truax-Traer's large mechanized stripping operation, the competition became much keener. Many operators supported the contention of A.C.M. Wilson, manager of Manitoba and Saskatchewan Coal, that Truax-Traer "upset the whole coal industry."[5] C.C. Morfit, consulting engineer at Western Dominion Collieries, stated that the deep-seam mines could never hope to compete against the prices established by the strip mine for slack, lump, cobble and other sizes of coal. He also warned that unless the practice of gradual and persistent reductions ceased, many mines in the district would face insolvency.[6] The Winnipeg *Tribune* carried an editorial that summed up the situation in the Souris coalfield:

> Deep-seam mines cannot compete with strip mines. A narrow seam cannot be worked by hand in competition with a seam which is thick enough to be worked by a mechanical coalcutter. These things are obvious to the bystander, but it is natural that the operator of a sub-marginal mine should resist seeing them. To admit that a mine is sub-marginal is to accept defeat. A coal mine that is operating at a loss is not a valuable property; it is a liability . . .[7]

Coal subventions also played an important role in the reduction in realization from the sale of lignite. By instituting a coal subvention, the federal government in effect assumed a portion of freight charges in an attempt to reduce the cost of transporting Canadian industrial coal to market. Prior to the establishment of a subvention, the freight rate per ton from British Columbia and Alberta coal fields to Winnipeg amounted to $4.95; from the Saskatchewan field it was $2.30.[8] In an effort to eliminate American coal and coke from the Winnipeg market, the government in 1929 granted a subvention of at least fifty cents per ton on coal being shipped into Manitoba. This subvention of one-eighth of a cent per ton mile gave Alberta coal a subsidy of $1.07 and Saskatchewan the minimum of fifty cents per ton, with the result, according to Morfit, that freight rates from the fields of the two provinces were practically equalized.[9]

H.N. Freeman, manager of National Mines, alleged that the Alberta operators lobbied the Department of Mines in Ottawa and eventually succeeded in obtaining an even larger subvention in 1931, one-seventh of a cent per ton mile.[10] Morfit claimed that this new arrangement gave Alberta producers an average subvention of $1.22 per ton while reducing their Saskatchewan competitors to forty cents per ton, no minimum being allowed. He stated that to remove this injustice and grant parity, Saskatchewan producers should receive a subvention of fifty-seven cents per ton into Winnipeg. Prior to the granting of subventions, according to Morfit, Bienfait ranked first in the Manitoba market with the Brazeau and Canmore fields of Alberta second and third, and the Fernie, British Columbia, field fourth. With the introduction of the 1931 subvention, the rating became Brazeau, Canmore, Fernie and then Bienfait.[11] The revised rates virtually eliminated a market that, it was claimed, would have insured almost year-round activity in the Souris field. Brodie observed that the people who had invested in the coal fields in the district certainly would not have done so had the subvention been in effect at the time.[12]

The decrease in realization accruing to the mine owners from the sale of lignite ultimately led to wage reductions, a major factor in the ensuing labour dispute. The companies maintained that reductions in wage schedules were necessary to cover at least a portion of the loss of revenue. The miners, of course, protested, asserting that cuts were out of proportion to the actual decrease in realization and to the decline in the cost of living.[13] George Wilkinson, a miner at Western Dominion Collieries, judged that reductions instituted at that mine deprived the workers of thirty to fifty dollars per month.[14] At Eastern Collieries, where the miners were paid twenty-five cents per ton, the average wage at the time of the strike amounted to only $1.60 per day.[15]

Although seemingly unrelated to the subject of wages, several other factors tended to depress the miners' net incomes and consequently, like the reductions, were sources of discontent. Mine operators were accused of placing maximum available limits on the gross tonnage of each car of coal loaded underground by their men, overestimating dockage for slack and the smaller sizes of coal, and using inaccurate scales. Complaints regarding non-payment for "extra work" were also widespread. In the majority of instances, individuals complained bitterly of loss of time—and, consequently, money—or of not being credited for the full amount of time expended in fulfilling certain duties. Dissatisfaction regarding non-payment for the performance of extra work centred around water removal, clearing clay falls, timbering and assisting in laying track.

A letter to the provincial deputy minister of Railways, Labour and Industries dated August 27, 1931, from A. Nelson, secretary-treasurer of Bienfait, leads one to conclude that wage levels were deplorable. According to Nelson, in the winter of 1930-31, the average monthly wage of the miners was nine dollars to twenty-five dollars, the latter being exceptional.[16] Nelson also stated that the men were facing an even lower wage scale. This lends credence to a subsequent statement by Harry Hesketh, a miner at Bienfait Mines: "There was a certain boast made a while back that they would have men working for twenty cents, before this reduction was made, that they were going to have another reduction and they would have it if we had not jumped up."[17]

All things considered, it is quite apparent from existing evidence that the income position of men working in the Souris coal field was not an enviable one. They had never enjoyed the same level of earnings as their counterparts in the Alberta and British Columbia fields. Between 1921 and 1929, a miner's average annual income in Alberta and British Columbia exceeded the Saskatchewan average by almost fifty per cent. Moreover, in the early years of the Depression, the economic position of Saskatchewan coal miners worsened considerably. Average annual earnings declined almost twenty-one per cent from 1929 to 1931.[18] The cost-of-living index meanwhile fell by only ten points, from one hundred to ninety.[19] Under such circumstances, it is not surprising that the reductions of 1930 and 1931 produced widespread discontent among those affected. Nor is it any wonder that, together with reduced opportunities for supplementary income and other matters pertaining to take-home pay, they tended to precipitate a reaction on the part of labour.

While dissatisfaction concerning take-home pay was a major factor in precipitating the Estevan strike, widespread discontent among miners and their dependents respecting working and living conditions was also an underlying cause. Working conditions in the "Big Six" were less than ideal.[20] Employees from both Crescent and Eastern Collieries told of working months—even years—in one to two feet of water.[21] In Western Dominion's eastern district, smoke from blasting hung in the air for long periods of time owing to the absence of adequate ventilating equipment. In addition to inadequate ventilation, black damp—a term used to indicate the presence in the air of an abnormal amount of carbon dioxide—was a serious problem at Bienfait Mines and Crescent Collieries. Several workers at these mines claimed they frequently had become seriously ill from breathing foul air. In addition, all the mines except National Mines failed to provide a sufficient number of underground manholes and did not keep these refuge places whitewashed and free of trash as they should have.[22] This failure to provide proper places of safety greatly increased the possibilities of injury and even death from blasting and from coal trips passing along the haulage ways. Western Dominion Collieries in particular also often failed to replace rotten timbers, with the result that instances of sections of the roof caving in were frequent. On one occasion, such a fall endangered the lives of a number of miners.[23] National Mines' slogan of "Safety First, Safety Always" was undoubtedly a factor in the relative absence of dissatisfaction with working conditions there. This mine posted a notice to its employees stating that management wished to avoid accidents: "Men protect themselves and confer a favour on the company by reporting to the mine foreman any dangerous places or defects in the mine."[24]

When working conditions in the Souris coal field are examined in the light of the Mines Act, numerous grievances voiced by labour are substantiated. The report of an inspection undertaken by Robert J. Lee, a consulting mining engineer and former dominion mines inspector, indicated that all but one mine were guilty of contravention of certain regulations contained in the act.[25] Yet the operators of the deep-seam mines were not prosecuted. Indeed, Samuel A. Lee, an inspector, stated that in the thirty years he had been around these mines, the Mines Act had never been completely enforced.[26]

During the period May 1930 to August 1931, Samuel A. Lee inspected the deep-seam mines every six weeks on the average. The departmental inspection form he completed contained his observations on general conditions in each mine in his inspectorate. Of the smaller mines inspected, many were found to be in "fair" or "poor" condition and a number of repairs were ordered. However, this was certainly not so in the case of the large mines. Lee's report of an inspection of Crescent Collieries undertaken on August 18, 1931, is representative of his reports on the deep-seam mines during the aforementioned period:

Condition of shaft	good
Condition of slope	good
Condition of roof	good
Condition of sides	good
Ventilation	good
Repairs ordered	none[27]

On the other hand, between November 1931 and January 1932 (after the strike and riot had occurred), he inspected each of the deep-seam mines at least once and each was ordered to initiate certain repairs—replace broken timbers, create additional refuge holes and whitewash them, or repair air passages.[28] It is inconceivable that conditions as recounted in his earlier reports could have suddenly deteriorated to such an extent while the mines were closed for a month by a labour dispute. It is equally difficult to accept the fact that not one deep-seam mine required a single repair during a fifteen-month period, when repairs ordered between November 1931 and January 1932 were so numerous.

If working conditions in the Souris coal field were bad, living conditions were worse. With few exceptions, the miners and their families living in company houses existed amid sordid surroundings. Annie Baryluk, the sixteen-year-old daughter of a miner at Bienfait Mines, described conditions that were quite general when she stated:

> One bedroom, two beds in there, dining room, no beds in there, kitchen, one bed, and eleven in the family . . . I think we need a bigger place than that. When it is raining the rain comes in the kitchen. There is only one ply of paper, cardboard paper nailed to about two-inch wood board . . . It is all coming down and cracked . . . When the weather is frosty, when you wake up in the morning you cannot walk on the floor because it is all full of snow, right around the room.[29]

Alice Robinson, wife of a Bienfait Mines employee, stated that the reason families lived in these hovels rather than in the village of Bienfait was that, by living in a mine house, a miner was recognized as a permanent employee and consequently guaranteed work.[30]

Of the 113 houses and bachelor shacks inspected by Thomas Douglas, district sanitary officer, in November 1931, fifty-three were reported cold, forty-three leaky, fifty-two dirty, twenty-five overcrowded and almost all in need of repair. Shower facilities for the miners were provided by only two mines, Manitoba and Saskatchewan Coal and National Mines. Bienfait Mines kept its camp free from garbage and rubble and Crescent Collieries provided refuse removal semi-annually. The remaining four companies made no provision for sanitation.[31]

An inspection of residences not the property of the mining companies presented an equally grim picture of the conditions under which the miners lived. Although Douglas found the village surroundings superior to those at the mining camps, of the twenty-five miners' residences in Bienfait inspected, he reported five cold, eleven overcrowded, eleven dirty and three infected with bedbugs.[32] The squatters' settlements that had grown up in the east and west valleys of Western Dominion Collieries' property he branded "a menace to community health" that should not be allowed to continue. The twenty-four shacks in the valleys were poorly lighted and ventilated, dirty and with a bad odour, and extremely overcrowded. Cattle roamed the property at will and refuse was scattered about unfenced wells.[33] It was this area that was most frequently described by the newspapers carrying accounts of the squalour and filth in which the miners of the Souris field lived.

Any discussion of discontent among employees arising from working or living conditions in the Souris coal field would be incomplete without reference to the stores operated by Western Dominion Collieries and Manitoba and Saskatchewan Coal. In respect to these stores, mine operators informed their employees that patronage was prerequisite to continued operation.[34] Compulsion was not explicit in the assertion, but was it implied? In the case of the Manitoba and Saskatchewan store, it may have been. A.C.M. Wilson, manager of the company, repeatedly denied ever having told mine employees that they had to deal at the firm's store,[35] and two members of a men's committee at the mine professed no knowledge of compulsory purchasing.[36] Likewise, another company employee said that, while he dealt at the store, he was not compelled to do so.[37] On the other hand, one miner stated that he was afraid to deal anywhere else because Wilson had warned him he would be fired if he did so.[38] Another claimed that he had been fired for purchasing eggs from another source and reinstated only after he promised to deal exclusively at the company store.[39]

Several Manitoba and Saskatchewan employees also told of having resorted to smuggling articles purchased elsewhere into the camp after dark. To have adopted such a course of action suggests that they too may have believed that future employment and patronage of the company store went hand in hand. But was that really the case? Edward

Edwardson, who served as night watchman at the gate, maintained that he never checked people returning to camp for possession of "smuggled" goods.[40] Wilson further claimed that the purpose of stationing a man at the gate was not to prevent the practice, but rather to prevent peddlers from "dumping" goods in the camp.

Employees of both mines also charged that prices at the company stores were exorbitant. One stated that the Western Dominion store sold cornflakes at eight boxes for one dollar, whereas Estevan merchants offered twelve for the same price.[41] Two others maintained that the prices of miners' supplies were ten to sixty cents higher at the same store than elsewhere. W. Bonchall said that the Manitoba and Saskatchewan store charged twenty cents per pound for meat when it was only fifteen cents in Estevan stores and ten cents from local farmers.[42] Another miner recalled paying three dollars for one hundred pounds of flour at that store and only $2.25 in Bienfait. Although company officials denied that prices were exorbitant, an inquiry after the strike into the operation of the company stores was to reach that conclusion, and led to prices being somewhat reduced.[43]

On the basis of existing evidence, it is all too apparent that the plight of the Souris miners and their families was not a happy one. Those men fortunate enough to be employed worked a minimum of ten hours per day under quite deplorable conditions for a very meagre wage. Many owed their soul to the company store, while others were denied even the opportunity of buying on credit. Families lived under conditions which were, for the most part, equally deplorable. Hence, it is not at all surprising that grievances concerning living and working conditions arose and persisted. Nevertheless, it was not these factors alone that ultimately precipitated the strike.

The absence of a grievance mechanism placed the miners in an extremely difficult position. Experience extending over many years indicated that any complaint—or even inquiry—regarding wages or working conditions would be met with the reply: "If you don't like it, pack your tools and get out."[44] The magnitude of this fear of dismissal was to be emphasized during the royal commission inquiry that followed the strike when J.H. Harris, a miner at Bienfait Mines and spokesman for the workers, requested protection against any friction or discrimination resulting from miners' testimony.[45]

Several miners alleged that blacklisting was another technique management employed in handling labour grievances. Wilbur Enmark, an employee at Eastern Collieries, claimed that when he protested the amount of compensation received as a result of an injury suffered in a mine accident, Edward Pierce Jr., the mine manager, told him he had better take what he was getting or he would get "a damned sight less." During the ensuing argument, Pierce reportedly said: "I will chase you out of the country."[46] Enmark went on to say that, after being without work for a year, R.J. Hassard hired him, saying: "I am going to give you a job, but Mr. Pierce asked me not to give you one."[47]

Several miners also alleged that they were subjected to abusive language by employers whenever a grievance was voiced. A shovel operator at Manitoba and Saskatchewan Coal reported that when he complained of not being credited with four hours' overtime, the pit boss answered, "God damn you, you are lucky you get one hour."[48] Another miner testified that the pit boss at Eastern Collieries cursed his men constantly. William Kushnerus, the man referred to, acknowledged that he used "rough language," but only to obtain results, not to silence complaints.[49] Although profanity exists in many working situations, this excessive verbal abuse was indicative of the treatment the miners were receiving at the hands of their employers, a treatment hardly designed to foster good employer-employee relations.

Under such circumstances, it is not surprising that the thoughts of miners in the Souris field turned to unionization. Evidence of this is sketchy, but there is no question that they took up the subject during the recession that followed World War I. It is highly probable that they then requested the newly formed One Big Union (OBU) to organize them and thereby improve their bargaining position when seeking improved wages and conditions. In any case, in 1920 the OBU assumed responsibility for doing so and an organizer from Calgary, P.M. Christophers, arrived in Bienfait on June 30, 1920, to organize a local branch of the union.

Unfortunately for the Souris miners, Christophers's visit was abruptly terminated—he was kidnapped, driven across the border, and promised "a real reception which would start with tar and feathers" should he ever return to Canada.[50] The matter was quickly taken up by the police, whereupon seven men were arrested and charged with kidnapping. These included Sam Dryden, president of the Estevan branch of the Great War Veterans' Association, Corporal George Hunter of the Saskatchewan Provincial Police (SPP), Tom Jones, Amos Gough, James Clarke, Tom Munroe and Ray Thompson. But only one of them was to be penalized in any way by the authorities for the alleged crime. The case against Jones, Thompson, Dryden and Gough was dismissed at the preliminary trial. After hearing eight prosecution witnesses and deliberating for half an hour, the jury returned a verdict of "not guilty" in the case of Hunter, Clarke and Munroe because "the evidence did not bear out the charge of kidnapping."[51] The commissioner of the SPP disagreed with the verdict but believed he could do little about it, except to have Corporal Hunter suspended from the force. In his annual report, he stated that, although the Crown felt there was sufficient evidence to obtain a conviction, "the state of the popular mind . . . was such as to make the securing of a conviction exceedingly difficult, if not impossible."[52]

After the abortive attempt at unionization in 1920, Souris miners apparently refrained from taking further action until the early thirties, when they set out anew by making representations to various labour bodies. However, the procedure proved unproductive. During the early summer of 1931, several attempts were made to secure an organizer. The matter was brought to the attention of various labour leaders in Saskatchewan, but "apparently no action was taken by trade unions affiliated with either the Dominion Trades and Labour Congress or the All Canadian Congress [of Labor]."[53] On one occasion a group of miners also approached M.J. McGrath, a mine inspector, and asked him to locate and send a union organizer to the district. This request, too, was unavailing. McGrath later asserted: "That is entirely outside the jurisdiction of the department and we paid no attention to the request at all."[54]

Having failed in their efforts to obtain the co-operation and assistance of either provincial labour leaders or the government of Premier J.T.M. Anderson, the miners undertook to form their own organization. During July and August of 1931, men from the various mines in the field met secretly to discuss the situation and to devise some form of local organization. In early August "men's committees" were formed at each of the larger mines. In addition, a "mines' committee" was established with John Loughran as acting president and Bernard Winn as vice-president. This committee consisted of twenty-eight members, twenty-five representing the employees of the six large deep-seam mines and three representing those miners employed at the smaller mines in the district.[55] Upon the formation of this committee, a letter was directed to the Workers' Unity League of Canada (WUL) requesting that an organizer be sent to the district. The league dispatched Martin Forkin, who counselled the men to join a mine union; after several meetings, the miners agreed to approach the Mine Workers' Union of Canada (MWUC). Upon request, the latter forwarded the requisite books and membership cards and organization of a local got underway.[56]

Even before the local branch of the MWUC was fully organized, Loughran, Winn and associates faced their first test of strength and enjoyed their first taste of victory over an employer. Perhaps this event facilitated organization of the union by demonstrating the value of unity; it also likely strengthened the miners for the greater confrontation which was soon to follow, and increased their confidence as to its outcome. If it did, it may to some extent have helped to precipitate the September strike. Be that as it may, the organizers of the mines' committee were evidently determined to be as strong as possible when they presented their demands to the operators for better wages and conditions. For this purpose, it would appear that they charged certain individuals with responsibility for organizing those men referred to as "foreign workers" at the various mines. This brought action from management. On August 21, John Adams was fired by Crescent Collieries for organizing that mine's foreign employees. A flurry of activity on the part of the mines' committee executive followed. It met with the Crescent men's committee and workers and then dispatched a delegation to Frank Newsome, the mine manager, to demand the man's reinstatement. Newsome refused to comply. Nor, while acknowledging that Adams was a capable miner, would he give any reason for dismissing him. Faced with such a response, the executive called upon Crescent employees to walk off the job, a procedure which proved much more effective. After a strike lasting two and a half days, Newsome capitulated and reinstated Adams, and the men resumed work.[57]

In the last week of August, under such propitious circumstances, organization of the union went forward rapidly. During the week both Sam Scarlett of the WUL and James Sloan, president of the MWUC, appeared on the scene to help with organization and were greeted with enthusiasm by miners and their families. Scarlett, an organizer for the WUL in Saskatoon, addressed a crowd of some 1200 people attending a picnic at Taylorton arranged by the mines' committee on August 23.[58] Sloan arrived from Calgary two days later and, after conferring with the men's committees at the various mines, arranged a meeting attended by more than one thousand people at Estevan that evening. It was at this meeting that Sloan announced that the MWUC had succeeded in obtaining a one hundred per cent sign-up and had a total membership in the Souris coal field of more than six hundred men.[59]

With the formation of a branch of the MWUC in the Souris coal field, a crisis arose that eventually culminated in the September 8 walkout. The operators of the large mines adamantly refused to recognize the new organization as a body with constituted authority to negotiate on behalf of the miners. The miners were equally adamant in their refusal to negotiate independently of their union. When requested by the union to attend a joint meeting of all operators and miners' representatives in the Estevan Town Hall at 8:30 P.M. on September 3 for the purpose of reaching an agreement on hours of work, wages and living conditions, only the operators of six smaller mines complied. The operators of the six deep-seam mines stated:

> We will not meet you [Sloan] or any representative of an organization such as yours which, by your own statement, boasts a direct connection with the "entire Workers' Unity League and the Red Internationale of Soviet Russia."[60]

Under these circumstances, the union decided to use its ultimate weapon and voted to cease work at midnight on September 7, 1931.

The sudden threat of a serious labour dispute in the Souris coal field probably came as no great surprise to provincial authorities. Mine inspectors had been intermittently reporting to their superiors the existence of considerable unrest among the miners. Provided officials in the Department of Railways, Labour and Industries promptly passed information on to their minister, the government must have been aware that trouble was brewing as early as January 1931. However, for undetermined reasons, they took no action. Perhaps they were preoccupied with the multitude of other problems resulting from the Depression and the drought. Or they may simply have believed that existing problems would either be settled locally, as they had been in the past, or their settlement facilitated by conditions produced by the Depression itself. When they finally did intervene, it was a case of too little, too late.

With only a few days remaining until the September 8 strike deadline, the Honourable J.A. Merkley, minister of Railways, Labour and Industries in the Saskatchewan government, dispatched his deputy, T.M. Molloy, to Estevan to assess the situation. On September 3 and 4, Molloy met with several Estevan citizens and civic officials, as well as with the operators of the deep-seam mines and with representatives of the union. Although many individuals expressed considerable sympathy with the miners' cause, they were opposed to the union owing to the revolutionary nature of the Workers' Unity League with which the MWUC was affiliated. Molloy's attempts to bring the disputants together were unsuccessful. The men insisted that their union be accorded recognition, and the coal operators adamantly refused to accede to their demand.[61]

In dealing with the immediate causes of the strike, one final factor must be taken into consideration—the antagonistic attitude of James Sloan, president of the MWUC, towards a board of conciliation that might have served as an alternative to a strike. Molloy discussed the invoking of such a board at the September 3 meeting with the union, and he telegraphed Sloan on September 7, urging him to advise the men to observe the law by remaining at work and to apply immediately for the establishment of a conciliation board under the Industrial Disputes Investigation Act. Commenting on the telegram from

Molloy, Sloan stated:

> We are not breaking any laws; we have a right to strike. As for a board of conciliation, our fight is right here with the operators and here we stay. That is the course the executive committee have decided upon.[62]

His reaction to a somewhat similar suggestion by W.W. Lynd, an Estevan lawyer, was even more explicit. When informed of Lynd's call for a conciliation board, Sloan reportedly replied: "To hell with the lawyers in Estevan, and to hell with the conciliation board, we don't want it and we are not going to have it."[63]

Where, then, does one place responsibility for the coming of the strike? A royal commission examining its causes was to state: "An organization in each mine with a committee authorized to represent the men in any difference or complaint . . . would have removed much of the [miners'] dissatisfaction."[64] The management of National Mines had consistently made a concerted effort to keep in touch with its men, and as a result this mine received little or no serious criticism from employees. According to Freeman, a men's committee to deal with grievances had been established at National Mines prior to the organization created by Loughran and Winn. Under this system, complaints were placed before the committee and discussed immediately. If it were felt that a matter warranted further consideration, a delegate approached management. Freeman stated that, in many instances, grievances were ameliorated by the committee without ever being referred to the employer.[65] The operators of the other mines would have been well-advised to have followed National's example and established mechanisms whereby labour could legitimately and easily seek rectification of any grievances.

The position adopted by the operators regarding recognition of the MWUC also helped bring on the strike. A statement issued by the United Farmers of Canada (Saskatchewan section) is pertinent:

> It would be just as logical for the owners to refuse to negotiate with the men as unionists because they were Liberals or Conservatives as because they are Communists . . . If, after a settlement has been effected on union lines, the owners find that any of their employees are attempting to foment discontent among the workers without just cause, and purely in the interest of a political party, then will be the time to take a stand against them as politicians.[66]

Several Alberta coal operators had recognized the new union as a constituted body with the authority to represent miners in any employer-employee negotiations. Despite its affiliation with the revolutionary WUL, the MWUC was also registered under the Trade

Unions Act.[67] It would appear that the anti-union sentiment of the Saskatchewan operators was at least as important a consideration in their stand against recognition as their professed anti-Communist beliefs. Even the offer of the Coal Operators' Association to negotiate with a committee of men is suspect. The history of labour-management relations in the Souris coal field clearly demonstrated that any employee grievance invariably was countered with a dictatorial "If you don't like it, pack your tools and get out." Obviously, past experience had taught the miners a lesson.

It is not inconceivable that the organization of the Estevan-Bienfait miners as a branch of the MWUC, an event that gave operators the opportunity to raise the issue of communism, could have been avoided. The union's success in organizing the men was a victory won only by default. It was only after their representations to the Trades and Labour Congress and the All-Canadian Congress of Labour failed to produce any results that the miners appealed to the MWUC. Only the MWUC responded to the request for assistance in organizing the coal miners; only the MWUC was prepared to assume the expense of the requisite organizational activities.

Although undoubtedly politically inspired, Norman McLeod's attack on provincial Labour Minister J.A. Merkley during the 1932 budget debate was not completely unfounded: "The minister of Labour [has] been placed in the House by the labour union, and yet he [has] not sent representatives of recognized unions into the field to assist the men in joining any recognized labour body."[68] Given its knowledge of the unrest in the Souris coal field—much of it a result of the miners' unorganized status and consequently weakened bargaining position—the provincial government acted unwisely, to say the least, in completely ignoring the miners' request that a union organizer be sent to the district.

When mine operators in the Souris coal field awoke on the morning of September 8, only one mine was in operation. Because Truax-Traer did not employ men underground and its employees were non-union, it was not directly affected by the work stoppage. Sloan intimated that the fifty men engaged in stripping coal and laying track there would be allowed to continue working despite the union's call for a one hundred per cent walkout. He warned, however, that there would be trouble if any attempt were made to have the men load or ship coal.[69] The union further stated that it was prepared to permit coal to be shipped to Dominion Electric Power and the Estevan Hospital, but would vigorously oppose any shipments destined for outside markets.[70] Provision was also made for local supply. Soon after the strike began, union officials granted the owners of several hillside mines permission to supply coal for local consumption, and to fill orders from farmers within a twenty-five-mile radius of Estevan.[71]

Despite the gestures of goodwill by the union towards those in the vicinity of the coal field who might require fuel, and despite the sympathetic response to the plight of the striking miners by workers and others elsewhere, suspicions quickly arose that the strike might not be altogether peaceful. Hence, to assist the two-man local detachment in quelling any future disturbance, a squad of four RCMP officers arrived in Estevan from Regina at noon on September 8.[72]

As the strike progressed and tension mounted, additional reinforcements were sent to the strike zone. A dozen RCMP under the command of Detective Staff-Sergeant Mortimer arrived and began operating twenty-four-hour-a-day patrols throughout the district for the stated purpose of maintaining law and order. In addition, the Saskatchewan Coal Operators' Association engaged a private force of thirteen special constables to assist police in protecting mine property.[73]

The strike was not a week old when the operators intimated that they might hire new men to operate the mines. Soon afterwards a third party also thrust itself into the dispute, announcing that it would recruit six hundred men in the Calgary area and move them to Estevan with the object of breaking the strike. Organized in early 1931, the Canadian Defenders' League allegedly was formed to fight the spread of communism and to protect British subjects. Lewis McDonald, president of the League and formerly a leader of the Alberta miners, telegraphed C.C. Morfit offering to supply as many men as were required to bring the strike to a halt.[74] At a meeting of the strikers, referring to McDonald as "the biggest scab herder in Canada," Martin Forkin said: "If he comes to Bienfait he will get what is coming to him . . ." "You bet he will," said a striker. "He won't go back," said another.[75] In the end, failure to arrange for transportation to Estevan prevented the Defenders from accomplishing their goal.

On September 16, Eastern Collieries, Western Dominion and Manitoba and Saskatchewan Coal attempted to reopen, using farm youths from the district. Because it was obviously impossible to work the mines with a small group of inexperienced men, it can only be concluded that these farm youths were brought in to provoke the strikers to some overt act of violence, thus creating a crisis situation demanding police interference. However, the ploy failed. Hundreds of miners assembled at these mines, met with the workers and demanded that management dismiss them. Management, on the advice of the police, complied with the miners' demands and the Big Six were again closed down.[76]

Despite the increasing number of law-enforcement personnel in the district, the coal operators were dissatisfied. Morfit in particular believed that the RCMP were handling the situation poorly. Morfit, "an American with extreme ideas who has had experience in the Pensylvania [*sic*] USA strikes,"[77] reportedly stated that "if this was in the States, it would soon be settled . . . the strikers would be mowed down with machine guns if they carried on the way they do up here."[78]

At the conclusion of a conference held September 18, the coal operators issued a statement charging that the absence of adequate police protection had prevented the reopening of the mines.[79] A few days later, the operators requested that additional police be sent to the strike sector "to insure protection to life, property and the peaceful operation of our industries."[80] Their plea fell on deaf ears. The acting attorney-general, the Honourable Howard McConnell, seemingly of the opinion that the Saskatchewan government was not responsible for breaking strikes, stated that the government had been and still was according the mine owners ample police protection in the Estevan district coal field.[81]

At about the same time, M.S. Campbell, chief conciliation officer with the Canada Department of Labour, arrived in Estevan. After a brief conference with the coal operators, he obtained their assurance that if the miners agreed to return to work pending an investigation of their grievances, they would be reinstated in their former positions without discrimination.[82] However, when it became obvious that the operators would not recognize the union, negotiations collapsed and Campbell proceeded to Regina to meet with provincial authorities. Testifying later before a royal commission, Dan Moar, a miner and officer of the MWUC local, stated that upon his arrival Campbell told the miners' committee that the royal commission, headed by Judge E.R. Wylie of Estevan, which had just been appointed to inquire into the labour dispute, could not proceed until the men resumed work. He quoted Campbell as saying that "the government wasn't going to spend money if we wouldn't go back to work . . ."[83] When told the men would not do so, Campbell allegedly said: "If that is your attitude, I am through with you, I leave this morning."[84] Thus, the stalemate continued and the stage was set for violence.

On September 28, information was conveyed to Estevan Police Chief McCutcheon that the miners intended to hold a "nuisance parade" in Estevan the following day. The parade was to be held for the purpose of dramatizing the miners' plight in order to gain local support, and to advertise a mass meeting scheduled for the evening of the twenty-ninth in the town hall, at which time Anne Buller, a WUL organizer from Winnipeg, would address the assembly.[85] As no application for a permit to hold the parade had been made, Mayor Bannatyne called a special session of the town council for the morning of the twenty-ninth to discuss it, as well as the matter of renting the hall to the strikers. After brief deliberations, council, it has been said, passed a resolution prohibiting the renting of the town hall to the miners, banning the parade and authorizing the Estevan police and the RCMP to prevent any such demonstration.[86]

While the meeting was in progress, McCutcheon received a long-distance call from Sloan regarding the proposed parade. Sloan was informed that council was in session and that resolutions had been adopted prohibiting any demonstration or meeting within the limits of Estevan. When asked what he proposed to do about the parade, Sloan stated that he was not going to commit himself.[87] Shortly after the session adjourned, Dan Moar, Harry Hesketh and James McLean, members of the mines' committee executive, arrived at the town clerk's office to pay for the rental of the hall on a previous occasion. McLean was handed a letter informing him of council's decision to ban the meeting slated for that evening, and Moar was given a copy of a telegram which read: "The Council have resolved unanimously that no parade be allowed in the Town of Estevan nor meeting in the Town Hall."[88]

After some discussion, a miners' committee at Bienfait concluded that while the council might prohibit a walking parade, the resolution would not apply to a motor cavalcade. On this basis, organization of the demonstration proceeded. It was not until the day following the riot that Moar received a letter confirming the contents of the telegram. The letter, dated September 29 and postmarked ten P.M., contained an additional piece of important information—the police would prevent any parade or demonstration. Testifying later before the Wylie Commission, Moar was to state that until this letter had been received neither he nor anyone else was aware that council had instructed the police to stop the parade: "Had there been any such knowledge of such an order to the police, the miners would never have attempted to hold either a parade or motor-car procession in Estevan."[89]

At 1:30 P.M. on the twenty-ninth, some two hundred miners, all of them evidently unaware that they would soon be confronted by the police, assembled in Bienfait intent on motoring to Estevan, accompanied by their wives and children, to interview Mayor Bannatyne regarding prohibition of the public meeting scheduled that evening in the town hall. At two o'clock the group departed for Crescent Collieries, three miles distant. That mine had been chosen for a rendezvous and soon cars and lorries bearing strikers and their families arrived from various points throughout the district. Here the men boarded lorries, a few of which were draped with Union Jacks, and the women and children entered automobiles for the seventeen-mile journey. The caravan, consisting of thirty or forty vehicles, extending for a distance of a mile along the highway and moving at a speed aptly described as that of a funeral cortège, then threaded its way through the idle mining district, picking up recruits en route. As it approached Estevan, banners proclaiming "We will not work for starvation wages," "We want houses, not piano boxes" and "Down with the company stores" were unfurled.[90]

Meanwhile, in Estevan the police were reportedly charting strategy to prevent any violation of the town council's edict forbidding any parade or demonstration. They are said to have decided that should any attempt to demonstrate occur, they would concentrate their forces at the limits of the town to prevent the striking miners from entering.[91] Reinforcements had arrived intermittently during the strike, and by the twenty-ninth Inspector Moorhead had forty-seven RCMP under his command. The police were equipped with thirty rifles (one hundred rounds of ammunition per rifle), forty-eight revolvers, forty-eight riding crops and four machine guns capable of firing three hundred shots per minute.[92] Rumours were prevalent that the police also were holding a stock of tear-gas bombs in readiness.[93]

Shortly before three P.M., three to four hundred striking miners plus members of their families reached the outskirts of the town. The motorcade approached Estevan from the east on Highway 39 and proceeded west along Fourth Street, the principal thoroughfare, to Souris Avenue, where twenty-two policemen had formed a cordon across the street. Chief McCutcheon approached the lead vehicle and told the strikers: "Now boys youse had better pull back home for we are not going to allow you to parade through town . . ."[94] During the ensuing argument, McCutcheon apparently grabbed hold of Martin Day and attempted to pull him down off the lorry. While some of his colleagues were engaged in holding Day back, another struck McCutcheon in the face and knocked him to the ground. It was at this point that McCutcheon ordered Day's arrest and the initial struggle began.[95] The strikers leaped from the lead truck and, led by Martin Day, who shouted: "Come on boys, come on, give it to them,"[96] rushed the arresting officers.

Almost simultaneously, the fire brigade was called to the scene. Their intervention, however, proved both unavailing and tragic. After a brief encounter, five miners succeeded in driving the firemen from the equipment and prevented the anticipated drenching. One striker climbed up on the engine and declared it "captured." He was shot dead on the spot.[97]

Striking miners and their women, wielding clubs and throwing stones and other missiles, then launched the final assault. Hopelessly outnumbered and unable to halt the advancing crowd, the police retreated step by step, firing warning shots above the heads of the demonstrators and at their feet. It was not until the police, "with blood streaming down their faces,"[98] stood with their backs to the town hall that Inspector Moorhead, accompanied by a squad of about thirty RCMP, arrived on the scene from Truax-Traer. The police then took the offensive and by 4:15 P.M. the mob had been dispersed, leaving in its wake some wounded, dead and dying, and sixty thousand dollars' damage to store fronts, light standards and the fire-fighting equipment.[99]

The grim toll of the battle consisted of three dead and twenty-three injured. Nick Nargan, a twenty-five-year-old miner from Taylorton, died instantly from a bullet in the heart; Julian Gryshko, age twenty-six, died of abdominal bullet wounds.[100] Pete Markunas, a Bienfait miner aged twenty-seven, died in Weyburn General Hospital two days later as a result of bullet wounds to the abdomen.[101] Eight other miners, four bystanders and one RCMP constable also suffered bullet wounds. In addition, eight RCMP personnel and Chief McCutcheon were injured by weapons wielded and thrown by the strikers.[102]

The Estevan riot was a tragedy of errors. Although council held authority under the Town Act to prohibit the proposed parade, their decision to do so proved most unwise. Parades and demonstrations designed to dramatize the plight of miners and acquire support in their fights for improved wages and working conditions were common throughout the coal-mining regions of North America. Had council issued a permit to the striking miners to demonstrate, it is unlikely that any violence or loss of life would have resulted. Although the situation in the Souris coal field was tense, it would appear that the town authorities over-reacted in banning the parade.

Nor were the strikers themselves blameless. Several miners and sympathizers were cognizant of the council's prohibition of any parade or demonstration. McCutcheon had informed Sloan by telephone and Moar, McLean and Hesketh had definitely been made aware of this fact at the town office. Detective Staff-Sergeant Mortimer of the RCMP had alerted another man, Chester McIlvenna, the morning of the riot: "I hailed him and said 'hello' and stopped him and I said I suppose you know about the parade being stopped. He said there was going to be a parade and he said he was going to be there."[103] The union's parade committee obviously discussed the ban because it concluded that the prohibition would apply only to a walking parade, not a motor cavalcade. This rather interesting rationalization indicates that the strikers were intent on proceeding with the demonstration regardless of its legality. But were they determined to proceed under any and all circumstances? Perhaps they were not.

Moar later testified that the parade would not have materialized had the men been aware of the fact that the local police and the RCMP had been instructed to prevent the demonstrators from entering the town of Estevan. If what he said was true, it is indeed unfortunate that the town clerk neglected to include this important piece of information in either of the communications he handed to Moar and McLean on the morning of September 29. And it is equally unfortunate that two of the senior men charged with carrying out the council's decision should likewise neglect to mention the matter when they had occasion to refer to prohibition of the parade. Indeed, it would seem that the town clerk, Police Chief McCutcheon and Staff Sergeant Mortimer were guilty of contributing to the tragedy by failing to mention something that might have averted it. Or were they?

Before such an accusation is made, one must be able to account for certain rather puzzling things which occurred at Estevan on September 29. Why did three men fail to mention council's instructions to the police? How could a telegram and its letter of confirmation differ markedly in detail? Why were sixty per cent of the police in the area absent from a place where trouble was expected strongly enough for plans to be made to meet it at the time such trouble arose? Why was a police cordon thrown across a downtown street when existing plans called for it being placed on the edge of town?

Evidence suggests that, when council ended its morning meeting, no one knew what would occur in the next few hours. Would the miners cancel their parade? Would they attempt to proceed with it? Or would they decide to do something else, perhaps close down Truax-Traer? In the light of both the evidence and the events it seems reasonable to conclude that, until early afternoon, the authorities believed that serious trouble if it developed would take place at Truax-Traer rather than Estevan. Why should they expect trouble in Estevan from demonstrating miners? A prime purpose of the proposed parade had been to advertise a meeting that could not now be held in the Estevan town hall since council had refused to rent it. Moorhead therefore kept the bulk of his forces stationed in the vicinity of Truax-Traer and left the balance in Estevan with Mortimer, just in case they were needed at some other location. Early in the afternoon, authorities in Estevan learned that a large number of miners were forming a motorcade and would be coming to the community. They could not have known this until some time in the afternoon, because the miners' decision to do so and to speak to the mayor about renting the town hall was made in

Bienfait "shortly after the lunch hour."[104] Somewhat later a hurried consultation among authorities in Estevan probably took place to decide what should be done. A decision was made to call out police to prevent the parade. But the decision came too late. It was likely made just as the miners' lorries began reaching the edge of town. The police could not run fast enough to set up their cordon on the outskirts, so they threw it up at the only place possible at such a late moment: across a downtown street. What followed was tragedy—three miners dead or dying and twenty-three persons injured, including four bystanders struck by bullets.

Viewing the carnage, the authorities, like normal individuals, were doubtless horrified lest they be regarded as having failed to take the necessary steps to head off violence, especially violence in which non-participants had been struck by flying bullets. Under the circumstances, they might well panic and begin asking what they could do to make themselves appear as innocent as possible, thereby placing as much blame as possible on the miners. It would appear that they opted for altering the original minutes to state that council, meeting in the regular manner earlier in the day, had specifically advised the police to prevent a violation of its edict. Such a change would be very useful. It would suggest that the town council was an alert body of men, making specific, even if unsuccessful, provisions to safeguard the lives and property of their citizens.

Only in the light of such an interpretation do certain events make complete sense: the failure of the town clerk, McCutcheon and Mortimer to mention council's instructions to the police, the difference between the telegram and letter received by Moar, the ill-chosen site for the police cordon and the retaining of three-fifths of the police at Truax-Traer rather than in Estevan. Consequently, the town clerk, McCutcheon and Mortimer should not be singled out for criticism. Rather they, together with the town council and Inspector Moorhead, should be charged with being parties to the falsification of official records and circulation of stories with which to shift responsibility for events from themselves to the miners. That the original council minutes were altered cannot be disproven by the records of Estevan. There is no account of the meeting of September 29, 1931, in the minute book. All that remains as a record of this meeting is what is purported to be a copy of the minutes filed as an exhibit at the trial of Anne Buller, a document bearing no notation stating that it is either the original or a certified copy of the minutes. At the same time, other details concerning the Estevan riot tend to increase the plausibility of this interpretation.

As is frequently the case in a confrontation such as this, the police came in for a considerable amount of criticism. W.H. Heffernan, defence counsel for many of those individuals charged in connection with the riot, accused the police of being "the aggressors in the whole affair" and of having "started the riot with their riding crops."[105] The riot began with the attempt to arrest Day, a move by authorities which resulted in intervention by his co-workers. It is conceivable that the officers had already provoked the miners or used more force than was necessary to prevent Day's being freed. If this were in fact the case, only a thin line separates attacker from defender. Heffernan also charged that: "Several of the police . . . were young and inexperienced men who were brought here before finishing training school, and who had lost control of themselves in the fight and had started firing."[106] Thirty-four of the forty-three RCMP constables on strike duty the day of the riot had less than one year's service with the force and twenty-six were only twenty-two to twenty-five years of age.[107] That several of these constables had served with the armed forces either at home or overseas does little to enhance their suitability for riot duty; soldiers are taught to shoot first and ask questions later. Did this happen in Estevan on "Black Tuesday"?

More than one policeman giving evidence at the trials stated that their revolvers were not drawn until they had their backs to the town hall.[108] However, John Munroe of the Estevan fire brigade stated: "They [the police] were retreating to the town hall and firing into the ground . . ."[109] Munroe was doubtless the one most nearly telling the truth. A photograph taken during the melee clearly indicates that the police had in fact drawn their revolvers prior to reaching the town hall. At the time this photograph was taken, the police had retreated from Souris Avenue down Fourth Street to Eleventh Avenue. It was evidently not until after the fire engine had been captured and a man shot that the striking miners launched their final assault on the police and drove them to the wall of the town hall.

In the evening after the riot, everything was quiet, but Estevan was like an armed camp. The RCMP, expecting reprisals from the strikers hourly, maintained a ceaseless vigil throughout the night. The Mounties, reinforced by a forty-five-man contingent rushed from Regina by special train, patrolled the community and mining sites steadily.[110] Sentries were on duty at different points throughout the town; machine guns were mounted at strategic locations, and tear-gas bombs were held in readiness for any outbreak.[111] The night was filled with rumours that Sloan, Forkin and Scarlett had fled Bienfait in a high-powered automobile headed north, and that a large group of Alberta miners were on their way to Estevan.[112] As further precautions, the Estevan militia, sixty strong, was called out in case its services were required to maintain law and order,[113] and arrangements were made to move the eighty-one members of the Winnipeg Strathconas to the strike zone if they were requisitioned by the attorney-general of Saskatchewan.[114]

The following morning the police moved out to take various people into custody. In accordance with their belief that Sloan, Forkin and Scarlett were being harboured by sympathizers in Bienfait, sixty RCMP descended on the village at noon on the thirtieth. Armed with rifles, revolvers, quirts and billies and accompanied by a patrol wagon on which a Lewis machine gun had been mounted, they surrounded and searched Boruk's boarding house but failed to find any trace of the three union officials. A systematic search of several miners' homes and a tour of the mining camps also failed to produce any results.[115]

During the early evening of September 29, Dan Moar approached an insurance salesman who had befriended some of the miners, and requested transportation to a farm just a short distance from Bienfait. Having extracted a promise of complete secrecy, Moar directed him to the farm where they were greeted by Annie Buller and Martin Forkin. Buller stated that "they would like to go to Oxbow to do some phoning as the local line was being watched."[116] Shortly before they reached their destination, Buller asked the driver if he would mind taking them to Brandon? Forkin said:

> Yes, that's my town and we will pay you well, sure you will help us comrade as we have to get in touch with our lawyers of the Canadian Defence League, you know a bunch of our boys got arrested, we got to get bail for them.[117]

Upon their arrival in Brandon in the early hours of the morning, Mrs. Buller paid the salesman ten dollars for the ride.

In the early evening of October 1, thirteen men arrested on charges of rioting were remanded for trial at a preliminary hearing in Estevan. Then, handcuffed and under heavy police escort, they entrained for Regina. Wives, sweethearts, friends and children of the men followed the solemn procession to the railway station to offer their encouragement and to say their goodbyes on a platform crowded with curious bystanders.[118] When they arrived in the capital, representatives of the city police and the CPR investigation branch were on hand, prepared to frustrate any attempt to release them from police custody. The arrested men were taken to RCMP station cells downtown, booked and held overnight prior to being transferred to Regina jail.[119] However, their period in custody was rather brief. Solomon Greenberg of Winnipeg, engaged by the MWUC as counsel for the miners, arranged the release of eight of the prisoners within the week. The remainder were released a few days later.

While preparations for the impending trials were in progress and an intense search for "the ringleaders" went on, those who died in the riot were laid to rest under a tombstone bearing the inscription: "MURDERED IN ESTEVAN SEP. 29 1931 BY RCMP." On Sunday afternoon, October 4, in flower-covered caskets borne shoulder high by eighteen comrades and followed by a procession of six hundred men, women and children, Nick Nargan, Julian Gryshko and Pete Markunas were buried in a common grave in the little cemetery half a mile north of Bienfait. Several mourners held aloft banners reading, "They Fought for Bread, but Got Bullets Instead," "Honor to Martyrs for the Workers' Cause" and "Murdered by the Bosses' Hired Police Thugs."[120] The brief graveside service, contained in the constitution of the MWUC and read by A. Gough, an official of the Canadian Labour Defence League of Winnipeg, was the only ceremony of the funeral.[121] Solemn Ukrainian funeral hymns and *Nearer My God to Thee,* sung unaccompanied by the huge gathering, were the only music.[122]

Despite a concentrated search in Canada and the United States, police were unable for a considerable period of time to discover any trace of the three strike leaders wanted on charges of rioting and inciting to riot—Sam Scarlett, James Sloan and Martin Forkin. Traced through a letter written by Mrs. James Sloan, Scarlett was finally arrested on C.W. Pavo's farm at Birsay, Saskatchewan, on October 15.[123] Judge Hannon set bail at ten thousand dollars, and Scarlett was released after electing to be tried with the other prisoners on March 3, 1932.[124] After "travelling all over the country," Sloan eventually surrendered to the authorities.[125] W.H. Heffernan, Sloan's counsel, telephoned the Crown prosecutor, W.J. Perkins, on November 11 and informed him that he and the fugitive would arrive in Estevan the following day, at which time Sloan would surrender for preliminary hearing. At the hearing, Magistrate Martin commented that Sloan, charged with rioting, "was undoubtedly in a position where suspicion would fall on him . . . but my feeling is that were I to commit for trial, I should be doing so on suspicion only."[126] Hence he dismissed the charge and released Sloan from custody. Forkin was arrested at Pembina, North Dakota, on a charge of illegally entering the United States. After his hearing at Grand Forks on June 10, 1932, he was deported, arrested immediately at Emerson, Manitoba, and brought back to Estevan by Detective Staff-Sergeant Mortimer of the RCMP to face trial.[127] Finding no evidence that Forkin had taken an active part in the riot, Magistrate Martin dismissed the rioting charge against him at the preliminary hearing.[128]

The first group of prisoners indicted on various charges appeared before Mr. Justice J.F.L. Embury on March 1, 1932. Counsel for the defence, W.H. Heffernan and F.J. Cunningham, entered pleas of not guilty on behalf of Martin Day, Alex Petryk and Peter Smarz, all three of whom were charged with rioting, and Joseph Bernatos, who faced an additional charge of assaulting and wounding a police officer. When the jury failed to reach an agreement in the cases of Day and Petryk, both men were ordered to stand trial at a later date during the March 1932 sittings of the Court of King's Bench. Smarz was found guilty and sentenced to three months at hard labour in Regina jail, where he was to be kept under medical observation for his "mental capacity." Bernatos was also found guilty as charged and sentenced to one year at hard labour in Regina jail.[129]

All members of the second group were charged with rioting and found guilty. Owing to their having had to be hospitalized as a result of injuries sustained during the riot, three of the accused, Fred Konopachi, Roy Buttazoni and Charles Grigalis, received special consideration. Extreme leniency was recommended for Konopachi, who was bound over to keep the peace for two years on his own recognizance of one thousand dollars and two sureties of five hundred dollars each. Leniency was urged for Buttazoni as well. He was fined two hundred dollars and bound over to keep the peace for two years on a personal recognizance of two thousand dollars and two sureties of one thousand dollars each. John Gryciuk, John Kolenkas and Grigalis were each fined $150.00 and bound over to keep the peace for two years on their own recognizance of one thousand dollars and two sureties of five hundred dollars each. Kolenkas and Gryciuk were also sentenced to two and three months respectively at hard labour at Regina jail, a jail term being deferred in the case of Grigalis.[130]

The third trial commenced on March 10 and concluded with the Crown dropping charges of rioting and unlawful assembly against David Rowsen when the jury failed to agree. Isadore Minster, found guilty of rioting, was sentenced to two years less one day in Regina jail at hard labour. William Cunnah was convicted on a charge of unlawful assembly and was bound over to keep the peace for two years on a personal recognizance of $250.00 and two sureties of $125.00 each. He elected to serve one month's hard labour at Regina jail rather than pay a fifty-dollar fine. James McLean was also convicted on an unlawful-assembly charge and was given eight months at hard labour in Regina jail.[131]

In the final group trial, Tony Stankovitch and Chester McIlvenna were acquitted on charges of unlawful assembly. Metro Kyatick and Louis Revay, meanwhile, were convicted on the same charge and each received suspended sentences. Both men were bound over to keep the peace for two years on personal recognizances of five hundred dollars and two sureties of $250.00 each. Day and Petryk were retried and again the jury was unable to reach a verdict. The cases were set over to the fall assizes, but the attorney-general's department dropped all charges against the pair.[132] A charge of rioting laid against Metro Uhyran was also withdrawn by the Crown.[133]

Convicted on charges of unlawful assembly and rioting, Scarlett was fined one hundred dollars and sentenced to one year's imprisonment in Regina jail. Hard labour was omitted from his sentence in consideration of his health—Scarlett suffered from a severe case of sciatica which he claimed caused him excruciating pain. Upon Scarlett's conviction, his counsel submitted a notice of appeal. Justices F.W.G. Haultain, W.M. Martin and George Taylor heard the appeal and, although they removed the fine, they upheld the jail term imposed by the lower court.[134]

Of the trials arising out of the Estevan riot, that of Anne Buller provoked the greatest interest. Arrested in Toronto in mid-December 1931, Mrs. Buller was brought back to Estevan by RCMP Staff Sergeant Metcalfe for preliminary hearing on a charge of rioting.[135] Magistrate Martin remanded her for trial and on February 23, 1932, W.J. Perkins, agent for the attorney-general, officially charged that:

> She, the said Anne Buller, at Estevan . . . on the 29th, September, A.D. 1931, with divers other persons, unknown, unlawfully and riotously and in a manner causing reasonable fear of tumultuous disturbance of the peace, did assemble together, and being so assembled together, did then and there make a great noise and thereby began and continued for sometime [*sic*] to disturb the peace tumultuously, contrary to the provisions of the Criminal Code of Canada.[136]

With the courtroom jammed to the limit of its seating capacity, the trial commenced at 3:30 P.M. on March 17, 1932. Mr. Justice H.Y. Macdonald presided, with Sampson and Perkins appearing on behalf of the Crown and Heffernan and Cunningham for the accused. Prior to pronouncing sentence, Macdonald asked Mrs. Buller if she had anything she wished to say. She replied in a clear, firm voice:

> Your Lordship, I appreciate the opportunity you grant me. I am prepared to receive your verdict and I want to state further that when I received the invitation from the miners to come and assist them in connection with their relief I felt it my duty to assist these miners. My speech on the Sunday afternoon before the disturbance was of no character to incite the crowd to riot. My intention was, and I state now on the basis of the analysis of the conditions of which I spoke, to make a speech of an educational character. As such it has since been commented upon by a number of miners. I am not of the

> destructive type. I aim to educate my class. Throughout my short life I have endeavored to be and I have been loyal to that class I belong to, and I emphasize to you that I did not incite, and my activities were all directed to the welfare of the men and women that toil. In some small way I have made an effort to assist the exploited workers and farmers of this country.[137]

The trial was interesting in that a great deal more was made of a speech before a mass meeting of the striking miners at Bienfait on September 27 than of her participation in the subsequent riot. Her own statement before the presiding judge would seem to indicate that she felt obliged to answer a charge of inciting to riot rather than riotous conduct. Although several witnesses testified to her being present and even urging on women participants, no one provided conclusive proof that she did in fact actively participate. Nevertheless, the jury found her guilty as charged and Macdonald sentenced her to one year at hard labour in the Common Gaol at Battleford and imposed a fine of five hundred dollars.[138] The conviction was appealed and on November 17, 1932, Justices Turgeon, Martin and McKenzie ordered and adjudged "that the appeal of the said Annie Buller be allowed and her said conviction be quashed."[139] However, the court further directed her to stand trial at the next sittings of the Court of King's Bench in Estevan "to answer to such charge as may then and there be preferred against her."[140] On March 10, 1933, she again appeared in Estevan before Justice J.F.L. Embury on a charge of rioting. She was found guilty and sentenced to imprisonment of one year less three months and eighteen days in Battleford jail. An appeal on this conviction was dismissed on May 9, 1933.

Despite the relatively light sentences handed out by the presiding judges, certain circumstances concerning the trials of the miners are puzzling, while other events make their fairness suspect. A sworn statement by a juror, R.J. Buckner, indicates that a rather blatant attempt to influence a jury was committed by W.W. Lynd, legal counsel for the coal operators. According to the statement, Lynd invited Buckner, Peterson and Erickson, jurors in the case of Martin Day *et al.*, to a hotel room for a drink and, in reference to Scarlett and Buller, stated: "We will have to get the whole bunch of red sons of bitches."[141] Lynd also referred to the lawyers for the defendants as "not having a ghost of a chance as they did not know the jurymen."[142] The attorney-general's repeated references to several of the accused as "radicals," "reds," "Communists," and "agitators" certainly must be recognized as prejudicial to the trials.

In certain instances, evidence presented by witnesses for the Crown was not the same at the trial as at the preliminary hearing. In another case, a witness—a police officer—gave evidence to suggest that at least one miner had been armed with a revolver. However, such testimony was not given at the trial of the miner so accused but at a different trial.[143] An odd procedure, to say the least. Even Justice Macdonald seems to have exceeded the bounds of propriety in the Buller case when he said, "I do not think you will have any difficulty coming to a conclusion that there was a riot."[144] Surely when an individual is on trial on a charge of rioting, the presiding judge should leave the jury to determine whether or not a riot occurred on the basis of the evidence submitted by counsel during the trial.

Mr. Justice J.F.L. Embury's charge to the jury in the case of Isadore Minster *et al.* also warrants mention. His lordship stated:

> Unfortunately we are not trying the man or the men, the individuals holding positions of authority, who withheld from the miners the information that the parade was forbidden and prohibited by the town council. I am sorry that we are not trying those men. They, having received this information, should have conveyed it to their people. They knew of the resolution of the town council and it makes one's blood boil to think that they kept this information secret.[145]

This statement clearly indicates that Embury had formulated a conclusion about the innocence or guilt of the strike leaders (Scarlett, Sloan, and Forkin) before these men had even been brought before the courts. This action raises two important questions. First, if in one instance, Embury could pass judgement on individuals who had not been brought to trial, could he not have done so in other instances? Consequently, although he displayed some sympathy for the men on trial, he could have been presiding over a case in which he had already determined the defendants to be guilty as charged. Second, because two of the presiding judges, in their charges to the jury, were obviously not unbiased, could the individuals charged in connection with the events of September 29, 1931, expect to obtain a fair trial? Given the circumstances, it is questionable whether justice could be served.

During the course of the strike, the governor general in council, under the provisions of the Inquiries Act, appointed Judge Edmund R. Wylie commissioner on September 18, 1931, "to make inquiry concerning the causes and circumstances which led to a cessation of work in various mining and other industries at or near Estevan or elsewhere in southeastern Saskatchewan during the early part of September 1931 . . ."[146] The lieutenant-governor of Saskatchewan, under authority of the Public Inquiries Act, issued a concurrent appointment on September 19, 1931. Although the strike had been called contrary to the provisions of the Industrial Disputes Investigation Act, the appointment was not conditional on the miners returning to work. Both governments, nevertheless, believed that the men should not be pursuing both a legal and an illegal solution to the dispute simultaneously.[147] For this reason, Wylie was requested to defer commencement of the inquiry pending the outcome of negotiations undertaken by M.S. Campbell, chief conciliation officer with the federal Department of Labour.[148] A few days later, on September 26, after Campbell reported that his efforts to effect a settlement had failed, Wylie was instructed to proceed.[149]

Advised by telephone of the individuals who were to participate most extensively in the inquiry, Wylie at once arranged for an organizational meeting to be held in the Estevan courthouse on September 30. W.W. Lynd appeared on behalf of the operators of the six deep-seam mines, W.J. Perkins as counsel for the commission, and John Galloway, coal operator, on behalf of twenty-two of the smaller mines in the district. However, as a result of the riot, Perkins was unable to contact any representative of the miners, and the inquiry had to be adjourned until October 5. On October 3, the miners asked to have Solomon Greenberg of Winnipeg retained as their counsel, but the government refused their request. It gave as its reason the fact that Greenberg was not a member of the Saskatchewan bar. Perhaps this was the cause of the refusal. Nevertheless, it is equally possible that the government did not want an inquiry into the riot and feared that Greenberg would press for one. If this was so, their fear was justified when, at the inquest into the deaths of the three riot victims, Greenberg strongly urged the jury to recommend a complete investigation of the whole affair.[150] As an alternative, the government agreed to provide the miners with any counsel they wished to name from the provincial bar. The mines' committee responded by agreeing that W.J. Perkins be assigned to the preparation and presentation of their case and that R.D. Newsome, an Estevan lawyer, be appointed associate counsel to the commission. It was further arranged that J.H. Harris, an official of the local branch of the MWUC, be in attendance during the inquiry to instruct counsel on behalf of the miners.[151] These arrangements completed, the commission adjourned to permit a conference between the coal operators and the miners.[152]

The Estevan riot, with its terrible consequences in dead and wounded, served as a catalyst to bring the warring factions together in an attempt to settle the dispute. As a result of a meeting with W.J. Perkins, the striking miners expressed a willingness to negotiate with the coal operators and to formulate a temporary agreement under which they would return to work pending the outcome of Wylie's inquiry. A preliminary conference of operators and miners was quickly arranged, and commenced at eleven A.M., October 6, in the Estevan courthouse with T.M. Molloy of the provincial Department of Labour acting as chairman.

When the meeting got underway, Dan Moar, speaking on behalf of the miners, submitted a proposed contract including a detailed wage schedule and enumerating twenty-seven conditions under which the men were prepared to return to work. The first condition called for recognition of the MWUC and the pit committees at each mine. The remaining twenty-six points dealt with specific working and living conditions.[153]

While this move by the miners at the conference suggests that they were prepared to bargain seriously and in good faith, it is by no means as evident that the other side was prepared to act similarly or that the miners were meeting their employers in the presence of an impartial third party. The miners placed their cards on the table by submitting a proposed contract. But the operators neither submitted any proposals for a contract, nor responded to the miners' representatives by indicating that they would meet certain of their proposed terms on the understanding that employees would resume work on a temporary basis. Rather, they viewed the commencement of negotiations thus: "We are hopeful that . . . our meeting will result in the only solution practicable at this time and that is, the immediate return to work of the employees . . ."[154] As well, they expressed their intention to consider those miners in attendance as individuals, not as representatives of the MWUC.[155]

Molloy apparently believed that the onus was on the employees to submit proposals to settle the dispute. He failed to require any submission or commitment from the operators. Quite the contrary, he suggested that the miners present their "minimum or maximum demands" and leave all other matters to subsequent negotiation.[156] Molloy's purpose in assuming this position casts some doubt on the impartiality of the government in the discussions. Since the miners' proposed contract obviously embodied their maximum demands, this procedure could lead them into disclosing the minimum that management would have to concede to resume operations. Management could then enter negotiations aimed at a temporary return to work with a distinct advantage. They could seek to have the men compromise on their minimum rather than their maximum demands. They would shortly proceed to do precisely that.

Responding to Molloy's request, the miners stated that, as a minimum, employers would have to agree to the appointment of checkweighers, an eight-hour day, payment on a mine-run basis, water removal by company men, all wage increases being retroactive to the commencement of work, and to refrain from intimidating or discriminating against employees connected with the strike. The miners compromised on what was probably their most important demand—recognition of the MWUC was reduced merely to a demand that pit committees for each mine be a recognized organization in each mine.[157] After four and one-half hours of discussion, Morfit, representing the operators, and Moar, representing the miners, signed a temporary agreement.

Short congratulatory speeches, handshaking and cheering marked the conclusion of the negotiations, throughout which a spirit of understanding and co-operation was said to have been clearly manifest.[158] The only point of the agreement that prompted prolonged discussion was one dealing with a change in the ten-hour day that had been in existence prior to the strike. The men pointed out that an eight-hour day for underground workers had been recommended by the League of Nations and was already insured by legislation in many countries. They also maintained that, owing to the unsatisfactory conditions and poor distribution of coal cars, eight hours a day was a sufficient period of time to work below the surface in any of the mines, and they assured the operators that an eight-hour day would increase production. The operators, citing the depressed economic conditions of the province, the reduction in realization from coal and the fact that the existing wage schedule was based on a ten-hour day, argued for a compromise of nine hours. In the end, primarily as a result of the intervention of Freeman, the manager of National Mines, the operators agreed to the eight-hour day for all underground employees.[159]

While the press reported cheering at the conclusion of discussions, it is questionable whether or not the reporter was paying much attention to the miners' representatives who were present. Had he done so, he may well have detected evidence of emotions other than pleasure. There is reason to suspect that the authorities had already decided to take action that amounted to breaking the strike. By the time of this meeting, they appear to have decided to blame the troubles on "outside agitators," to remove those agitators and consequently to place the men in the position of having to meet the bosses face to face without the advice and support of union officials or individuals from outside the coal field.

October 3 seems to have been an important turning point in the dispute. It was on this day that the provincial government apparently began putting into effect what may well have been a plan to smash the miners' union, deprive the miners of any outside support and silence militants. On October 3, Premier J.T.M. Anderson stated that the mine strike was most unfortunate and that the trouble could have been averted had not "outside agitators" been able to persuade the men not to go back to work.[160] On the same day, Attorney-General M.A. MacPherson replied to a Saskatoon Trades and Labour Council resolution criticizing the government for its handling of the dispute. MacPherson branded the MWUC as "Communistic in its attitude, prepared to carry on a wide agitation and propaganda of the principles of revolutionary class struggles" and charged union leaders with avoiding government ministers who had endeavoured to effect a settlement of the dispute.[161]

On the morning of October 7, the day the miners were to ratify the agreement, James Bryson, a former miner from Lethbridge and organizer for the MWUC, was arrested at the Bienfait hall where he was "alleged to have been making a statement inciting interference with guns should the miners go back to work . . ."[162] He was apprehended on a charge of vagrancy. On that same day, T.M. Molloy, speaking at a meeting of the Estevan branch of the Canadian Legion, outlined the provincial government's attitude to trade unions affiliated with the Red Internationale and stated that, because the organization behind the MWUC was revolutionary in character, it "could not be recognized by the government."[163]

While the miners were gathering in Bienfait for a meeting to ratify the temporary agreement, the authorities put on a show of force. Forty armed RCMP were in attendance to insure that only miners carrying union cards entered the meeting and "to prevent agitators from outside points getting into the meeting."[164] Although the police returned to Estevan before the meeting adjourned, their presence probably was not without effect. The miners, by an oral vote delivered before Harry Hesketh, decided 130 to 41 in favour of returning to work. The WUL alleged that out of some four hundred strikers, only a minority were permitted to vote on the question. According to the league, anyone whose name did not appear on lists supplied by the operators was denied the right to signify his agreement or disagreement with the temporary settlement arrived at by labour and management representatives.[165]

Early the following morning, a patrol of forty RCMP was again on hand, reportedly "to nullify possible attempts on the part of agitators at preventing the recommencement of work."[166] However, perhaps because all of the so-called agitators were in custody, no such disturbances occurred and, at seven A.M. on October 8, the strike ended. Some three hundred miners then returned to the pits and shipment of coal was resumed the same day.[167] A short time later, it was agreed that the operators and the men would meet on October 19 to attempt to draft a permanent agreement covering wages and working conditions.

With the dispute temporarily settled and the miners back at work, the Wylie Commission sat for a couple of days and then adjourned, first because W.W. Lynd's father was taken seriously ill, and then while management and employees again conferred. During the interval, the miners maintained that they would not continue working under the "old" conditions and would demand a substantial wage increase. The operators in turn declared that they would be severely handicapped by shrinking markets and falling prices in meeting the men's demands. Evidence also came to light that one of the companies was apparently not keeping faith with its men. In a letter to Molloy dated October 13, W.J. Perkins warned of a "fly in the ointment, which promises immediate trouble." He went on to state that, according to reports reaching him, Eastern Collieries, while observing the letter of the temporary agreement, was violating its spirit, with the result that the men were again speaking of striking.[168] When questioned by Molloy, Herbert Wallace denied the allegations: "As usual, your information from this field regarding ourselves is garbled and incorrect."[169]

That Eastern might violate the articles of the temporary agreement is not surprising. Could not all the operators have believed that, by its actions in arranging a temporary settlement, the government was firmly on their side? If this were indeed the case, the operators had little to fear from the authorities, even if their side of the agreement were not fulfilled.

With work in the coal field having been resumed, actions by government officials and the police to isolate the men, smash the MWUC and keep the mines operating continued apace. On October 12, a week before the second conference was to be held, Premier Anderson journeyed to Bienfait and spoke as the guest of honour to those assembled at a "smoker" held in connection with the founding of a branch of the legion in Bienfait. The premier had not gone to the area to attempt to avert the strike, had visited neither the wounded nor the bereaved, and had not attended the funeral of the slain miners. However, he took time to make a special trip to Bienfait to mark the establishment of an organization that would assist in destroying unity among the miners. Anderson "strongly urged the men to keep away from another revolutionary movement in their organization."[170] Scarlett observed that the type of union the premier advocated in place of affiliation with the MWUC was comparable to "a meal ticket found on the sidewalk with all the nourishment punched out of it."[171]

Two days later, on October 14, several of the men held in custody on charges arising from the riot were released on bail. Two of those granted bail, Isadore Minster and D. Rowsen, were evidently looked upon by the court as "outsiders." Both men were ordered to return to Manitoba and to remain there pending their trials, which were to be held at King's Bench sittings in Estevan on March 1, 1932.[172] On October 19, against this background, the coal operators and miners met for a second time. T.M. Molloy, representing the provincial government, was also in attendance, as was W.J. Perkins, counsel to the Wylie Commission, who chaired the meeting.

The operators scored two important victories before the negotiations even began. The miners' committee, stating that the public had been "kept in the dark too much already," requested that the meeting be open and the press allowed to be present. The operators, alleging that their competitors would obtain certain valuable information to be tabled during the conference, refused.[173] After two hours of sporadically heated exchanges, public and press were expelled. The second victory came with the expulsion of L. Maurice, vice-president of the MWUC, who had journeyed from Calgary to act in an advisory capacity to the miners.[174] Because T.M. Molloy was present at this meeting, one is led to conclude that the government favoured not only a complete news blackout but also the expulsion of men considered to be "outside agitators." Negotiation on terms then commenced.

At the conclusion of the first day, a spokesman for the miners stated that the strike might resume because management appeared unwilling to grant any concessions in those matters which meant more money for labour. The owners had agreed to have materials delivered by company men to places required by the miners, to a reduction in the price of blasting powder from $3.65 to $3.50 per keg, to refrain from discrimination against or intimidation of employees purchasing goods at private stores, to the appointment of a checkweigh-man at each mine, and to sell coal to miners at $1.50 per ton rather than the former rate of $2.00. Although the operators had agreed on October 6 to recognize pit committees of the men, they again refused any recognition of either the miners' committee or the MWUC. They were obviously as determined as ever to prevent any type of organization arising that would enable the miners to bargain collectively with all operators. Other questions still at issue were the interpretation of the eight-hour day, which had also supposedly been settled on October 6, a minimum wage of four dollars per day, and pay for timbering.[175]

The attorney-general, M.A. MacPherson, fresh from a speaking engagement the night before in Bienfait where he had "exposed" the MWUC as being directly affiliated with the Communist Party of Canada, arrived in time to attend the October 20 meeting.[176] When negotiations concluded that day, both sides intimated that the outlook for a settlement was not promising. Dan Moar, spokesman for the miners, stated that he believed the men would refuse the conditions, which represented only a slight improvement over what they had formerly.[177] In the event that negotiations failed and the strike resumed, an additional twenty-six RCMP were sent to the area on October 18 "to preserve peace."[178]

With police still very much in evidence, the men returned to work on the morning of October 21, despite a lack of any agreement to the negotiated settlement at a mass meeting of miners held in Bienfait the previous evening. Many miners withdrew from the meeting upon finding that a vote on the proposed contract was to be given to everyone holding a MWUC membership card—the majority felt that only those men employed in the mines on September 7 should be permitted to vote.[179] The pit committees met the operators separately during the day and, on the evening of the twenty-second, the men voted 221 to 83 in favour of a continuation of work.[180] Although the agreement was ratified by a majority of 138 out of a total vote of 312, L. Maurice, vice-president of the MWUC, legitimately claimed:

> The vote was a directly intimidated one, intimidation being carried on not only by the RCMP and the operators, but by Hon. M.A. MacPherson, attorney-general, who openly fought against the Mine Workers' Union of Canada at a Bienfait meeting which was called under the auspices of the Canadian Legion.[181]

After the miners were back at work and the RCMP had been withdrawn, Maurice warned that "all is not clear sailing yet," and accused Molloy and MacPherson of "holding meetings with anxious miners and non-sympathizers to smooth the situation up in favour of the coal operators . . ." He further charged that they had influenced "the men to vote for practically the same destitution"[182] as they had faced before the strike. Meanwhile, MacPherson, referring to the "overwhelming vote of the men to accept the proposals of the operators," reported his satisfaction that the self-appointed leaders of the strike had been eliminated by the men themselves. He also expressed the opinion that the miners' grievances "might readily have been adjusted by the operators had not the field been infested by members of the Red Internationale of Trade Unions and representatives of other communistic organizations."[183] The evidence already put forth clearly indicates that Maurice's appraisal of events was much more perceptive than that of the attorney-general. It was the RCMP and the courts who "eliminated" the "self-appointed leaders" by arresting them, imprisoning them or driving them out of the district. It was government officials who, greatly aided by the police, dedicated their efforts to eradicating all vestiges of the union.

Of the twenty-seven demands contained in the proposed contract submitted at the October 6 conference, almost all were officially granted by management. However, few were apparently conceded with any real degree of sincerity. Three conditions were refused by all six deep-seam mine operators—elimination of bunkhouses, pay every two weeks and recognition of the MWUC.[184] This failure to obtain recognition of their union meant that the final agreement signed by the operators and their employees can scarcely be considered even a partial victory for the miners. In addition to this serious setback, certain operators refused to concede various other demands and still other items were to be adjusted at individual mines.

With the dispute supposedly settled and the men back at work in the district's coal mines, Judge Wylie reopened the public hearing, which continued for about three weeks. By the time its work was completed on November 17, 103 witnesses had appeared and given 2533 pages of testimony and evidence. In addition to these proceedings, thirty-seven exhibits were entered on behalf of the commission, ninety by the coal operators and thirteen by the miners. Twenty-two miscellaneous documents were also filed with the commission. Wylie then proceeded to complete his report, which was transmitted to the governor general of Canada and the lieutenant-governor of Saskatchewan on January 25, 1932. That report, consisting of 147 pages, dealt in considerable detail with each aspect of the dispute in the six deep-seam mines, as well as with matters generally applicable to all lignite mines in the Souris coal field.

The report submitted by Commissioner Wylie presented seventeen recommendations designed to enhance the various aspects of the Saskatchewan lignite industry. In his first two recommendations, Wylie advocated that the October 19-20 agreement continue in force until September 1, 1932, and that during the summer of that year, a new wage schedule be formulated at a conference of the coal operators and miners. In recommendations 3, 4 and 5, the commissioner advocated payment on a mine-run rather than screened-coal basis, payment for additional timbering in any abnormal conditions, and a differential wage scale for a partnership consisting of an experienced and an untrained miner.

Having put forth his conclusions regarding the wage schedule, Wylie turned his attention to health and sanitation, living conditions and working conditions. He advocated better enforcement of health regulations, repair and maintenance of company houses, a sufficient supply of good drinking water, a more thorough inspection of the mines and a more detailed inspector's report, strict enforcement of the

Mines Act and accompanying regulations, and a regular inspection of all tipple scales.

Other recommendations pertained to the marketing of Saskatchewan coal. The commissioner advocated that specific heat values and other properties of all coal mined in the province be ascertained by government analysis, that these values and properties also be established by the same method for coal produced by all mines with a specified annual ton output, that coal produced by these mines be sold under a trade name and that the Canada Fuel Board re-examine the existing subvention rate.

Judge Wylie also advocated some twenty-five amendments to the Mines Act. These pertained to the licensing and certification of mine employees, wages, hours of work, ventilation, safety measures, mine inspections, first-aid facilities and wash facilities. As a result, on March 17, 1932, the minister of Labour introduced Bill No. 64, an act to amend the Mines Act, in the Saskatchewan legislature.[185] The bill was given second reading on the twenty-eighth and referred to the Select Standing Committee on Law Amendments.[186] Royal assent was granted and the Coal Mines Safety and Welfare Act became effective November 1, 1932. Almost without exception, the amendments advocated by the Wylie Commission became law under the new legislation. Its passage, however, was not unopposed. On March 31, a delegation of miners' representatives and coal operators representing both the large and small mines of the Souris field appeared before the amendments committee. The operators strenuously objected to several clauses in the proposed legislation. Making it compulsory for all miners to hold certificates would, they claimed, prevent farmers from obtaining employment in the mines during the winter season, necessitate importing labour during the busy months and create unemployment during the slack periods. Ordering all mines employing less than six men to provide a certified manager would mean that many owners who managed their own mines would have to close. Paying the men every two weeks would be impossible because coal was sold on terms of thirty, sixty or ninety days. Finally, instituting an eight-hour day would in fact result in a working day of seven hours or less because the miners would be paid from the time they reached the shaft until the time they returned to the top.[187] Although their protestations resulted in a minor amendment to the clause relating to certification of miners working at the coal face, the operators failed to convince the committee that their objections to the proposed legislation were valid.

The recommendations submitted by Commissioner Wylie clearly indicate that he accepted the evidence put forth by the miners to substantiate their grievances of September 1931. Without exception, his suggestions, if accepted by the federal and provincial government and put into effect, were designed to improve the lot of coal miners in Saskatchewan. Wylie advocated an improved wage schedule, better working conditions in the mines and more congenial living conditions. Even his recommendations pertaining to the marketing of Saskatchewan lignite would benefit the miners indirectly. Nevertheless, Wylie failed to provide for what was undoubtedly the most important single factor in insuring a decent standard of life for the Souris coal miners—union organization. The testimony before the commission of miners and operators alike should have convinced him that pit committees could not possibly serve the men as well as union organization. Either the evidence he heard failed to convince him that a strong voice representing the miners was required, or the government prevailed on him not to recommend unionization. By not recommending that the miners be permitted to organize into the union of their choice and that management be compelled to recognize such a union, Wylie left the miners in essentially the same unhappy position they had previously occupied.

It is equally unfortunate that the commission was not also endowed with the requisite powers to undertake a thorough investigation of the riot. When the question of an inquiry arose during the commission's public hearings, Judge Wylie stated that: "Unless there is some particular demand [to investigate] those riots, I wasn't intending to do it. In that case I will get instructions from the Government to extend the scope of the Commission."[188] Why was the commissioner not requested by the authorities to inquire into and report on the events that had precipitated the violence of September 29? In the light of the evidence, it would appear that the authorities believed it was in their interest to suppress the facts, to insure that the public remained totally ignorant of the official blunders which were in part responsible for the tragedy. Although the cases brought before the courts shed a certain amount of light on the causes and events of the September 29 melee, a full investigation undoubtedly would have removed much of the mystery that surrounds aspects of the confrontation.

The coal operators' refusal to recognize the union left the miners with little choice but to sever connections with the MWUC. Thus, the dramatic days of September 1931 seemed to have had no permanent impact on the industry of the Souris coal field. With the demise of the MWUC, the organization of miners in Estevan fell apart and for the next decade they remained powerless in their dealings with the operators. The miners flirted with a variety of unions and affiliated with a number of parent bodies; the operators usually refused to recognize any of them. By 1945, when an American union, the United Mine Workers of America, finally succeeded in organizing the miners, the spirit and militance of 1931 and the Mine Workers' Union of Canada was only a memory.

Notes

1. Saskatchewan Department of Railways, Labour and Industries, *Fourth Annual Report* (Regina, 1932), p. 7.

2. Archives of Saskatchewan (AS), Royal Commission on the Estevan-Bienfait Mining Dispute, 1931 (hereinafter referred to as Wylie Commission), *Proceedings,* vol. 2, p. 55.

3. *Ibid.,* vol. 3, p. 30.

4. Wylie Commission, *Report,* p. 109.

5. Wylie Commission, *Proceedings,* vol. 7, p. 31.

6. *Ibid.,* vol. 8, pp. 293-294.

7. Winnipeg *Tribune,* 10 October 1931.

8. Wylie Commission, *Proceedings,* vol. 8, p. 302.

9. *Ibid.,* pp. 302-303.

10. *Ibid.,* p. 437.

11. *Ibid.,* pp. 303-305.

12. *Ibid.,* vol. 2, pp. 40-41.

13. Wylie Commission, *Report,* p. 62.

14. Wylie Commission, *Proceedings,* vol. 8, pp. 23-25.

15. Regina *Leader-Post,* 14 October 1931.

16. A. Nelson to T.M. Molloy, 27 August 1931, Estevan Coal Strike, 1931 (hereinafter referred to as Estevan Strike File), Deputy Minister's Office, Saskatchewan Department of Labour, AS.

17. Wylie Commission, *Proceedings,* vol. 2, p. 113.

18. Canada, Dominion Bureau of Statistics, "Coal Statistics for Canada, 1931" (Ottawa, 1932), p. 67.

19. Canada, Royal Commission on Dominion-Provincial Relations, *Report* 1 (Ottawa, 1940): 144.

20. The "Big Six" deep-seam mines were: Bienfait Mines, Manitoba and Saskatchewan Coal, National Mines, Eastern Collieries, Crescent Collieries and Western Dominion Collieries.

21. Wylie Commission, *Proceedings,* vol. 5, pp. 88, 217; vol. 10, pp. 83-115, *passim.*

22. Wylie Commission, *Exhibits,* no. C-21.

23. Wylie Commission, *Report,* p. 70.

24. Wylie Commission, *Proceedings,* vol. 11, p. 13.

25. Wylie Commission, *Exhibits,* no. C-21.

26. Wylie Commission, *Proceedings,* vol. 11, p. 41.

27. Wylie Commission, *Exhibits,* no. C-18.

28. Mine Inspection Files, Coal Administration Branch, Saskatchewan Department of Natural Resources, AS.

29. Wylie Commission, *Proceedings,* vol. 3, pp. 77-78.

30. *Ibid.,* p. 74.

31. Wylie Commission, *Exhibits,* no. C-26.

32. *Ibid.*

33. *Ibid.*

34. Wylie Commission, *Report,* p. 50.

35. Wylie Commission, *Proceedings,* vol. 6, p. 370; vol. 7, pp. 8, 50.

36. Wylie Commission, *Report,* p. 49.

37. Wylie Commission, *Proceedings,* vol. 6, p. 195.

38. *Ibid.,* pp. 242-248.

39. *Ibid.,* p. 360.

40. *Ibid.,* p. 316.

41. *Ibid.,* vol. 8, p. 170.

42. *Ibid.,* vol. 6, pp. 165-166.

43. Wylie Commission, *Report,* p. 72.

44. This phrase, with only slight variations, was evidently popular with the officers of most of these mines. Its use was particularly common at Bienfait Mines (Wylie Commission, *Proceedings,* vol. 1, pp. 72, 95), Crescent Collieries (*ibid.,* vol. 10, p. 35; vol. 11, p. 168) and Eastern Collieries (*ibid.,* vol. 5, pp. 122, 135).

45. *Ibid.,* vol. 6, p. 51.

46. *Ibid.,* vol. 5, p. 124.

47. *Ibid.,* vol. 2, p. 155.

48. *Ibid.,* vol. 6, p. 147.

49. *Ibid.,* vol. 5, p. 101; vol. 6, p. 23.

50. Official Report of Proceedings at Trial of Those Alleged To Be Concerned in the Kidnapping of One P.M. Christophers, p. 35342, Papers of W.M. Martin, AS.

51. *Morning Leader* (Regina), 13 October 1920, p. 9; 19 August 1920, p. 9.

52. Saskatchewan Provincial Police Annual Reports, 1920, Saskatchewan Attorney-General, AS.

53. T.M. Molloy to M.A. MacPherson, 2 October 1931, Estevan Strike File.

54. Wylie Commission, *Proceedings,* vol. 10, p. 14.

55. *Ibid.,* vol. 11, pp. 165-166, 243.

56. *Canadian Miner* (Calgary), 12 October 1931, p. 3; Wylie Commission, *Proceedings,* vol. 11, pp. 165-166.

57. Wylie Commission, *Proceedings,* vol. 11, pp. 168-169.

58. *Western Miner* (Lethbridge), 8 September 1931.

59. Estevan *Mercury,* 27 August 1931.

60. *Ibid.,* 10 September 1931.

61. Wylie Commission, *Proceedings,* vol. 10, p. 3.

62. Estevan *Mercury,* 10 September 1931.

63. Wylie Commission, *Proceedings,* vol. 11, p. 246.

64. Wylie Commission, *Report,* p. 93.

65. Wylie Commission, *Proceedings,* vol. 8, p. 474.

66. Regina *Leader-Post,* 19 September 1931.

67. Director of the Corporation Branch, Canada Department of Consumer and Corporate Affairs, to the author, 24 June 1971. The MWUC was registered by a certificate dated 19 March 1926. This certificate of registry was cancelled by the Department of the Secretary of State on 22 August 1935.

68. Estevan *Mercury,* 25 February 1932.

69. Regina *Leader-Post,* 9 September 1931.

70. *Western Producer* (Saskatoon), 17 September 1931.

71. Regina *Leader-Post,* 11 September 1931.

72. *Ibid.,* 9 September 1931.

73. Regina *Daily Star,* 9 September 1931.

74. Regina *Leader-Post,* 19 September 1931.

75. *Ibid.*

76. Source not for publication; information in the hands of the author.

77. *Ibid.*

78. *Ibid.*

79. Regina *Leader-Post,* 16 September 1931.

80. *Ibid.,* 24 September 1931.

81. *Ibid.*

82. M.S. Campbell to H.H. Ward, 21 September 1931, Papers of R.B. Bennett, Public Archives of Canada (PAC) no. 267263.

83. Wylie Commission, *Proceedings,* vol. 11, p. 189.

84. *Ibid.,* p. 177.

85. Estevan *Mercury,* 8 October 1931.

86. Minutes of Estevan Town Council, 29 September 1931, p. 1, File of documents relating to the trial of Anne Buller (hereinafter referred to as Anne Buller File), Estevan Judicial District (EJD).

87. Estevan *Mercury,* 8 October 1931.

88. A.B. Stuart to Dan Moar, 29 September 1931, Anne Buller File.

89. Wylie Commission, *Proceedings,* vol. 11, p. 173.

90. Regina *Leader-Post,* 29 September 1931; 30 September 1931.

91. *Ibid.,* 29 September 1931.

92. *Canadian Labor Defender* (Toronto, April 1932), p. 5.

93. Regina *Leader-Post,* 28 September 1931.

94. Source not for publication; information in the hands of the author.

95. Interview with Pete Gemby, Bienfait, 21 June 1973.

96. Regina *Leader-Post,* 1 October 1931.

97. Regina *Daily Star,* 5 October 1931.

98. Regina *Leader-Post,* 29 September 1931.

99. *Ibid.*; T.S. Belcher to R.B. Bennett, 20 September 1931, Papers of R.B. Bennett, PAC no. 267264.

100. Regina *Leader-Post,* 30 September 1931.

101. *Ibid.,* 2 October 1931.

102. *Ibid.,* 30 September 1931; 1 October 1931; and *Canadian Miner* (Calgary), 12 October 1931.

103. King v. Chester McIlvenna *et al.,* King's Bench (Criminal), EJD.

104. Regina *Leader-Post,* 30 September 1931.

105. Estevan *Mercury,* 10 March 1932.

106. *Ibid.*

107. King v. Chester McIlvenna *et al.,* Exhibit D9, EJD.

108. King v. John Kolenkas *et al.,* KB #284, EJD.

109. King v. Isadore Minster *et al.,* KB #285, EJD.

110. Regina *Leader-Post,* 30 September 1931.

111. *Ibid.,* 1 October 1931.

112. *Ibid.,* 3 October 1931.

113. Regina *Daily Star,* 5 October 1931.

114. A.G.L. McNaughton to A.W. Merriam, 30 September 1931, Papers of R.B. Bennett, PAC no. 267369.

115. Regina *Leader-Post,* 30 September 1931.

116. Source not for publication; information in the hands of the author.

117. *Ibid.*

118. Regina *Daily Star,* 2 October 1931.

119. Regina *Leader-Post,* 2 October 1931.

120. Winnipeg *Tribune,* 5 October 1931.

121. Regina *Leader-Post,* 5 October 1931.

122. *Ibid.*

123. *Ibid.,* 16 October 1931.

124. *Ibid.,* 23 October 1931.

125. Estevan *Mercury,* 12 November 1931.

126. *Ibid.,* 19 November 1931.

127. Regina *Leader-Post,* 19 April 1932; 11 June 1932.

128. Estevan *Mercury,* 23 June 1932.

129. King v. Martin Day *et al.*, KB #283, EJD.

130. King v. John Kolenkas *et al.*, EJD.

131. King v. Isadore Minster *et al.*, EJD.

132. King v. Chester McIlvenna *et al.*, EJD.

133. King v. Metro Uhyran *et al.*, KB #291, EJD.

134. King v. Sam Scarlett, CA #53, Saskatchewan Court of Appeal (SCA).

135. Estevan *Mercury,* 17 December 1931.

136. King v. Anne Buller, CA #52, SCA.

137 Estevan *Mercury,* 24 March 1932.

138. King v. Anne Buller, CA #52, SCA.

139. *Ibid.*

140. *Ibid.*

141. *Canadian Labor Defender* (Toronto), November 1932, p. 4.

142. *Ibid.*

143. In a similar vein, Joe Bernatos was convicted of assaulting and wounding Chief McCutcheon—a charge initially laid against Martin Day who allegedly had perpetrated the riot by striking McCutcheon!

144. King v. Anne Buller, CA #52, SCA.

145. Regina *Leader-Post,* 10 March 1932.

146. Wylie Commission, *Proceedings,* vol. 1, p. 4.

147. Wylie Commission, *Report,* p. 3.

148. Wylie Commission, *Exhibits,* no. C-19.

149. *Ibid.*, No. C-20.

150. Regina *Leader-Post,* 10 October 1931.

151. Wylie Commission, *Report,* pp. 4-6.

152. Wylie Commission, *Proceedings,* vol. 1, p. 127.

153. Estevan Strike File, "Preliminary Agreement," pp. 4-6.

154. *Ibid.*, p. 3.

155. *Ibid.* The *Leader-Post,* 7 October 1931, states that recognition of the union was temporarily waived by the miners and was not an issue at this meeting. However, from the statement by the operators it would appear that the miners made that decision at the meeting rather than earlier.

156. Estevan Strike File, "Preliminary Agreement," p. 9.

157. *Ibid.*, pp. 10-11.

158. Regina *Leader-Post,* 7 October 1931.

159. "Preliminary Agreement," pp. 35-36, Estevan Strike File.

160. Regina *Leader-Post,* 3 October 1931.

161. *Ibid.*

162. Estevan *Mercury,* 8 October 1931.

163. *Ibid.*

164. *Ibid.*

165. Wylie Commission, *Exhibits,* No. C-24.

166. Estevan *Mercury,* 8 October 1931.

167. *Western Producer* (Saskatoon), 15 October 1931, p. 7.

168. W.J. Perkins to T.M. Molloy, 13 October 1931, Estevan Strike File.

169. H. Wallace to T.M. Molloy, 19 October 1931, Estevan Strike File.

170. Estevan *Mercury,* 15 October 1931. See also Regina *Leader-Post,* 13 October 1931.

171. Regina *Leader-Post,* 17 October 1931.

172. *Ibid.,* 14 October 1931.

173. Estevan *Mercury,* 22 October 1931.

174. *Ibid.*

175. Regina *Leader-Post,* 20 October 1931.

176. Estevan *Mercury,* 22 October 1931.

177. Regina *Leader-Post,* 22 October 1931.

178. *Ibid.,* 19 October 1931.

179. *Ibid.,* 22 October 1931.

180. *Ibid.,* 23 October 1931.

181. Estevan *Mercury,* 29 October 1931.

182. Regina *Leader-Post,* 24 October 1931.

183. *Ibid.*

184. Wylie Commission, *Exhibits,* no. C-21, 0-83, 0-86, 0-89; Wylie Commission, Miscellaneous Documents, no. 2, 12.

185. Saskatchewan, Legislative Assembly, *Journals, 1932* (Regina, 1932), p. 84.

186. *Ibid.,* p. 105.

187. Estevan *Mercury,* 31 March 1932.

188. Wylie Commission, *Proceedings,* vol. 10, p. 218.

3

Aid to the Civil Power: The Stratford Strike of 1933

by Desmond Morton

The sight of Canadian soldiers in full fighting order in the streets of Montreal in October 1969 and again, a year later and in much larger numbers, in Montreal, Ottawa and Quebec City was a disturbing spectacle for many Canadians. It was, indeed, a throwback to an earlier era.

For most Canadians, the notion of "calling out the troops," like the even more confused concept of "martial law," is a source of vague apprehension and misunderstanding. One happy reason is that practical experience of such necessities has been rare and remote from our own time. Prior to the recent crises in the province of Quebec, one had to look back more than a third of a century, to the Stratford strike of 1933, for the most recent example of Canadian troops being called out in peacetime to defend the authority of the civil power.

The old post-Confederation Militia Act, like its successor, the National Defence Act, contained detailed provisions for military assistance to the civil authorities. Law and order was a provincial responsibility under the British North America Act. Local officials, acting through the attorney-general of the province, asked for the troops. The request was passed to the local military commander and the necessary soldiers were called into service. Thenceforth, they acted under the command of their own officers, although military regulations were explicit in insisting on the participation of a civilian magistrate to authorize such dire acts as an order to open fire. A key provision, the subject of long court conflicts and much legislation, was that the entire cost of military assistance be borne by the requisitioning municipality or, in later years, by the provincial treasury.[1]

That financial requirement, together with considerable experience of the unwieldiness, unpopularity and inevitable delays involved in summoning the militia, led to a steady decline in the number of incidents in which the troops were used. During the Winnipeg General Strike, the sole military role was to patrol the empty streets of the city after the riot on June 21. The last occasion before the thirties when Canadian troops were employed in large numbers was in 1925. In that year, most of the available men of the permanent force in eastern Canada were sent to Glace Bay in Cape Breton Island during a prolonged and bitter strike of coal miners. Both troops and police, according to Eugene Forsey, "acted with vigour and, the miners thought, with brutality."[2] One result was a rash of sympathetic strikes throughout the province's mining industry. Thanks in part to disavowal by their own international union, the Cape Breton miners were eventually crushed, but the massive deployment of troops was widely criticized in Parliament and in the press. The government of W.L. Mackenzie King took the hint. In any case, most provinces now had the services of the Royal Canadian Mounted Police or of their own provincial police forces. Military assistance ceased to be the only available resource for frightened magistrates or attorneys-general.

The Depression years inevitably brought the civil authorities to remember the military resources at their disposal. The onslaught of massive unemployment, the apparent collapse of the economic system and the unfamiliar experience of poverty for millions of Canadians seemed to open a seedbed for revolution. So it seemed to many on the radical fringes of politics; so it seemed equally to those in authority. While government economy drives slashed the strength of the Royal Canadian Navy and the Royal Canadian Air Force, militia manpower was left untouched.[3] On the inspiration of the chief of the General Staff, Major General A.G.L. McNaughton, relief camps were established under the auspices of the Department of National Defence to siphon off unemployed single men from the welfare rolls. While McNaughton's concern for the welfare of these young men may have been wholly charitable, it is hard to believe that the government did not feel that it would rest easier if such a potentially explosive element were removed from the city streets.[4] Meanwhile, local military staff officers dusted off plans to aid the civil authorities in the event of disorder and set their intelligence officers to keep in touch with the activities of local subversives. Any peacetime army longs for real work and foiling the plots of putative revolutionaries was the most congenial task available to Canadian soldiers in the early Depression years.[5]

While radicals were expected to flourish in such traditional hotbeds as Vancouver and Winnipeg, the impact of the Depression extended official anxiety to Ontario and to Toronto. During April of 1932, officers at the headquarters of Military District No. 2 at Toronto were busy planning counter-measures against anticipated Communist demonstrations on May Day. The chief constable of Toronto, the redoubtable Brigadier Frank Draper, was certain that he could manage any troublemakers in his city but plans were made to send men of the local permanent-force units, armed with pick helves, to Oshawa and Hamilton.[6] The threat failed to materialize. Eight months later, in January 1933, the military authorities were warned of an alleged Communist plot to seize militia armouries in Toronto. The district officer commanding, Major General E.C. Ashton, responded by hiring extra caretakers and arming them with small-bore rifles and axe handles. Arrangements were made to bring a hundred men from Camp Borden in trucks and private cars should an emergency occur, and Chief Draper stationed a few of his men in each of the military buildings. Once again, nothing happened.[7]

Although all their plans and arrangements had proved unnecessary, they were evidence of the readiness, even the eagerness of the military authorities to respond to any possible threat.[8] This enthusiasm doubtless struck a responsive chord among the officials of the Ontario government, such as Lieutenant Colonel William Price, attorney-general in the Henry cabinet.

Neither Price nor the senior military officers in Ontario could ever have predicted that the "Red Menace" would first manifest itself in the sleepy little city of Stratford, halfway between London and Kitchener. The limits of political activity in the town seemed to be expressed in occasional alternations between the Liberals and the Conservatives. Trade-union organization had barely spread beyond the employees in the CNR shops. When labour organizers appeared in Stratford in August 1933, they apparently faced a hopeless task.[9]

However, 1933 was a bumper year in Ontario for both industrial organization and disputes. The provincial Department of Labour recorded 109,240 aggregate days lost through strikes, compared to 50,401 the year before.[10] At least some of the new militancy was due to the Workers' Unity League, the self-proclaimed Canadian section of the Red International of Labour Unions. At a time when the traditional craft unions affiliated to the Trades and Labour Congress were shrinking in numbers and militancy, the WUL set out to organize some of the most difficult sections of the working community and succeeded. A precursor of the methods of the Congress of Industrial Organizations (CIO), the league ignored traditional craft jurisdictions and formed unions among shoe workers, lumbermen, coal and bread drivers and in the building trades. In July 1933, it won its first victories after a series of strikes in Toronto furniture factories and it was this success that probably brought the WUL's Chesterfield and Furniture Workers' Industrial Union to Stratford.

As in several other western Ontario towns, furniture manufacturing provided Stratford with a major industry. There were seven furniture factories in the city, including a branch of the Kroehler Manufacturing Company, the Preston-Noelting Company and the McLagan Furniture Company, whose president, David M. Wright, was the local MP.[11] The Depression years had reduced the already traditionally low wages of the industry and the WUL organizers, fresh from their Toronto achievements, found it unexpectedly easy to sign up members for their union. Although the chief organizer, Fred Collins, was based in Toronto, he shrewdly brought some former Stratford men with him to break the ice. Collins, a war veteran and former Glasgow policeman, painted a military image as he explained to his new members what strike action was all about:

> The front-line trenches will be your picket line. A strong front line is essential. The war is a just war and a right one—fought for the benefit and safeguarding of your homes. You are the troops.[12]

With the precipitate haste that characterized WUL strike tactics, union demands were formulated and presented to five of the local employers on the morning of September 13, 1933, with directions to reply by six P.M. Next morning, the furniture workers were on strike and Collins could announce that the stoppage was ninety per cent effective.[13] The ensuing days saw a pattern of activity familiar in such disputes. The strikers manned their picket lines, organized a few processions and devised new slogans. For their part, the employers refused to recognize the union and generously agreed to take back their workers at their former wages. The mayor offered to mediate while the local newspaper protested that the wage demands were unreasonable and would cost the town business. Ontario's minister of Labour, who also happened to be Stratford's member of the legislature, Dr. J.D. Monteith, proclaimed himself a friend of labour and then urged the strikers to consider the difficulties of their employers.[14]

The first sign of violence occurred on the night of September 18-19. The Preston-Noelting Company was determined to ship out its stock of unfinished radio cabinets for completion elsewhere. Angry strikers invaded the factory to eject three strikebreakers who were engaged in readying the cabinets for shipment. Then, long before dawn, a crowd of three hundred tried to stop two trucks from leaving the plant. Members of the local police force and of an imported detachment of Ontario Provincial Police proved unable to make a single arrest.[15]

After a week, the strike seems to have entered a calmer phase. A conciliation officer arrived from Ottawa and Monteith sent his deputy minister of Labour to open negotiations. Local employers expressed a guarded willingness to recognize the union, although they balked at allowing a closed shop. For Collins and the strikers, this demand was not negotiable. Talks broke down, the conciliators departed and Stratford got ready for the second round of the struggle. Meanwhile, with the restless energy which distinguished it, the WUL had begun to organize the women employed at the Swift's plant in Stratford. It was a remarkable achievement, for the women, largely country girls employed at chicken plucking for two cents a bird, must have had all the traditional rural suspicions of trade-union activity. Moreover, in such hard times, there were many others who would have welcomed the work, even at such meagre wages. On September 21, the strike began at Swift's.[16]

The willingness of the "chicken pluckers" to come out on strike was symptomatic of a rising mood of bitterness in Stratford. A meeting of strikers and strike sympathizers at the city hall on Saturday, September 23, heard the chief WUL organizer, Isadore Minster, warn that the RCMP was likely to be brought in to crush the strike. Later, a crowd of strikers again prevented the Preston-Noelting Company from sending out its unfinished radio cabinets. Three major radio manufacturers replied with a published threat to place their contracts elsewhere if the strike was not settled promptly. Faced with the prospective loss of business, the local factory operators appealed to the Stratford Police Commission for protection in reopening their plants.

The need for protection became apparent after an angry scene at the Swift's plant on Tuesday, September 26. From the beginning of that strike, public opinion had been chiefly concerned about the fate of 12,000 chickens, trapped by the work stoppage. Although the strikers were willing to have the birds fed, they began to suspect that the feeding operation was being used as a cover for strikebreaking. On Tuesday, the women on the picket line were reinforced by hundreds of striking furniture workers. In turn, the local police and members of the OPP arrived to protect the factory and cars bringing non-strikers to work. As the day wore on, the crowd became increasingly unruly. A photographer from Toronto was attacked, thrown to the ground and beaten. Stones and bricks began to fly through the air, directed at the plant and its defenders. On three separate occasions, police charged into the crowd to drive it back. By nightfall, the police were backed against the factory wall, trying to identify their assailants from the glare of security lights on the building. Eventually, after four policemen had been injured and the situation had become very tense, a delegation of strikers was allowed to inspect the plant and to search for signs of strikebreaking.[17]

That night, Mayor G.I. Graff and the other members of the police commission formally asked the attorney-general's department for assistance. The request was conveyed through Joseph Sedgewick of the department, already stationed in Stratford for just such an eventuality. Ever since Dr. Monteith's overtures had been rejected by the men, it had seemed apparent to him and to some of his fellow cabinet ministers that the Stratford strikers were under the sway of violent Communist revolutionaries like Collins and Minster. It was time to be firm. Only a few weeks before, the federal government had faced up to a strike of relief-camp workers at Long Branch, near Toronto. Despite radical leadership and much militant rhetoric, the men had submitted without a blow when their camp was closed and the occupants ordered to leave.

Graff's request offered the attorney-general the opportunity to display the full authority of the Crown. Perhaps anticipating the repressive reputation they would soon acquire, Price's colleagues were reluctant to act. In a letter to a Conservative stalwart, Premier George Henry confessed that the government's hands were tied by the municipal request: "The Statute requires that we send a detachment of the Militia whenever the municipal authorities and the police commission of the area request it. We were loath to send them, and rather sought to avoid it, but once the demand was made, we had no alternative."[18] With its provincial police seriously under-strength, the Ontario government formally called for troops.

Since Stratford was located in Military District No. 1, the request was forwarded from Toronto to Brigadier J.M. Ross, the district officer commanding at London. Ross's only available permanent troops were those stationed at the headquarters and a weak company of the Royal Canadian Regiment at Wolseley Barracks. Another company of the RCR was stationed at Toronto, under the jurisdiction of Military District No. 2. General Ashton was delighted to oblige his brother commander's request for reinforcements.[19]

The first company of troops, four officers and fifty-six men under Lieutenant Colonel R.J.S. Langford, arrived from London on Wednesday, September 27, on the morning train. The soldiers, in full battle order and armed with rifles and Lewis guns, marched from the station to the armouries of the Perth Regiment in Stratford. Later that afternoon, an equally small "B" Company arrived from Toronto in chartered buses. The most sensational arrivals were four small Carden-Lloyd machine-gun carriers, ancestors of the more familiar Bren-gun carriers of the Second World War. An evil genius must have persuaded Langford to bring those vehicles from London as part of his regiment's equipment. It took most of the day to make the trip and the crews were sick from exhaust fumes when they arrived. The faulty design of the machines meant that carbon monoxide was being pumped into the drivers' faces throughout the journey.[20]

The strikers and their sympathizers had greeted the marching troops with jeers and catcalls, but the arrival of what the Toronto *Daily Star* reporter described as "baby armoured military tanks" seemed the veritable symbol of the iron heel. To both reporters and bystanders, they spelled power, their clanking treads presumably designed to be driven over any resisting object, be it man, woman or child.

The military had been summoned as a guarantee of peace and order when the furniture factories were reopened on September 28. Peace there was, and the soldiers remained confined in their armouries, but no workers appeared.[21] The strike was still on. From every standpoint, the call for military assistance had been a mistake. Although older workers had reportedly been wavering after two weeks of unemployment, and although the furniture companies had offered better wages and "plant assemblies" in lieu of unions as an attempt to entice their employees back to work, the arrival of the troops and their "tanks" had introduced a new bitterness and determination in the ranks of the strikers.[22] At a mass outdoor meeting of strikers, Isadore Minster made a telling point when he congratulated Colonel Price and the prime minister, R.B. Bennett, "for organizing the workers of Stratford in their efforts to bring better conditions to the working man."[23] Alderman O.J. Kerr, himself on strike from one of the chair factories, claimed that Joseph Sedgewick had thrown the power of the provincial government against the strikers while the employees of Preston-Noelting insisted that no further negotiations would take place until the soldiers left town.[24]

The military intervention drew attention to the strike from the rest of Canada. A meeting of 1700 people in Toronto raised $591 for the workers and demanded the withdrawal of the troops and the OPP. The radical and erratic former judge, L. St. George Stubbs, on a tour through Ontario on behalf of the infant CCF, claimed that all the strikers were seeking was "a chance to live."[25] Across Ontario, pro-Liberal newspapers subordinated their suspicions of organized labour to criticize the introduction of military forces. In the view of the *Globe*, "neither mob demonstrations on one side nor military displays on the other are likely to bring an atmosphere conducive to a mutually satisfactory understanding . . ."[26] The Toronto *Daily Star* agreed that law and order must be maintained but went on to comment:

> The strongest characteristic of Canadian law has been its entire confidence in its own power to handle any condition that might

arise. Experience has shown that in Canada a few policemen can handle a situation which, in the United States, the arrival of a battalion of soldiers would inflame into a battle.[27]

Perhaps surprisingly, the voice of the established Canadian labour movement was at least as equivocal as that of the Toronto press. The *Canadian Unionist,* official organ of the All-Canadian Confederation of Labour (ACCL), condemned the use of troops largely as a blunder on the part of the authorities and of management. The workers, it maintained, would simply be blinded to the hopelessness of continuing their struggle. "If the unequal nature of the contest at Stratford was realized, as it should have been, common sense would have prevented the rejection out of hand of the niggardly wage increase and incidental concessions offered by the furniture firms . . ."[28] The executive of the Trades and Labour Congress, fresh from an annual convention at Windsor which had rejected affiliation with the CCF, was even more blunt. On October 3, Tom Moore, the president of the TLC, announced to the press that the Workers' Unity League was a Communist affiliate and that if the Stratford workers wanted a union, the congress would help them only through official channels.[29] Fred Collins, the WUL organizer, promptly denied the charge of Soviet affiliation and the Toronto and District Labour Council, a TLC affiliate, took a more independent line in demanding the immediate withdrawal of the troops.[30]

Meanwhile, the men of the RCR and their "tanks" remained in the Stratford armouries, emerging only for occasional games of softball on a neighbouring field. Colonel Langford's suggestion that the strikers might do battle with the soldiers in a game of soccer was not well received. With the exception of Alderman Kerr, the Stratford city council endorsed the mayor's action in summoning help. When it was apparent that the factories could not resume work, a new attempt was made to ship out the unfinished radio cabinets. This time, the strikers did not interfere. While the troops stood by in reserve, confined to the armouries, city police and the OPP oversaw the loading of trucks and boxcars.[31] At Kitchener, one of the cars was found to be on fire and the contents were badly damaged. If this was sabotage, it was of little direct benefit to the strikers. With their warehouses now empty, the Stratford manufacturers settled down for a long wait.

So did the troops. Members of the regimental band were sent to Stratford and band concerts were arranged in the hope of improving community relations. Indignation against the soldiers themselves rapidly subsided and people gathered at the armouries to talk with the men and to inspect the Carden-Lloyd carriers.[32] In only a few days, it had become apparent that the troops were irrelevant in the prevailing industrial conflict. The furniture companies found the charge that the union was Communist-led to be sufficient justification for withdrawing their earlier offer of recognition. The Kroehler Manufacturing Company dismissed its foremen and office staff and announced that it would be closing indefinitely. On October 12, there was a minor skirmish on a picket line outside one of the factories when office staff and strikebreakers were pelted with rotten apples, tomatoes and plums. For the first time, the police made an arrest and a crowd of a thousand marched in protest when the young striker was refused bail.[33]

The first break in the strike occurred on October 18, more than a month after it had begun. The Preston-Noelting Company announced that it had reached a settlement with its employees. It allowed only tiny pay increases for the worst-paid workers and recognition of a company union. Growing desperate, the remaining strikers were prepared to see even this agreement as a victory. A hastily produced "Code" of the Canadian Furniture Manufacturers' Association, earlier rejected out of hand, now seemed to be the only basis for getting back to work.[34]

Meanwhile, the military authorities wanted their troops back. Their regular program of duty and training was being disrupted, morale was sagging once the first excitement had worn off, and it was increasingly apparent that the men were not really needed. The provincial government, which bore the cost and the odium for having called the military into service, would also have been glad to see them go, but Colonel Price was caught in a trap at least partially of his own making. To critics of the use of troops, he had replied that he was consitutionally bound to meet the wishes of the mayor and police commission. His hands were tied, and Mayor Graff and his supporters continued to insist that the soldiers were needed. On October 27, the four Carden-Lloyd carriers were sent back to London. With winter approaching, a garage would have had to be hired for them and they were plainly not needed.[35] According to Colonel Langford, it was the furniture manufacturers who insisted that the remainder of the troops be kept in Stratford. They had assured Sedgewick and the police commission that "they still felt they needed protection, that the situation had in no way changed and they considered that if the troops were withdrawn, serious trouble would again break out."[36]

The Preston-Noelting settlement had not brought an immediate end to the strike. Other managements and employees proved more intransigent and it was early November before agreements were signed in the other plants. The interval brought few concessions from management.

The non-negotiable principle of union recognition was abandoned and most plants accepted shop committees, a forty-four- to fifty-hour week and a ten per cent increase in wages, a raise which did little more than bring levels up to the furniture manufacturers' own code.[37] As for the striking poultry dressers at Swift's, their treatment was similar. By November 4, all were back at work and a plant committee, composed equally of management and workers, was expected to settle the dispute. If the committee approved, the women might look forward to a ten per cent increase on their rate of two cents a plucked chicken.[38]

At last the troops were allowed to go home. The federal and provincial governments were left to haggle over the bills, and growing files debated such arcane matters as whether the Gray Coach Company had overcharged for its chartered buses and how much damage was actually inflicted on the officers' mess furniture of the Perth Regiment by their permanent-force guests.[39]

The political consequences were much more significant. In Stratford, Mayor Graff resigned at the end of his term and Alderman Kerr won the ensuing mayoralty contest at the head of a predominantly labour-endorsed slate of councillors. For the Ontario Liberal leader, Mitchell Hepburn, the Stratford strike was an occasion to declare that his sympathies lay "with those people who are the victims of circumstances beyond their control, and not with the manufacturers who are increasing prices and cutting wages at the same time."[40] Such sentiments did Hepburn and the Liberals no apparent harm in Stratford. In the 1934 provincial elections, the Conservative candidate in Perth went down to defeat by a substantial margin.[41]

Obsessed by "agitators and organizers of revolutionary bodies," the minister of Labour and his Conservative colleagues had done little to settle the strike in Stratford.[42] Instead, by calling in the troops, they had dramatized their ineffectiveness and their panic. Moreover, the presence of the soldiers and their "tanks" aroused the basic antimilitarism of Canadians in the interwar years and won the strikers a degree of sympathy that they could not otherwise have secured. Moreover, having called out the troops, the government found that they could hardly be used.

Politicians learned their lesson. The use of troops in the traditional peacetime role of "strike duty" was now recognized as a hopeless anachronism. With that realization, a chapter in the history of the militia and of the Canadian labour movement was closed.

Notes

1. See Desmond Morton, "Aid to the Civil Power: The Canadian Militia in Support of Social Order," *Canadian Historical Review* 51, no. 4 (December 1970). See also Major J.J.B. Pariseau, *Disorders, Strikes and Disasters: Military Aid to the Civil Power in Canada 1867-1933* (unpublished manuscript, Directorate of History, National Defence Headquarters, 1973).

2. Eugene A. Forsey, *Economic and Social Aspects of the Nova Scotia Coal Industry,* McGill University Economic Studies, no. 5 (Montreal, n.d.), p. 61.

3. On the reductions and their effects, see James Eayrs, *In Defence of Canada,* vol. 1, *From the Great War to the Great Depression* (Toronto: University of Toronto Press, 1964), chapter seven.

4. On the relief camps, see *ibid.,* pp. 124ff; John Swettenham, *McNaughton,* vol. 1, *1887-1939* (Toronto: Ryerson Press, 1968), p. 269ff.

5. For evidence of military attitudes, see "Disturbances in Unemployment Relief Camps" [Unpublished manuscript in Canadian Forces Historical Section (CFHS)].

6. Colonel H.F.H. Hertzberg to Colonel C.H. Hill, 22 April 1932, and attachments in CFHS file 162.009 (D 24).

7. Major General E.C. Ashton to Chief of the General Staff, 16 January 1933, and attachments in CFHS file 162.009 (D 24). (The precautions became public knowledge after a reporter revealed that an army officer had been attending meetings of the police commission at city hall.)

8. The enthusiasm of militia officers for General Draper as an upholder of authority was demonstrated at a mess dinner on September 21 when the chief constable was received with repeated cheers. At the time, he was under attack for alleged favouritism to prominent offenders. (Toronto *Globe,* 22 September 1933). See also *Saturday Night,* 23 September 1933.

9. On the Workers' Unity League and many aspects of the Stratford strike, see the valuable article by James D. Leach, "The Workers' Unity League and the Stratford Furniture Workers: The Anatomy of a Strike," *Ontario History* 59, no. 2 (June 1967). See also *Agents of Revolution: A History of the Workers' Unity League,* published by the Ontario government in 1931 on the authority of Colonel Price.

10. Province of Ontario, "Report of the Department of Labour," *Sessional Papers* 66, no. 10 (1934): 68. The *Canadian Forum* attributed much of the militancy to backwash from Roosevelt's proclamation of the NRA (November 1933).

11. "A revolutionary organization," according to the Department of Labour. (*Ibid.*, p. 11.) On the WUL, see Leach, "The Workers' Unity League," p. 39; Stratford *Beacon-Herald*, 18 October 1933.

12. Stratford *Beacon-Herald*, 12 September 1933.

13. Toronto *Globe*, 16 September 1933.

14. Stratford *Beacon-Herald*, 14-18 September 1933; Toronto *Globe*, 16 September 1933; Leach, "The Workers' Unity League," pp. 41-42.

15. Toronto *Globe*, 20 September 1933; Stratford *Beacon-Herald*, Toronto *Daily Star*, 19 September 1933.

16. *Ibid.*, 23 September 1933; *Labour-Gazette* 33, no. 10 (October 1933): 986. The organization responsible was the Food Workers' Industrial Union of the WUL.

17. The trouble allegedly began when the company brought a boxcar up to the plant with the intention of removing the chickens. See Toronto *Globe*, 27 September 1933; Toronto *Daily Star*, 26 September 1933; Stratford *Beacon-Herald*, 26-27 September 1933.

18. G.S. Henry to J. Harry Meighen, 2 October 1933, Henry Papers, Archives of Ontario.

19. Brigadier General Ross to Major General Ashton and Colonel Hertzberg (record of telephone conversation), CFHS file 162.009 (D 32A). See also file 161.009 (D 56).

20. The medical officer of the Perth Regiment found that the drivers suffered from headaches, nausea and diarrhoea but had largely recovered by the following day. [Captain H.G. Kenner to DMO, MD 1, 7 October 1933, CFHS file 161.009 (D 56).]

21. Langford to Defensor (National Defence Headquarters), 27, 28 September 1933, *ibid.*

22. The *Globe* correspondent reported evidence of wavering among the strikers on September 27.

23. Toronto *Globe*, 28 September 1933.

24. *Ibid.*, 2 October 1933.

25. *Ibid.*

26. *Ibid.*, 29 September 1933.

27. Toronto *Daily Star*, 28 September 1933. For other views see *Saturday Night*, 7 October 1933, and *Canadian Forum*, November 1933.

28. The *Canadian Unionist* 7, no. 5 (October 1933).

29. Toronto *Globe*, 3 October 1933.

30. *Ibid.*, 4 October 1933. A.R. Mosher of the ACCL also announced that the WUL was neither affiliated with nor recognized by the ACCL.

31. Brigadier General Ross to Secretary, Department of National Defence, 6 October 1933, CFHS file 161.009 (p. 56); Toronto *Globe*, 5 October 1933.

32. Leach, "The Workers' Unity League," p. 44, n. 10.

33. Stratford *Beacon-Herald*, 12 October 1933; Toronto *Globe*, 13 October 1933.

34. *Ibid.*, 19-20 October 1933.

35. Ross to Secretary, Department of National Defence, 26 October 1933, CFHS file 161.009 (p. 56).

36. Langford to Defensor, 30 October 1933, *ibid.*

37. *Labour Gazette* 33, no. 11 (November 1933): 1075.

38. *Ibid.*, p. 1076.

39. See CFHS file 325.009 (D 155). The original requisition was served on Brigadier General Ross at 10:30 P.M. on September 26. Troops entrained at London at 7:05 A.M. on the 27th and reached Stratford by 8:20 A.M. Notice to withdraw the troops was received on November 4 and the remaining soldiers returned to London on the morning of November 6 after a total of forty days' service. [Ross to Secretary, Department of National Defence, 23 February 1934, CFHS file 161.009 (D 56).] Troops were called out on the authority of the Militia Act cap. 122, RSC, 1927, sec. 75-9.

40. Neil McKenty, *Mitch Hepburn* (Toronto: McClelland & Stewart, 1967), p. 49.

41. The Conservative candidate won only 10,811 votes to the Liberal's 16,371.

42. "Report of the Department of Labour" (1934), p. 11. [The report of the Ontario Provincial Police attributed the strike to the work of "paid agitators." See Province of Ontario, *Sessional Papers* 66, no. 51 (1934).]

4 Oshawa 1937

by Irving Abella

As a landmark in the history of the Canadian labour movement the Oshawa strike of 1937 stands next only to the Winnipeg General Strike. In many ways, however, the two-week walkout of some four thousand General Motors workers in Oshawa, Ontario, in April of 1937 had the more permanent impact. Though it lacked the blood and violence—but not the passion—of the Winnipeg strike, the Oshawa strike must be regarded as perhaps the most significant labour event of the past fifty years. Not only did it mark the birth of industrial unionism in Canada but, perhaps as important, it had a convulsive and lasting effect on the Canadian political scene.

Oshawa in the 1930s was a trim, bustling, middle-size community situated less than thirty miles east of Toronto, not yet the commuter suburb it has since become. People who lived in Oshawa then tended the work there as well. It was the market centre for a good farming district, but its basic industry was, as it still is, automobiles.

In the early 1920s the giant General Motors Company of the United States purchased the struggling McLaughlin Carriage Works of Oshawa and built a huge assembly plant on the outskirts of town. Within a few years more than three thousand men were employed there producing more cars for the Canadian and Empire market than the combined output of the rest of Canada. The relationship between workers and management was never harmonious. Low wages, unsafe working conditions and lack of job security finally prompted a walkout of most of the company's employees in March of 1928. Within a week the company submitted to the workers' demands and the strike was called off.

Encouraged by the success of this display of muscle, the workers then organized themselves into a union and applied to the Trades and Labour Congress for a charter. Instead of affiliating this huge four-thousand-man local, the craft-obsessed TLC ordered the union to be broken up into its component crafts. Many of the workers rebelled at this decision and opted instead to join the Communist Auto Workers' Industrial Union of Canada, which was also organizing in the Oshawa area. A vicious struggle between the two unions ensued, with the inevitable result that by the early 1930s there was no union at all in the General Motors plant at Oshawa.

Of course, in the early 1930s, during the depth of the Depression, workers needed jobs, not unions. What employment General Motors provided went to men who promised not to join a union. Capitalizing on this opportune moment, the company fired most of the union leaders and promoted others—those too valuable to release—to managerial positions where they were beyond the ambit of the trade-union movement.

This situation was, of course, not merely restricted to Oshawa. Throughout Ontario in the early 1930s both jobs and unions were scarce. The TLC, the Canadian counterpart of the American Federation of Labor, was too timid and reactionary to organize unskilled, unorganized workers. The All-Canadian Congress of Labour, the only other national labour organization, was weak, both organizationally and financially, while the Workers' Unity League, the labour arm of the Communist party, had disbanded, its organizers and unions flocking back into the TLC. It was exactly at this time, late in 1935, that a group of disgusted American unionists intent on furthering industrial unionism created the Committee for Industrial Organization, the CIO, in the United States.

Its birth coincided with the end of the worst of the Depression. Jobs were becoming less scarce; companies were stepping up production; and optimistic politicians and industrialists were prophesying a quick return to prosperity. Simultaneously, workers were becoming increasingly restive. Wages were still lower than they had been in the 1920s, working conditions unbearable and job security non-existent. It was to mitigate these conditions that Canadian workers in the 1930s turned in large numbers to the CIO.

The CIO's first steps into Canada were hesitant. Created in 1935 by John L. Lewis out of unions that had split with the American Federation of Labor over its refusal to organize on an industrial basis, the CIO by 1937 had several million members. In Canada, however, membership at the beginning of 1937 was negligible. Lewis and his colleagues were loath to organize in Canada; too much remained to be done in the United States. But unofficial CIO representatives, most of whom were Communists who had received their experience in the Workers' Unity League, began appearing in Canada and organizing locals for various

CIO unions. Their efforts were nugatory. The CIO campaign in Canada did not catch fire. It needed, it seemed, a spark.

The spark was to come from Oshawa.

At the beginning of 1937 there was no union at the GM facilities in Oshawa. Consequently, while the workers were subject to their fifth consecutive wage cut, the General Motors Company announced that its profits in both the United States and Canada were the highest in the history of the company.[1] And there was little the company employees in Oshawa could do. Across the border GM workers had taken matters into their own hands. They had left the AF of L and created a new union—the United Automobile Workers of America. Then, under the aegis of the CIO, they had taken over several GM plants until the company agreed to recognize the new union and negotiate with them. Their Canadian colleagues in Oshawa looked on enviously. Conditions in Oshawa were as bad or even worse than those in the GM plants in Flint and Detroit. Wages were lower, hours of work longer and jobs were less secure; rarely were older workers, men in their late forties and fifties, rehired after the long seasonal layoff for re-tooling.

Since the unhappy events in 1928, a few spasmodic and invariably futile attempts had been made to organize a union in Oshawa. By the beginning of 1937 there existed in the plant only a clandestine committee, known as the Unity Group, of some few dozen men who met secretly and regularly to discuss ways of improving working conditions. Though they probably would have achieved little in any case, they spent most of their time debating the virtues of socialism and communism; understandably, they achieved nothing.

But what the men in the plant could not do for themselves—organize a union—the company helped them to do. On February 15, 1937, acting on the advice of efficiency experts from the United States, the General Motors management announced a speed-up in the assembly line from twenty-seven to thirty-two units per hour. The workers were infuriated. For years they had complained that the line was already too fast. Now the company had the gall actually to increase its speed. Almost immediately the workers in the body shop—the most skilled and thus the least replaceable in the plant—decided to lay down their tools to discuss the new system. The plant's general manager, Harry Carmichael, rushed down to speak with them. But when he announced the company's decision was irreversible, the men in the body shop warned that unless the speed-up were revoked they would strike on Friday, February 19. In addition, one of the workers in the plant phoned the UAW office in Detroit for help. At about the same time one of the CIO organizers in the province also phoned UAW headquarters at the urging of Joe Salsberg, the trade-union organizer of the Communist Party who had long taken an active interest in developments at the Oshawa plant. On Friday, February 19, the body-shop workers, about 250 men, struck, thus halting production in the entire plant. On the same day Hugh Thompson arrived in Oshawa.[2]

Thompson was a UAW organizer sent from Detroit in response to the two phone calls. Fortuitously, he arrived while Louis Fine, a mediator from the Ontario Department of Labour, was addressing the striking body-shop workers, urging them to return to work. When the workers were informed that the UAW representative was outside the hall, they invited him to address them despite Fine's protest that the strike was an issue between the company and its workers, and that "outsiders would only complicate matters."[3]

Thompson's speech was short and to the point. He outlined to the men the success of the UAW below the border, and the necessity of organizing in order to improve their situation. His speech must have been effective. All the men in the room voted to join the UAW and, on Thompson's advice, to go back to work.

On the following day Thompson set up an office in downtown Oshawa and opened up Local 222 of the UAW for business. Within three days the union had enrolled 650 workers. Within a week, over a thousand had joined and after a month it had four thousand members, making it the largest local in Canada. Even the mayor of Oshawa, Alex Hall, and most of the city council were enrolled as honourary members. Charlie Millard, a forty-year-old war veteran and chairman of the CCF in Oshawa, was elected president of the local, and stewards were nominated from each department to represent the men on the union's negotiating committee.

Naturally, General Motors took an avid interest in what the union was doing. The company hired several undercover investigators to attend union meetings and report back on its plans and activities, and most importantly to supply a list of names of those attending the meetings.[4] In addition, the company transferred Millard from the body shop, where militancy was highest, to a position on maintenance where he was required to work a double shift. Nonetheless, neither Millard nor other union members were intimidated and the rapid growth of the union continued undiminished.

More surprising than the company's activities and interests were those of the premier of Ontario, Mitchell Hepburn. That the busy premier of Canada's most populous province should concern himself with an apparently insignificant labour dispute seems fatuous. Yet only a few days after Thompson arrived in Oshawa, the Ontario premier had phoned his friend Ian Mackenzie, the federal Defence minister, asking him to persuade Thomas Crerar, the minister of Immigration, and Norman Rogers, the minister of Labour, to deport Thompson. But Crerar and Rogers demurred, on the sensible grounds that Thompson had entered Canada legally and had not yet committed any crime. Undaunted, Hepburn ordered his own attorney-general, Arthur Roebuck, to investigate Thompson in the hopes that some evidence could be uncovered which could be used to deport Thompson as "an undesirable immigrant." Despite an intensive investigation, Roebuck found nothing. At the same time, at the personal request of Hepburn, Crerar ordered a complete investigation of Thompson by an inspector from the Immigration Department. Predictably, after a long and complete investigation that included an interview with Thompson, the Department of Immigration concluded that Thompson could not be legally deported. This, of course, was not what Hepburn wished to hear; if no legal way could be found to get Thompson out of the country, then Hepburn would find another.[5]

What was most astonishing about Hepburn's attitude was that three years earlier he had come to power on a radical slogan: "I swing well to the left, where some Grits do not tread." He further entrenched his support amongst the working people of Ontario by denouncing Conservative Premier George Henry's decision in September of 1933 to send in troops and tanks to break a strike in Stratford, Ontario. "Toryism stands for oppression," he said. "The provincial government has seen fit to send artillery, machine guns and tanks to Stratford because the citizens are objecting to the treatment given them by wealthy manufacturers . . . They take all they can from the people and give as little as they can to the workers. My sympathy lies with those people who are victims of circumstances beyond their control and not with the manufacturers who are increasing prices and cutting wages at the same time."[6]

Once in office Hepburn matched his rhetoric with his actions. Despite the objections of the mayor of Toronto, he cordially received a large group of "hunger marchers" at Queen's Park and fired two members of the Toronto Board of Police Commissioners who had refused the men permission to march on the legislature. He introduced enlightened labour legislation and a minimum-wage law. So overwhelmed were the province's labour leaders that one remarked that Hepburn cabinet members were "not Liberals, they are socialists and labour men from the ground up." And a visiting official of the British Labour party remarked how "fortunate" Ontario was "in having an administration that is going to see justice done to the workers."[7]

But in February of 1937 justice for the workers seems to have been the furthest thing from Hepburn's mind. From the day he took office,

Hepburn had fallen more and more under the influence of those "fat cats of business" against whom he had campaigned, particularly George McCullagh, the editor of the *Globe and Mail*. In addition he had formed close relationships with such mining magnates as Sir James Dunn of Algoma Steel and J.P. Bickell of MacIntyre-Porcupine Mines, men who not only gave the Ontario premier useful advice about stocks he might add to his investment portfolio, but also advised Hepburn of the deleterious impact that a powerful union movement would have on these stocks, as well as on the entire mining industry of the province. As a small-town farmer Hepburn was in any case naturally suspicious of organized labour. It took the arguments of his big-business friends, especially McCullagh, to turn these suspicions into an active antipathy, particularly when the Ontario premier became convinced that the demands of organized labour would harm the province's resurgent economy. Thus, by February of 1937, when the CIO was beginning to take its first hesitant steps into the province, the labour movement no longer had a friend—if it ever had—in the premier's office in Queen's Park. In fact, the office was now occupied by its most important and hostile enemy.[8]

Hepburn viewed the Oshawa activity with a great deal of alarm. He was determined that the violence and bloodshed that had marked CIO organizing in the sit-down strikes in Michigan and other states would not spill across the border into Ontario. Yet he seemed helpless to do anything about it. The federal government had rebuffed his efforts to stop the CIO at the border. And there seemed little else he could do. Already CIO representatives were actively organizing auto workers in Windsor, rubber workers in Kitchener, steel workers in Hamilton and, worst of all, at least from Hepburn's point of view, mine workers in the north. And though all of these campaigns were peaceful and non-violent, it was in the premier's mind only a matter of time before the CIO shed blood in Ontario.

On March 2, 1937, the time arrived. On that day, against the advice of their CIO organizers, some seventy workers at the Holmes Foundry in Sarnia—all of whom were recent immigrants from eastern Europe—sat down at their machines in protest over the company's refusal to recognize their new union. At once, for reasons that had more to do with racial bias than anti-labour feeling, a mob of about three hundred of Sarnia's "best" citizens descended on the plant with an assortment of weapons. After a short but bloody battle the battered strikers were evicted from the factory while the Sarnia police stood outside the foundry, refusing to rescue the grossly outnumbered strikers. Yet once the strikers were outside the plant the police moved in and arrested them on charges of trespassing, though none of the several hundred strikebreakers were charged.

When this apparent disparity of justice was raised in the Ontario legislature by the lone CCF member, Sam Lawrence, Hepburn immediately jumped to his feet and shouted: "My sympathies are with those who fought the strikers... Those who participate in sit-down strikes are trespassers, and trespassing is illegal in this province... There will be no sit-down strikes in Ontario! This government is going to maintain law and order at all costs."[9]

Several days later Hepburn announced: "We are not going to tolerate sit-down strikes, and I point that out to these people now in this country, professional agitators from the United States—to agitate and foment unrest in our industrial areas... I shall put down the sit-down strikes with the full strength of the provincial police if necessary and other resources at the government's disposal."[10] No doubt he meant the tanks, artillery pieces and machine guns that he had denounced Premier Henry for using against strikers in Stratford.

Undaunted, Hugh Thompson continued his activities, not only in Oshawa but in other Ontario centres such as St. Catharines, where he helped organize UAW locals in several of the GM subsidiaries in that city. But it was Oshawa that required most of his attention. Since his arrival the city had become almost totally unionized. As the newspaper of the Communist party, the *Daily Clarion,* rapturously described it: "The change in attitude of the workers is one of the remarkable things to be seen. They walk with squared shoulders and a smile on their faces for they no longer fear for their jobs and they are proud of the union button they wear openly. Owing to the increasing demand for the union button there has been a shortage. This is the only time when workers pull long faces. This seems almost incredible in what was once a company town. But Oshawa is rapidly becoming a worker's city."[11]

The first meeting between the new union and the GM management took place on March 18 in the office of Colonel J.B. Highfield, the company's personnel manager. The union was represented by Charlie Millard and stewards elected from each department in the plant. Highfield and George Chappell, a company vice-president, represented management. According to the union negotiators' own description of themselves, they were "merely a bunch of amateurs." They thus sat silent and attentive while Chappell told them that the company was in no way bound by the UAW contract signed in the United States, and while Highfield added that the company would negotiate only with its own workers and not with any representative of the UAW. With that, after only fifteen minutes, the meeting was adjourned.[12]

Fearing that this rebuff would demoralize the union, Thompson decided that a show of strength would be fitting. He decided to call a general union meeting for March 20. Unfortunately, he found it impossible to rent a hall large enough to accommodate the union membership. His attempts to rent the hockey arena were rejected since Colonel R.S. McLaughlin, the GM president, was a major stockholder in the arena company. The Department of Defence refused to rent the armoury, and the school board rejected his application to rent a high-school auditorium on the grounds that he was not a "local resident." Undaunted, Thompson announced that the union would hold its meeting in downtown Oshawa at "the Four Corners," the busiest intersection of the city, during the height of the Saturday rush hour. Almost at once the school board reversed its decision and decided that perhaps renting the school auditorium to the union was not such a bad idea after all.[13]

Naturally the meeting was a rousing success. When Thompson related to the membership—most of whom were outside the auditorium since even that hall proved too small—that he had succeeded in renting the auditorium only because the power of the union was now "as great as that of the General Motors Company," they roared with approval. In addition, both Thompson and Millard promised the workers that the union negotiating committee would settle for nothing less than what the UAW had received in the United States. And indeed, shortly thereafter the power of the union was immeasurably enhanced, as was the morale of its membership, when a GM subsidiary in Oshawa, Coulter Manufacturing, signed a contract with the union, recognizing Local 222 as a full bargaining agent for the company's 260 workers.

At the next meeting between the company and the union negotiators, the newly confident Millard demanded that Thompson be allowed to sit in on the negotiations as a union representative. Highfield categorically refused. Since Thompson was not a company employee, he said, the company would never negotiate with him. On that note, barely ten minutes after the meeting started, the union negotiators walked out, bringing the meeting to an abrupt end.[14]

Later that week a UAW vice-president from Detroit, Ed Hall, addressed a large rally of the Oshawa workers and announced that Millard had been appointed as a full-time CIO organizer. In addition, he promised the local the "full support" of the international. In fact, however, Hall had privately warned Thompson that the UAW treasury was empty and could afford Local 222 nothing more than its best wishes.[15]

Negotiations were now deadlocked, despite the efforts of Labour

Minister David Croll. On Wednesday, March 31, Croll met with Chappell and Thompson at his Queen's Park office. Chappell emphasized that his company would never negotiate with non-employees. Croll then turned to Thompson and said: "Well, this narrows the issue down to one thing. It looks as if the people would get along nicely if it were not for one person, and I would suggest that you withdraw out of the picture." Thompson countered that it was the wish of the men and of the international union that he stay in his present position, but after an hour of discussion he agreed to Croll's proposal that Charlie Millard should do the negotiating for the union. Chappell also agreed, and a meeting was scheduled for the following day at Croll's office.[16]

Early the following afternoon, Chappell and Highfield came to Croll's office to discuss Millard's new status. Highfield protested that all that had been done was "to change the name of Thompson to Millard" and emphasized that the company would have no dealings with the CIO nor its representative. Croll reproved the two men for their "childish stubbornness" and then remarked: "I can read men, and as I look at that bunch in the next room I can tell by the eyes of most of them that they are a bunch of fanatics; . . . as for Millard . . . I think he's a weakling who can't do anyone any harm . . . I don't want a strike, and they shouldn't either, because I'll have to feed them and they won't get fat on what they get from this department." With that he ushered Highfield and Chappell into the adjoining room where Louis Fine and the union negotiating committee were waiting, and the meeting began.[17]

Millard spoke first and presented Chappell with a list of the union demands. These included:

1. An eight-hour day.
2. A steward and grievance committee modelled on the one agreed to by GM in the United States.
3. A seniority system.
4. Abolition of the new efficiency system.
5. A minimum wage.
6. Payday every other Friday.
7. A contract that would terminate at the same time as that with the GM plants in the United States.
8. Factory bulletin boards to be made available for union notices.
9. Five-minute rest periods every two hours.
10. Vending machines for chocolate bars, etc., to be set up around the plant.

Chappell agreed to study these demands and present the company's answers at a meeting on the following Monday. Fine then adjourned the meeting on an optimistic note, stating that he was sure an agreement could be reached shortly so that Croll, who was leaving on Friday for a two-week vacation, would not have to postpone his trip.

Yet for the following three nights the GM company shipped an average of fifteen hundred cars from the Oshawa plant to an emergency storage depot on the Canadian National Exhibition grounds in Toronto; this was more than ten times the usual number.[18] Evidently General Motors did not share Fine's optimism.

After three more meetings with the union, on Tuesday, April 6, the company agreed to negotiate all the union's demands and to recognize Millard as the representative of Local 222. When Millard announced this to the men at the plant they were jubilant. They had been primed for a strike for weeks and only the indefatigable efforts of Millard and Thompson had kept them in line. Now it appeared that the strike would not be necessary.

While these negotiations were taking place, Hepburn had been on vacation in Florida. He returned to Queen's Park on Wednesday, April 7. On that same day, just hours after Hepburn's arrival home, General Motors once again changed its mind and announced that it would neither negotiate with Millard, as long as he was "a representative of the CIO," nor would it sign a written contract with the new union. It would undertake only to make verbal commitments to the workers.[19]

This sudden hardening of the company's position caught both Millard and Fine by surprise. Fine met immediately with Highfield and Chappell to try to moderate the company's stand. He was informed by them that Hepburn had phoned Chappell and had urged the company to take a firm stand against recognition of the CIO. Naturally, with the premier's promise of "total support," the company refused to reconsider its position. At the meeting with the union that evening, Chappell broke off negotiations with the statement that the GM position was firm, and there was nothing left to discuss.[20]

The union now had no alternative but to strike. Both Thompson and Millard were aware that a strike might destroy the union since few funds were available to support the strikers, but the workers were growing increasingly impatient and it had required all of Thompson's and Millard's efforts to keep them from walking out on their own. Thus, when the company refused to continue negotiations, both Thompson and Millard saw the futility of further discussions. On Thursday, April 8, Thompson ordered the morning shift to report as usual at seven A.M. At 7:05, on a prearranged signal, the shop stewards ordered the men out of the plant. By 7:15 that morning, for the first time in ten years the General Motors facilities in Oshawa were at a standstill. The strike had begun.

The news from Oshawa did not seem to surprise Hepburn. Indeed, his actions indicated that not only did he expect a strike, he in fact welcomed it. At once he wired the federal minister of Justice, Ernest Lapointe, requesting Royal Canadian Mounted Police reinforcements for Oshawa. He told Lapointe that although he was prepared to induct special police, he feared that they would not suffice since he had already received reports that the situation in Oshawa was "becoming very acute and violence was anticipated at any minute." He then ordered General Victor Williams, chief of the Ontario Provincial Police, to cancel all leaves, to put his entire force on a twenty-four-hour alert and to mobilize one hundred constables from the area surrounding Oshawa. In turn, Williams informed him that the OPP had an undercover constable in Oshawa "to keep an eye on developments." E.G. Odette, chairman of the Ontario Liquor Control Board, acting on the recommendation of Mayor Hall and the union's executive, received Hepburn's permission to close all liquor and beer outlets in Oshawa for the duration of the strike. Hepburn also ordered the Department of Welfare not to issue relief to the strikers because "these employees are rejecting the opportunity to work at fair wages and fair hours and as a result they need not look to the government for relief assistance."[21]

Hepburn then called a press conference to outline his position to the Ontario public. He told the newspapermen that he regretted "very much that the employees of General Motors have seen fit to follow the suggestion of the CIO-paid propagandists from the USA to desert their posts at a time when both employees and the industry itself were in a position to enjoy a prosperity not known since 1929." He claimed that the conditions in the automobile industry were good and he saw no need for the men to strike. The strike itself, he claimed, was "the first open attempt on the part of Lewis and his CIO henchmen to assume the position of dominating and dictating to Canadian industry." He further added that his government completely supported the attitude of the company, that the time for a showdown with the CIO had arrived and that he fully expected the support of "the law-abiding citizens of Ontario." As he put it: "The CIO's demands are merely the first step in a policy of ever-increasing and impossible demands, culminating in the loss of a tremendous and ever-increasing export trade now being enjoyed by the automobile industry in Ontario." He warned the union against resorting to violence and promised to protect "all those workers desiring to resume their duties." He concluded emphatically: "The entire resources of the province will be utilized to prevent anything in this country resembling that which is taking place at the present time across the border due to the failure on the part of constituted authority to take adequate action." For the first time since he'd been elected, Premier Hepburn had, in the words of the Toronto *Star*, "openly turned his back on labour and the considerable liberal element in Ontario . . . whose votes in 1934 had elected him." Hepburn had publicly announced for all to hear that he would willingly use government power on the side of employers against the working man.[22]

Hepburn's request for RCMP aid was received coldly by a distraught Mackenzie King. According to the prime minister, the Oshawa situation was very delicate and "in dealing with it, Hepburn was going entirely the wrong way about it." Nevertheless, King gave into the demands of Lapointe, who enthusiastically supported Hepburn's pleas for assistance; he agreed to send one hundred RCMP officers, though the province would have to bear all their expenses.[23] Hepburn immediately phoned the RCMP Commissioner, J.H. MacBrien, to alert him that he would need many more reinforcements as he did not expect the "main crisis" for two or three days. The commissioner informed him that he'd already dispatched sixty-seven men and that thirty-three others would be "moving up by fast freight and passenger train" by the morning. Another fifty men from the Toronto division, he added, would also be made available. On Lapointe's instructions, MacBrien ordered the RCMP commanding officer in Toronto to keep his forces "in the background as much as possible" so that they would be used only to support provincial and municipal police.[24]

Despite these frantic activities, Oshawa itself was calm. As the Toronto *Star* put it, "A city more peaceful than Oshawa under the shadow of the walkout cannot be imagined. It is neither grim nor gay but placidly ordinary, showing signs neither of industrial strife nor of holidaying workers." To keep order on the picket line the Oshawa chief of police, Owen Friend, had enrolled fifty strikers to act as deputies. In fact, it seemed that the only unusual activity was the continuous procession of cars along the road to the nearby town of Whitby, where the beverage rooms were recording a record business. Indeed, so placid was the town, and so complete was the support for the strike, that when the train from Ottawa carrying the RCMP officers rolled into Oshawa, Mayor Hall rushed to the station to warn them that he wouldn't allow them off the train since he was the only person who could call them into the city. The RCMP continued on its way to Toronto.[25]

In Oshawa, Hepburn's behaviour met with almost total disapproval. In an official statement, issued on behalf of the city of Oshawa, Mayor Hall condemned Hepburn for his "impulsive and irrational action" and praised the "peace-abiding, respectable citizens of Oshawa who are on strike." But in the same breath he refused to grant relief to the strikers, since this would mean "taking sides in a strike." Hugh Thompson warned Hepburn that until the strike was settled, General Motors would never build another car in Canada, "and the moment they attempt to bring one automobile to Canada from the United States in an attempt to beat the strike here, they will never make another automobile in the United States."[26]

Most of the Ontario press, however, supported Hepburn. The *Globe and Mail,* published by Hepburn's good friend, George McCullagh, praised Hepburn for checking the CIO before "it can extend into all the major industries of Ontario and wreak havoc in its wake." The Toronto *Telegram* cried: "The time to check the foreign invasion is now. Premier Hepburn is to be commended for the prompt steps he has taken to make sure that any resort to violence will be speedily suppressed." The Hamilton *Spectator* warned: "If the CIO wins, it will not stop until it has gained the control it has been seeking across the line." And even the Oshawa *Times* cautioned that the Communists "are taking advantage of the situation." Indeed, all the Ontario press, with two significant exceptions, totally supported Hepburn's position. Only the Toronto *Star* and the Ottawa *Citizen* censured Hepburn for his actions. The *Citizen* called him "impetuous." But more trenchant in its criticism was the Toronto *Star,* which claimed that "no Government is warranted in forcibly interfering with labour so long as labour is doing only those things which the law sanctions." It asserted that Hepburn "cannot logically fight international labour while at the same time [supporting] international capital." But perhaps the clearest insight into Hepburn's behaviour came from the Communist *Daily Clarion,* which editorialized: "Hepburn fears the CIO unionism will mean the ultimate invasion of the mines . . . and Hepburn's close association with certain big mining magnates of northern Ontario has been a source of much gossip during the past year."[27]

On the afternoon of Friday, April 9, the second day of the strike, Millard phoned Hepburn and asked him to meet with a group of workers to hear "their side of the story." When Hepburn agreed, Millard and some members of the bargaining committee met in the premier's office for over an hour. According to Millard, Hepburn listened attentively to what each union man had to say, and when they were finished he told them that there was no reason why the strike could not be settled within an hour.[28]

After they emerged from the premier's office, Hepburn told the press gathered outside that he thought everything would be "straightened out fairly soon." Millard agreed, but added significantly:

"Things look brighter, but in any settlement that is reached, we expect recognition of our status as an international union." Notwithstanding Millard's qualification, Hepburn expressed confidence that the strike would be over by the following day and added that he was inviting union and management to meet with him Saturday afternoon in his office. Hepburn now obviously saw himself as a mediator. He also announced that Millard had agreed to allow company trucks to cross the picket line to pick up spare parts, something the union had not agreed to before.

Then the optimistic, cheerful Hepburn dismissed the strikers and the press and immediately went into conference with Chief Williams of the Ontario Provincial Police. He soon emerged, angry and shaken, again called in the press and in a strained, angry voice told them: "We now know what these CIO agitators are up to. We are advised only a few hours ago that they are working their way into the lumber camps and pulp mills and our mines. Well, that has got to stop and we are going to stop it! If necessary we'll raise an army to do it."[29] This was Hepburn's declaration of total war on the CIO. He had announced publicly that he was willing to call out the armed forces to protect the mines of northern Ontario from the CIO.

Meanwhile, Thompson was disturbed when he heard of Millard's actions. He stated that Millard had neither the authority to discuss a settlement with Hepburn nor to assure the premier that General Motors had the right to cross the picket line to pick up spare parts. He then called a meeting of the stewards and after a short conference announced that the union "would take no responsibility for accidents which may happen to any strikebreaker."[30]

Mayor Hall was outraged at Thompson's statements. To him, it seemed that Thompson was threatening violence. He publicly urged Thompson to retract his statement, and asked the union to disown Thompson's "menacing declaration of war." Privately, however, he called in Inspector Feiling of the provincial police and pleaded with him to arrest Thompson on a charge of intimidation. The inspector declined, suggesting that Hall present his evidence to the Crown attorney before taking action, since he would have "to be prepared to accept the responsibilities for developments if Thompson were arrested."[31]

A chastened Thompson soon retracted his statement "because of the danger of its being misinterpreted." However, that night, at a rally in St. Catharines, Millard told his audience of auto workers that "no attempt to stop any strikebreaker will be made, but we will find out where these men live and we will visit them and have a nice long talk."[32]

The first incident occurred early in the morning of April 10, a Saturday. Since the beginning of the strike the company had demanded the right to enter the plant and ship out spare parts. Hepburn supported this demand and threatened that the union's refusal to allow company trucks into the grounds would be met by force. Despite Millard's assurance that the trucks would be allowed to enter, Thompson had been adamant in his refusal. Nevertheless, after a lengthy, acrimonious discussion with Millard and other union officials, Thompson reluctantly submitted.[33]

At 10:30 that morning, the company sent several trucks to pass through the picket line in front of the plant gates. There the strikers were gathered seven deep and refused to let the trucks through. Within minutes, Mayor Hall was on the scene and, jumping on top of a car, urged the men to let the trucks in "because your leaders have ordered you to do so." The strikers ignored Hall and began rocking the trucks. It seemed that the riot Hepburn had predicted was finally underway. At just this moment Thompson arrived, jumped up beside Hall and shouted: "General Motors has been trying to arouse some sort of disturbance to get an excuse for bringing the Mounties in here and taking power out of your hands. Why let them?" He urged the men to let the trucks pass through the gates. Someone shouted that the trucks might contain machine guns, whereupon Hall begged the men to search the trucks if they wished but to let them pass. Thompson reminded the men that "as long as you maintain discipline you have the public on your side and you can't lose!"[34] The men cheered lustily and the trucks only had to fight their way through an army of catcalls and huzzahs to get into the plant. So the affair ended and it seemed certain that despite Hepburn's concern—or perhaps his hope—the strike would remain peaceful.

Just about this time, Harry Carmichael and J.B. Highfield were being ushered into Hepburn's office in Queen's Park. There they spent the entire morning planning strategy with the premier for the afternoon meeting with the union.

At 2:00 P.M. the union bargaining committee entered Hepburn's office. Significantly, Hugh Thompson was left outside in the corridor. Millard immediately asked Hepburn to admit Thompson to the negotiations, not as a member of the committee but as its solicitor. Hepburn refused. Millard then left the room to consult with Thompson and, on his return several minutes later, asked Hepburn if Thompson would be accepted as a member of the delegation. Hepburn again refused, declaring that he would not meet Thompson under any circumstances. Millard then walked out of the room and announced that "there was nothing left to discuss." Understandably ruffled at the turn of events,

Hepburn told newsmen outside his office that he would never negotiate with Thompson "or any of those men who are trying to dominate Canadian industry and inciting the same state of anarchy that exists below the border."[35]

The union negotiating team meanwhile went to the office of J.L. Cohen, a Toronto labour lawyer who had just been appointed the union's legal adviser. After a short discussion at Cohen's office the men left for Malton airport to welcome UAW President Homer Martin, who was arriving from Detroit to inspect the Oshawa situation. Several carloads of strikers had also driven to meet Martin, and it was in a cavalcade of more than a dozen cars that he was conveyed to the battleground over forty miles distant.

By the time this procession reached Oshawa, there were more than fifty cars behind the flag-draped convertible bearing Martin. As they moved down the main street, thousands of people who had been standing on the sidewalks to catch a glimpse of the smiling, waving UAW president fell in behind the cavalcade. A hastily assembled band gave forth with attempts at harmony; hundreds of cars parked along the main street tooted their horns. In the words of an observer, "men, women, children and babes in arms all shouted and cried themselves hoarse . . . This vast mass of humanity filled the street from side to side and stretched back for four or five blocks." As one of the participants remarked twenty-five years later: "It was a spectacle I shall never, never forget!" And Felix Lazarus, in an article for *Canadian Forum,* wrote: "Veteran labour leaders almost wept when they saw this amazing display of enthusiasm . . . never in all the history of the Canadian labour movement had a town been so completely captured by the sentiment of unionism."[36]

After circling the General Motors plant, the parade stopped in front of the Genosha Hotel where the slight, bespectacled ex-Baptist minister and newly chosen president of the UAW stood on the hood of his car and exclaimed: "Never have I seen such enthusiasm and unity . . . With me I bring the greetings of four hundred thousand auto workers in the United States who are with you in this your first step in creating a great brotherhood of auto workers throughout North America." According to the chief of police in Oshawa, it was the largest demonstration in that city's history.

At a huge rally of the strikers that evening, Martin warned that "if General Motors doesn't make cars in Canada under union conditions, they won't make cars in the United States at all." He called Hepburn "a puppet of General Motors . . . a little two-by-four who is trying to sweep aside the traditions of a thousand years." As for the premier's remarks about foreign agitators, the ex-minister found an analogy in the Holy Book. As he put it: "In the Bible we read of a man who stirred up the people. He was an agitator, a foreign agitator according to some because he came from heaven. I would be glad to introduce him to the premier." Martin spoke for more than two hours, encouraging the workers and promising them the full support of their UAW brothers in the United States. The rally ended with the exuberant workers in a mood of defiance. They had heard their leader's response to Hepburn's declaration of war and they were more determined than ever to see the strike through to the very end.[37]

For the next few days the morale of the strikers was kept at a peak level by the unusually warm spring weather, the backing and material support offered by the Oshawa business community and the thousands of letters and telegrams of support from various labour groups, churches and individuals throughout Canada. The strikers were also heartened by the large numbers of tourists from Toronto and the surrounding district who drove through Oshawa "to take a peek at the strike," and stopped to talk and encourage the pickets. The competition between the Young Communist League and the Co-operative Commonwealth Youth Movement also benefited the strikers. Every day, a truck from Toronto arrived at the plant carrying that day's edition of the *Daily Clarion,* which was handed out free to the strikers. It also brought a host of active Young Communists eager to help wherever they could. Similarly, cars and trucks bearing equally enthusiastic young CCYMers from Toronto arrived regularly to add to the number of young people anxious to help the pickets by marching, making coffee and doing odd jobs.[38]

Meanwhile, on Saturday, April 10, the federal minister of Labour, Norman Rogers, had wired Mayor Hall offering the services of his department to settle the strike. Earlier in the day, Rogers had announced that he would intervene in the Oshawa strike even if only one party to the dispute would agree to federal intervention. He added, of course, that it would be better "if both sides were willing." Hall had immediately taken Rogers's offer to the General Motors officials. When Hepburn learned of the offer he angrily wired Mackenzie King that he "deeply resented the unwarranted interference" of Rogers and that he believed that the General Motors Company would "not be a party to such treachery." He added gratuitously that "this action is quite in common with the treatment that this government has received from most of your ministers."[39]

When he received Hepburn's telegram, King was beside himself with rage. From the beginning he had felt that the Oshawa situation was "a delicate one." Although he also believed that Rogers had not acted wisely in offering to negotiate before a request had been made to his department by both parties, he felt that Rogers was only doing his duty. King, however, was totally opposed to any federal intervention. The "greatest danger," as he saw it, "was being drawn into the controversy . . . The moment Rogers or officers of his department intervene, they would have to say at once whether they favoured or did not favour recognition of the CIO local organization. The poker would immediately be in the fire. We would be linked up in opposition to the Ontario government and said to have lent the aid of the federal government to the forces of communism."[40]

Even though he felt that Hepburn "had become pretty well beside himself in the attitude he was taking towards the Oshawa situation," after consulting with Rogers, King sent a conciliatory telegram to Hepburn informing him that the federal government "has neither the intention nor the desire to intervene in any way without the consent of both parties to the dispute and so long as the matter is being dealt with by the authorities of the province of Ontario."[41]

Feeling that he had the federal government on the run, Hepburn was quick to press his advantage. Despite the fact that the city seemed relatively peaceful, on April 13 Hepburn informed Lapointe that the situation in Oshawa was desperate and that at least another hundred RCMP reinforcements would be required as he had received word that the Communists were about to foment "disturbances." At the same time, Hepburn called in the press and told them that it was absolutely necessary to increase the number of police in Oshawa because he had a conclusive secret report proving that the CIO was working "hand-in-glove with international communism." He affirmed that there had been "no real trouble in Oshawa yet, but the situation is becoming more tense . . . it appears that the Communists are anxious to take an active part in case of disturbance." He then stated that he had ordered the provincial police to enroll two hundred "or if necessary" four hundred special police officers. So were born the infamous Hepburn Hussars, or Sons of Mitches as they were irreverently known in Oshawa.[42]

Colonel Fraser Hunter, a Toronto Liberal MPP, was appointed to aid General Williams in recruiting and mobilizing this special police force. Within hours of Hepburn's announcement the Toronto *Star* reported that Queen's Park was "swarming with men ready to volunteer and be sworn in." Despite his remarks to the press about the need for this new force, Hepburn does not seem to have been motivated by the deteriorating situation in Oshawa. The secret reports that he got several times daily from undercover agents in the city indicated that "the strike is proceeding smoothly . . . with no threat of violence in sight." In fact, the strike was so peaceful that an American movie cameraman had offered two strikers five dollars each if they would stage a mock fight "to add some local colour to his story." He was quickly removed.[43]

When informed by Lapointe of Hepburn's request for more RCMP reinforcements, King was furious. He feared that Hepburn's activities "would cut the Liberal Party in two if not into four." He disliked Hepburn's statements equating the CIO with communism because "in this way he has gone out of his way to raise a great issue in this country, the frightful possibilities of which no one can foresee. The truth of the matter is he is in the hands of McCullagh of the *Globe* ... The situation as he has brought it into being has all the elements in it that are to be found in the present appalling situation in Spain. Hepburn has become a fascist leader and has sought to have labour in its struggle against organized capital put into the position of being under communist direction and control. Action of this kind is little short of criminal."[44]

On the following day, April 14, King met with his cabinet to discuss Hepburn's request for the RCMP reinforcements. He began the discussion by saying that the Oshawa situation had "all the elements in it of the Spanish situation, the creating of a fascist and a communist party in Canada, and a conflict between the two when nothing more in reality was at stake than the right of men to organize in recognition of their chosen organization." According to King, "Lapointe seemed to feel that he should send more police, and his whole sympathies seemed to be against the men because they were associated with Lewis's organization. He kept repeating that they had organized sit-down strikes in the States, etc. I pointed out that nothing of the kind had been attempted in Canada. There was not evidence of any overt act of any kind. The cabinet was solidly behind me in the view that no more police should be sent. We discussed at the time as to whether we should not direct Hepburn's attention to the act which enables municipalities and provinces to call out the militia in case of need. It was wisely decided not to direct attention specifically to this feature which is already known to the provincial government. What we suggested should be done was to point out that with the circumstances what they at the present time are, the government, having regard to its responsibilities generally throughout the Dominion, did not send any further police. With the kind of fight Hepburn is shaping up there is every possibility that strikes may take place at St. Catharines, Windsor, and other points and disorder may become more or less general. Lapointe did not like sending the wire but said he would carry out the wishes of the council and did so."[45]

Immediately following that meeting, King and Rogers held a press conference. They announced that there would be no federal intervention in the strike until Hepburn himself requested it. King maintained that his "only desire is to be helpful and that we couldn't help if the Ontario government opposed our efforts." Rogers also issued a statement stressing his support of "the right of workmen to organize for every lawful purpose . . . The right of association for legitimate purposes should not be denied, and labour should not be refused the means of organizing for collective bargaining." It was clear from that press conference that King was disturbed over the behaviour of Hepburn. As the New York *Times* reporter in Ottawa put it, King feared that "Hepburn's antics would bring to a head forces in Canada which many have predicted may ultimately divide this democracy into left and right extremism."[46]

These statements of King and Rogers, in the words of the Toronto *Star,* "made Hepburn's pot boil over." He immediately sent Lapointe a telegram condemning the federal government for its "vacillating attitude." He also requested the removal of all RCMP reinforcements as he had decided that he could no longer depend on federal aid "and would take necessary actions to preserve law and order within the province on his own." In place of the RCMP Hepburn announced that he would increase his special police force to four hundred men, half of whom were already on hand at the legislature building and the balance of whom would be mustered at once, "many of them to be university lads." It seemed that a goodly number of University of Toronto students had crossed the road to Queen's Park and enrolled in Hepburn's special police force. Hepburn also informed the press that he had been advised by Major Fletcher of the RCMP that his men were to take no active part until it was shown that provincial police were unable to cope with the situation. As Hepburn put it: "We were paying for a police force that was of little or no assistance to us. I want to tell the people of Ontario that the Dominion police were brought in here at our own expense and instructed not to take any part, but to stand by until our fellows had their heads broken."[47]

The response to Hepburn's plea for more police recruits was overwhelming. Shortly after the recruiting office opened, "standing room only" signs were posted and within two hours, Colonel Hunter, the head of the force, announced that Hepburn's quota had been reached. Hepburn then delivered a pep talk to his new "Hussars." He told them that they would be issued regular provincial police uniforms and would be paid twenty-five dollars a week. He also related to the men that the Eglinton Hunt Club had offered the force sixty of their horses. Then, to loud cheers, Hepburn announced that he would continue to use their services even after the Oshawa strike was over as he could no longer depend on the federal government to maintain law and order in Ontario.[48]

During these manoeuvres, Hepburn still found time to fire two members of his cabinet who had opposed his actions during the strike, Arthur Roebuck, the attorney-general, and Labour Minister David Croll. Hepburn had originally taken Roebuck and Croll into his cabinet because they represented the significant urban, radical, left-Liberal and pro-labour element that had elected him in 1934. Now there was no longer room for this element in the Hepburn cabinet. Both Croll and Roebuck had been out of Toronto for the first few days of the strike; when they returned, Hepburn had refused to meet them. Immediately upon his return, Croll had contacted Chappell to learn what had gone wrong with the negotiations, which had been proceeding so smoothly before he left on his vacation. Chappell told him that the premier's return from Florida on April 8 had changed the situation drastically and that the company had decided to break off negotiations since Hepburn had promised that he would do all in his power "to break the union in Oshawa."[49]

On Wednesday, April 14, Hepburn sent both ministers letters asking for their resignations as they were "not in accord" with his policy of "fighting against the inroads of the Lewis organization and communism in general." At the same time Hepburn called in the press and told them: "There is absolutely no turning back now . . . this is a fight to the finish and we must have solidarity in our ranks." He then told reporters that he had taken such firm action against the CIO not only because Ontario was facing an economic and industrial crisis but also because, "if the CIO wins at Oshawa it has other plants it will step into . . . it will be the mines, [it will] demoralize the industry, and send stocks tumbling."[50]

Later that day Croll and Roebuck sent Hepburn their letters of resignation. Both complained that they had not been consulted before they were fired. Both stated that the CIO had absolutely nothing to do with communism and both expressed their support for the workers and condemned Hepburn's position—as Croll memorably phrased it: "My place is marching with the workers rather than riding with General Motors." Croll bluntly accused Hepburn of "having passed the borders of Liberalism," and Roebuck summarized: "There is no disagreement as to the maintenance of law and order. If there is settled divergence of opinion it is as to the display of unnecessary or provocative force, . . . the maintenance of impartiality by the state in industrial disputes, . . . the right of labour to such forms of organization [as it] may choose, . . . its freedom to speak through such channels of representation as it may name, and its right to collective bargaining."[51]

The reaction to these dismissals was predictable. The *Globe and Mail* asserted that "Croll and Roebuck must fall in line enthusiastically or give way to others who will uphold the integrity and good name of the province in this fight for principle." On the other hand, the Toronto *Star* editorialized that Hepburn had "lost his two most outstanding cabinet ministers . . . because they refused to sacrifice their conscientious beliefs and adherence to the welfare of the workers to Hepburn's impetuous, unfair and unwise attacks on the rights of labour." Graham Spry, a leading member of the CCF, invited both men to join his party. The Toronto and District Labour Council called Hepburn "Canada's Hitler" and charged that he had fired Croll and Roebuck because they believed in and fought for "the rights of the common worker and organized labour." The humour of this situation, however, was not lost on one political pundit who, noting that Hepburn had taken over Croll's portfolios of Labour, Welfare and Municipal Affairs, commented: "Hepburn is now Prime Minister, Minister of Labour, Minister of Public Welfare, Minister of Municipal Affairs and Provincial Treasurer. If anyone sees him talking to himself he will be able to conclude that the Ontario cabinet is having a meeting."[52]

With all these activities in Queen's Park and on Parliament Hill, the workers in Oshawa must have wondered whether anyone remembered the strike. Certainly Hepburn seemed to have other things on his mind, at least until he was informed that at a meeting with the General Motors executive in Detroit, Homer Martin had agreed that the Oshawa strike "should be settled on a Canadian basis without recognition of the CIO . . . and that it should be settled between company officials and the various representatives of the local unions involved." Hepburn rapturously termed Martin's decision "a surrender of the CIO of its attempts to extend [its] mass product industrialization drive into Canada," and a victory for his own attempt to "root communism out of the Canadian labour movement." He then phoned Millard and invited him to resume negotiations at his office. The latter demurred until Martin, who was due in Oshawa that same day, could explain to the angry members of his union why he had reneged on his promises.[53]

Early Friday morning, April 16, Martin arrived in Oshawa to explain to the strikers his "surrender" in Detroit. He explained to them that he had accepted a four-point program to settle the strike. This involved opening negotiations at once, establishing a seniority system similar to the one accepted by the UAW in the United States, agreeing to a contract that would run concurrently with the one signed in the United States and finally, drawing up individual contracts with the local unions in Windsor and St. Catharines. The key point to the UAW, of course, was the third, which meant that in future, American and Canadian contracts would be negotiated at the same time to cover plants on both sides of the border. To bolster the morale of the strikers further, Martin arranged the first conference telephone call in Canadian history in which he spoke to the presidents of all the forty-five UAW locals in the United States from San Francisco to Atlanta. The call lasted for twenty minutes and at its conclusion the UAW president announced that the Oshawa local had been promised all the support necessary to win the strike.[54]

Immediately after the call, Millard, Thompson and J.L. Cohen left for Queen's Park to continue negotiations with Hepburn. At two P.M. Cohen was ushered into Hepburn's office and was enthusiastically greeted by the confident, jubilant premier. Already in the office were J.B. Highfield and Harry Carmichael, who had arrived there earlier in the day. Hepburn told Cohen that he had been asked to do all the negotiating for the company. Consequently, he led the union's lawyer into another office where they argued for over an hour over the status of Charlie Millard. At one point Hepburn left the room to allow Cohen to place a long-distance call to Martin in Oshawa for further instructions. Hepburn then handed Cohen a document which he demanded must be signed before negotiations could continue. The document contained one sentence: "J.L. Cohen and Charles Millard are negotiators for the employees' union of the General Motors Company of Oshawa, and are no way connected or instructed by the CIO." Cohen agreed that he and Millard would sign the document and then discussion turned to the seniority clause. Hepburn presented the company proposal which Cohen thought was acceptable but the lawyer wished to consult with Millard before committing himself.[55]

He then went out into the corridor and placed the company's proposals before Millard and Thompson. Both agreed that they were reasonable but Millard suggested that they phone Martin before accepting. They were directed by a reporter to a nearby vault which contained a phone. It was just as the three men entered the vault and Thompson began to dial that Hepburn hurried out of his office, rushed to the vault, took one quick look at the three men, turned, hastened back to his office and announced to the reporters gathered in the corridor that as far as he was concerned the negotiations were over. "We aren't going to settle this by remote control!" he shouted.

The three union men were as bewildered as the newspapermen by the sudden turn in events. Hepburn soon came out of his office and told reporters that it was "nothing but a complete double cross to have Thompson and Martin try to run this conference by remote control... Thompson showed great temerity to even appear here, let alone to enter my private vault where my personal, valuable and top-secret papers are stored . . . Inasmuch as I have repeatedly asserted my determination never to negotiate with the hirelings of J.L. Lewis there was nothing left to do but to bid these gentlemen goodbye!''

This statement only added to the confusion of the reporters, as they had often used the phone in the premier's vault. Indeed, on Hepburn's orders, tables had been placed in the room so that reporters in their spare time could ''sit around, drink tea, or play cards.'' It seemed that Hepburn had used the incident only as an excuse to break off talks he never had any intention of completing. The three union negotiators then met Homer Martin again at the Royal York Hotel in Toronto. At this meeting, according to Millard, Martin promised the local the full financial support of the UAW. He also phoned Charles Wilson, the vice-president of General Motors in the United States, and warned him that if the strike were not settled soon, the UAW would close down all General Motors facilities in the United States.[56]

Hepburn had two reasons for not wishing to continue negotiations that day. Firstly, he had received secret reports from his undercover police agent in Oshawa informing him that ''the pickets are half-hearted, most of the strikers are impatient and unhappy . . . and everyone around here is demanding an immediate settlement.'' The workers, according to this source, also felt ''betrayed by Martin's surrender.'' Hepburn believed that if the company would hold off negotiating for a short period, the workers would soon be on their knees begging for a settlement on management terms.[57]

But perhaps the major reason Hepburn called off the talks was the ominous secret reports he was receiving from his agents in northern Ontario of increased CIO activity in the gold mines. These reports informed him that a CIO organizer, George Anderson, had threatened to call a strike if the mine owners refused to meet union terms. It seems that Hepburn was now more than ever convinced that the CIO had to be totally crushed at Oshawa before it succeeded in organizing the mines of Ontario. As the general manager of the Hollinger Mine privately warned him: ''The CIO is only waiting for the Oshawa results before mobilizing the mines.'' The premier therefore issued a statement declaring that his Oshawa stand had greatly handicapped ''the CIO's drive to dominate Canadian industry'' and that he was ''more concerned with the CIO threat in the mine fields than in the automobile industry . . . for Oshawa is only an attempt by the CIO to pave the way for its real drive against the fundamental wealth of the province—its mine fields.'' He then issued his battle cry: ''Let me tell Lewis here and now that he and his gang will never get their greedy paws on the mines of northern Ontario as long as I am prime minister.'' He was immediately supported by his mine-owner friends Joe Wright, Jules Timmins, Jules Bache and J.P. Bickell, who warned that they would "close the mines before they would negotiate with the CIO." More emphatically, Timmins of the Hollinger Mine warned: "Under no circumstances will we recognize the CIO and should the CIO interfere with our operations we have the assurance of the government that ample protection will be given our men who are desirous of continuing to work."[58]

The fears of Hepburn and the mine owners, whose profits in 1936 had reached fifty per cent on total production, were underscored by a major gold-stock collapse on the Toronto Stock Exchange on Monday, April 19—a collapse due largely to the rumours of CIO activities in the gold fields. On the same day, however, it seemed that the Oshawa strike had been settled. All day long Mayor Hall had been running between the offices of Highfield and Millard carrying proposals and counter-proposals. By evening these "remote-control" negotiations had succeeded, with Highfield agreeing to the four points of the Detroit agreement and Millard and Thompson agreeing that the men would return to work before the contract was signed. All that remained was for the strikers to ratify the agreement. That night, however, at a large rally the men repudiated their own strike leaders. Even the union stewards, when told of the settlement, voted to a man to turn the proposals down. When Hall got up to announce the settlement, he was hooted off the stage by the strikers, who were determined to hold out in their demand for a signed contract before they returned to work. Tears streaming down his face, Hall attempted to argue with the men. He failed, and the strike continued.[59]

It was obvious to Thompson and Millard that the strike had to be settled quickly. They would accept any reasonable terms because there was absolutely no financial support coming from the UAW in the United States. Homer Martin had made promises to the strikers that he had neither the intention nor the ability to fulfil. He had not consulted John L. Lewis nor any CIO or UAW official before promising the Oshawa men full financial support. In fact, the entire strike was carried on without "one cent" of aid from the American unions. Yet on Tuesday, April 20, Thompson announced that the first instalment of the hundred thousand dollars promised by Martin had arrived and the Oshawa *Times* carried a photograph of Thompson depositing the money at the union's bank. Unknown to everyone but Thompson and Millard, the union treasurer had withdrawn all the local funds from the bank the preceding afternoon. It was this money that Thompson with a great deal of publicity and fanfare had deposited as the "first instalment from the USA." In this way, the company, Hepburn and the men on the picket line were led to believe that the strikers were receiving the fullest support from the international.[60]

In fact, the strikers were totally on their own. They had no savings, nor was there any strike pay to tide them over. Their earlier jubilation had worn off, and they were becoming increasingly desperate. Nevertheless, they rejected the Hall proposal even though it was supported by their own leaders. But their leaders were unsure how much longer they could hold out.

To buoy up the strikers, the UAW executive board held a special meeting in Washington to discuss the strike. Martin presented his report and, reneging on his promise to the strikers, stated that he was "personally against a sympathy strike" as this would "jeopardize our entire union." Walter Reuther, UAW vice-president, suggested that the Oshawa local sign a temporary agreement that would be in effect until the termination of the General Motors pact in the United States; when a new contract was signed with the company, all Canadian workers would be included. The executive finally decided to leave negotiations to the men in Oshawa. The board also agreed that it would be impossible to support the strike financially as the union treasury was empty. Nevertheless, for purposes of publicity, Martin wired Thompson that the executive had "unanimously voted necessary financial aid"—a telegram which both Martin and Thompson released to the press.[61]

Hepburn was not completely fooled; he had been informed by his agents in Oshawa that the union was in trouble. When Thompson announced that he was going to Washington "to discuss union matters," J.J. McIntyre, one of Hepburn's informants and a *Globe and Mail* reporter, wired the premier that "Thompson is hi-tailing it to Washington as it is obvious he needs help . . . he is running out to get his hand strengthened." Hepburn had also met secretly with a delegation of strikers who told him that most of the men wished to return to work at once. Thus, when he was informed by Highfield that the company was anxious to re-open negotiations, a frantic Hepburn took the almost unbelievable step of wiring Colonel McLaughlin, the president of GM in Canada, who was vacationing somewhere in the Caribbean on his yacht, to order management to suspend negotiations with the strikers as he had "confidential reports that a 'total collapse' of the strike was imminent."[62]

The union negotiating committee, however, was ready to sign an agreement on almost any terms and General Motors was anxious to begin producing cars again. Realizing the union's precarious situation, Millard and Thompson decided that the strike must be settled at any cost. Therefore Millard phoned Highfield to request a reopening of negotiations. Highfield was naturally agreeable and a meeting was arranged for Hepburn's office on Wednesday, April 21 at two P.M. Hepburn now had the upper hand. He made Cohen and Millard sign a document stating that neither of them was "instructed by or represented a committee known as the CIO." Cohen further signed a statement that he had definite word from Homer Martin that "neither he nor Thompson would return to Oshawa or Toronto during the negotiations." When Hepburn got word from his undercover agents that "Claude Kramer, a CIO agent, was in Oshawa agitating the men" and that even if the negotiating committee repudiated the CIO, "the men at a mass meeting will take matters out of the hands of the negotiating committee and hold out for recognition of the international union," the Ontario premier asked Millard and Cohen to sign a statement that neither knew Kramer nor had any intention of discussing the agreement with him. It seemed that Hepburn had finally achieved his goal. The agreement would be signed by the local union only, and the CIO had been effectively excluded.[63]

After another meeting with Cohen and Millard on the following day a smiling Hepburn emerged from his office late in the afternoon and told newsmen that the strike was over, subject to the ratification of the union. He then arranged with Defence Minister Ian Mackenzie for the strikers to use the Oshawa armoury for their vote.

The vote was scheduled to begin at ten A.M. Friday, April 23. By nine that morning a cheerful throng of two thousand strikers was already assembled outside the armoury, four abreast in a line stretching several blocks, anxious to get in. By noon, just before the voting began, Millard announced that he was so sure of the results that he had already instructed pickets to leave their posts and begin moving tents and other equipment. At 1:45 Cohen announced that the vote to end the strike was 2205 in favour and only 36 against. To the joy of all, Mayor Hall then announced that he would ask that all the bars in Oshawa be reopened immediately. Then, to the strains of *For He's a Jolly Good Fellow,* Police Chief Owen Friend was carried to the stage where he announced that the fifteen days of the strike had been the most peaceful in Oshawa's history. No one had been arrested in connection with the strike. Arrangements were also made for boxing matches, parades and dances to celebrate the end of the strike.[64]

At 2:45 that afternoon Millard and Cohen arrived at Hepburn's office and signed the contract to end the strike. After fifteen days, the Oshawa strike was officially over.

The question of who had won the strike now became as prickly as the issues of the strike themselves. In order to justify his somewhat extraordinary activities on behalf of management, Hepburn strove desperately to prove that he had held the CIO at bay. There was no doubt that Hepburn had won a semantic victory. The CIO had been repudiated in writing by the union negotiators and the agreement had been signed between "General Motors Company of Canada and the employees of the company at Oshawa." Nowhere was there any mention of the CIO, nor even of Local 222 of the UAW. Millard, in the company's view, was simply "an employee on leave of absence." As the *Globe and Mail* put it: "The settlement . . . was a permanent defeat for Lewisism and Communism in Canada . . . no matter what false and flimsy claims may be put forward by Lewis agents and their comrades, the Reds, the CIO is repudiated."[65]

In fact, it was anything but a victory for Hepburn and his anti-CIO forces. As the *Daily Clarion* correctly pointed out, the Oshawa strike was "the dawn of a new era . . . for the CIO victory in Oshawa . . . has broken into the hitherto unorganized and terrorized mass-production industry." At a rally of the strikers, both Millard and Cohen stated that the settlement was a tremendous victory for the CIO and that any attempt to claim that the union had not been recognized was, in Millard's words, "just child's play." J.L. Cohen added that "the agreement was so worded and the interpretation was so planned that there can be no doubt about the union's recognition." He further emphasized that the company had met every single one of the union's demands—the forty-four-hour week, wage increases, the seniority system, a grievance committee, a minimum wage, and the promise never to discriminate against an employee for union activity, past, present or future. The strikers then passed a resolution "affirming the alliance with the UAW and the CIO with which our union is affiliated" and sent it on to Hepburn as an expression of their feelings.[66]

That the settlement was less than a victory even Hepburn was ready to admit. In the words of the *Financial Post*, he had hoped to demolish the CIO in one great stand, but had succeeded merely in "holding it at arm's length." Even George McCullagh (who later took the credit for Hepburn's anti-CIO stand) admitted that the settlement at Oshawa was not the body blow to the CIO he had hoped for. Ironically, McCullagh and Hepburn did not realize how close they had come to striking that fatal blow. According to Millard and Thompson, the union was "lucky" to get any type of settlement. It was their feeling that, had the strike not been settled that Friday, it would have fallen apart within a few days. In fact Thompson had told Millard to agree to any proposal the company made since the union was totally bankrupt and the men now realized that they had been "bamboozled" by Martin's lavish promises. Fortunately for the union, Hepburn's espionage system had failed him at a most critical moment and the premier actually believed, as he later told his personal aides, that he had got "the best he could under the circumstances." Had Hepburn been able to keep the company away from the bargaining table for several more days, he would likely have achieved a complete victory, totally crushed the strike and, perhaps with it, the CIO in Canada.[67]

The Oshawa strike was a turning point in the history of the Canadian labour movement. It marked the birth of industrial unionism in Canada. The achievements of the Oshawa strikers in fighting and defeating both the power of big business and the provincial government inspired workers throughout the country, and gave the CIO the impetus it so badly needed to begin organization in the mass-production industries in the country. Just as Roosevelt became "the best organizer" for the CIO in the United States, so, in a negative way, Hepburn became the CIO's most successful organizer north of the border. The Oshawa strike, and particularly Premier Hepburn's antics during it, suddenly turned the rather limited CIO organizing campaign into precisely the kind of violent crusade Hepburn and his mine-owner friends had feared. The Oshawa strikers had won a great victory for themselves but, even more important for the CIO, they had created the psychology of success and the enthusiasm needed for a massive organizing effort. What Akron and Flint had inspired south of the border, Oshawa was to inspire north of it. It was a landmark in Canadian labour history.

What is perhaps most significant about the Oshawa strike is that it was conducted by Canadians without much assistance from the CIO. Although Hugh Thompson was ostensibly in charge of organization, most of the organizing was in fact done by Canadians. Whatever financial assistance the strikers were given came from churches and neighbours. Not a penny of aid came from the United States. Both the CIO and the UAW concluded that neither had the men nor the money to help the strikers; they even refused to call a sympathy strike of GM workers in the United States to support the strikers in Oshawa. Though the UAW had publicly promised to send one hundred thousand dollars, in the end all it could deliver was its best wishes. Thus, what the Oshawa strikers achieved, they achieved on their own. The General Motors Company agreed to a settlement in Oshawa not because of the threats of the CIO but because it desperately needed cars for the Commonwealth markets, and these could only be built in Oshawa. Fear of losing those markets to Ford and Chrysler, rather than fear of John L. Lewis and Hugh Thompson, forced General Motors to recognize the union.

Thus the role of the CIO in the Oshawa strike seems ambiguous. The strike was conducted, financed and settled by Canadians. In fact, when the settlement was finally reached, Thompson was back in the

United States. The final negotiations were handled by Canadians. The CIO played no actual role in the strike except in the minds of Hepburn, the mine owners and, of course, most importantly, in the minds of the strikers themselves. Though the victory at Oshawa was a victory for Canadians, it was immediately hailed across the country as a great CIO triumph. Because Hepburn had defined the enemy as the CIO, the CIO was given full credit for a struggle it had done little to win.

With the victory at Oshawa, the CIO began a successful crusade to organize the industrial work force in Canada. Thus for the Canadian working man, perhaps no event in the history of the Canadian labour movement in the past fifty years is more important than the Oshawa strike. That fifteen-day walkout of some four thousand workers marks the birth of the labour movement in Canada as we know it today.

The political ramifications of the strike were equally significant. Hepburn was obviously displeased with the settlement. He had hoped to demolish the CIO in Ontario by smashing the strike at Oshawa, but he had failed. For this failure he attributed much of the blame to the hated Mackenzie King who, he felt, had undermined him at every step during the strike. So profound was his contempt for King and for the CIO that any scheme, no matter how outlandish or shocking, that would cripple both, was acceptable to the embittered premier. Just such a scheme was suggested to him by George McCullagh. It was a plan that would destroy Mackenzie King, break the CIO and perhaps, if Hepburn had his way, end the two-party system in Canada.

Unfortunately for Hepburn, it was also a plan that required absolute secrecy. But to Hepburn's chagrin, the Toronto *Star* had learned about it and, by publishing the details of the scheme, aborted it. On May 1 the *Star* carried the incredible story that Hepburn, who led "a party with 70 seats in Queen's Park," had offered to form a coalition and indeed turn over the premiership to Earl Rowe, the Conservative "who leads a party with only 14 seats." The premier, realizing that the scheme could never come to fruition now, heatedly denied it.[68]

But his denials were something less than candid. The *Star* report was accurate. It appears that on the day the strike ended, Friday, April 23, Hepburn informed the lieutenant-governor of the province, Herbert Bruce, that Ontario was in serious trouble and that it might be necessary to dissolve the House and to form a Union government. He later gave Bruce a list of Conservatives he would accept into his cabinet and arranged to meet the leader of the opposition, Earl Rowe.[69]

On April 27, he met Rowe in the Royal York Hotel. He told the wary Conservative leader that because of the great threat posed to the Ontario economy and especially the gold mines by the CIO and the

Communists, George McCullagh and other "interested parties" had proposed to him a solution. As Rowe recollects: "Hepburn stated that the only way to beat the CIO and stop them from getting into the mines would be to form a strong and united government, and that this could only be done if the Conservatives and Liberal parties formed a coalition." According to Rowe, Hepburn said: "Earl, I am prepared to resign and turn the office of prime minister over to you . . . I will help, and be your minister of Agriculture . . . if you think you need me, but I would like to spend more time throughout Canada selling this idea . . . You can name half the cabinet . . . I have also been advised to assure you that all your debts will be covered, and an honorarium of several hundred thousand dollars will be provided . . . Now how can you refuse such an offer?" He also told Rowe that such a coalition would be the "best way" to "get rid" of Mackenzie King.[70]

The flabbergasted Rowe left the meeting to consult other prominent Tories, though he did inform Hepburn that he was opposed to the idea since he was "named leader of a great party one and a half years ago to serve it and maintain its place in Canadian affairs . . . not for a short and easy road to the prime-ministership." After consulting various prominent federal and provincial Conservatives, most of whom opposed the scheme, Rowe officially rejected it, but not before his own lieutenant and the party's chief organizer in the province, George Drew, resigned in protest over Rowe's decision. As Rowe recollects, Drew told him at a private meeting that "the time had come to end the two-party system of government in Ontario since only a strong government could destroy communism." When Rowe spurned his plea, Drew resigned.[71]

Though Hepburn's scheme had failed, it indicated the extent to which he was ready to go to destroy the CIO and, of course, Mackenzie King. The plan had originated and been sponsored by George McCullagh and several of his mining-magnate friends. In order to protect their province, and naturally their mines, from the CIO they were ready to end the two-party system. It indicated the depth of the hostility the CIO would have to overcome in Canada before it became a viable force.

The events in Oshawa also had a more far-reaching political impact. Totally disillusioned with King's behaviour during the strike, Hepburn decided that the time was ripe to break with the prime minister and to look for new political allies. On June 3, speaking to a meeting of the Canadian Life Assurance Association in Toronto, the Ontario premier condemned King for his "vacillating" attitude towards the CIO and communism and proudly proclaimed that only his actions in Oshawa had saved Canada from the CIO "criminals." He then announced that he was "no longer a Mackenzie King Liberal" and he pointedly praised "the forceful and praiseworthy" activities of Premier Maurice Duplessis of Quebec. He looked forward, he said, to working more closely in the future with the Quebec premier. This speech was a harbinger of the notorious "unholy alliance" of Hepburn and Duplessis, which would bedevil Canadian politics for the next few years and whose goal was the destruction of Mackenzie King.[72]

Naturally, neither the break with King nor the alliance with Duplessis were direct results of the Oshawa strike. Both had been in the making long before the CIO arrived in Canada. But according to Hepburn, King's behaviour during the strike was "the final straw"—the breaking point between the two. There had never been much love lost between them, but a *modus vivendi* had been built up during the first few years of Hepburn's premiership. It was this that was destroyed by the Oshawa strike.[73]

The strike also became the major issue in the Ontario elections that fall. Campaigning on an anti-CIO ticket, Hepburn swept the province. The helpless Rowe was overwhelmed. So popular was the premier's position on the CIO that fully fifty per cent of the people of Ontario —including many workers and even the riding of Oshawa—voted Liberal. It was obviously a vote of confidence from the people of Ontario for Hepburn's behaviour during the strike, and perhaps for his attacks on Mackenzie King.

But the 1937 election was the high-water mark of Liberalism in Ontario. Never again, at least to the present time, would the Liberal party be a serious contender in Ontario politics. With the physical and mental deterioration of Hepburn, the Liberal party fell apart. In the 1943 election it won only 15 seats compared to 34 for the CCF and 38 for the Conservatives. In 1945, it managed to hold only 11. In neither of these elections did the Liberals win any urban or working-class seats and in every election since, they have managed to win only a handful. In an urban and industrial province, failure to win more than a few such ridings has doomed the Liberal party to opposition.

In this, the story of the strange death of Liberal Ontario, the Oshawa strike plays a prominent role. Until the strike, Hepburn and the Liberals had a corner on the labour, progressive and left-wing vote in the province. But Hepburn's conduct during the strike had, in the words of the *New Commonwealth*, "in one fell swoop lost the Liberals the support of labour throughout the province." Hepburn's magic and the anti-CIO hysteria swept the province in the 1937 election, but the Liberal party emerged as a right-wing, anti-labour party. As Professor Dennis Wrong commented, "Hepburn . . . faced the electorate in 1937 as an anti-labour candidate. He and his party were therefore not in a position to win over the rising labour movement that emerged as a new force in Ontario politics in the war and postwar years."[74]

In his "swing to the right," Hepburn had taken the Liberal party with him. A vacuum was created on the left which, following the 1937 election, was rapidly filled by the rejuvenated CCF. Thus, even though the party failed to win a seat in the 1937 provincial election, the Oshawa strike was also a turning point in the fortunes of the CCF in Ontario. For the first time it became the party of the left and of labour in Ontario, and particularly of the vastly expanding industrial work force that was organized following the victory in Oshawa.[75]

Today, more than a generation later, the impact of the strike on the Canadian labour movement and on politics in Ontario is still unmistakable. Certainly the birth of industrial unionism in Canada, and to some extent the growth of the CCF and the decline of Liberalism in Ontario, are all legacies of the Oshawa strike.

Notes

1. New York *Times,* 14 February 1937.

2. Interviews with Charles Millard, Joseph Salsberg, George Burt.

3. Interviews with Charles Millard, Louis Fine, Art Schultz.

4. Interviews with Charles Millard, "Tommy" Thomas.

5. Hepburn to Ian Mackenzie, 25 February 1937; Hepburn to Arthur Roebuck, 26 February 1937; Thomas Crerar to Hepburn, 4 March 1937, Hepburn Papers, Archives of Ontario.

6. Toronto *Daily Star,* 1 October 1933.

7. Toronto *Daily Star,* 1, 14 August 1934; 4, 12 September 1934.

8. Interviews with David Croll, Arthur Roebuck. For an excellent study of the relationship between Hepburn and McCullagh see Brian Young, "The Leadership League," (M.A. thesis, Queen's University, 1966). Also see N. McKenty, *Mitch Hepburn* (Toronto: McClelland & Stewart, 1967), pp. 92-93.

9. Toronto *Daily Star,* 4 March 1937; *Canadian Forum,* April 1937; Toronto *Telegram,* 5 March 1937.

10. Toronto *Telegram,* 8 March 1937.

11. *Daily Clarion,* 20 March 1937.

12. Minutes of meeting, 18 March 1937, Hepburn Papers.

13. Oshawa *Times*, 21 March 1937.

14. Minutes of meeting, 24 March 1937, Hepburn Papers.

15. Interview with Charles Millard; Letter to the author from Hugh Thompson, 19 February 1968.

16. Minutes of meeting, 31 March 1937, Hepburn Papers.

17. *Ibid.,* 1 April 1937.

18. Oshawa *Times,* 4 April 1937.

19. Minutes of meeting, 7 April 1937, Hepburn Papers.

20. Interviews with David Croll, Charles Millard, Louis Fine.

21. Hepburn to Ernest Lapointe, 8 April 1937; Hepburn to E.G. Odette, 8 April 1937; Hepburn to Miss H.N. Ward, assistant deputy minister of Public Welfare, 8 April 1937, Hepburn Papers.

22. New York *Times,* 9 April 1937. Strangely, the *Times* was the only paper to print the premier's entire statement. See also Toronto *Daily Star,* 9 April 1937.

23. The Mackenzie King Diary, 8 April 1937, Public Archives of Canada (PAC). I am grateful to Mr. Colin Read for drawing this to my attention.

24. Lapointe to Hepburn, 8 April 1937; J.H. MacBrien to Hepburn, 8 April 1937; MacBrien to officer-in-command, RCMP, Toronto, 9 April 1937, Lapointe Papers, PAC.

25. Toronto *Daily Star,* 10 April 1937.

26. Oshawa *Times,* 10 April 1937.

27. Toronto *Globe and Mail,* Toronto *Telegram,* Oshawa *Times,* Ottawa *Citizen, Daily Clarion,* 10 April 1937; Toronto *Daily Star,* 10, 12 April 1937; Hamilton *Spectator,* 12 April 1937.

28. Toronto *Daily Star,* 10 April 1937.

29. Toronto *Telegram,* 10 April 1937.

30. Oshawa *Times,* 10 April 1937.

31. *Ibid.;* Secret report from Inspector Feiling to Hepburn, 9 April 1937, Hepburn Papers.

32. Toronto *Globe and Mail,* 10 April 1937.

33. Interviews with Charles Millard, Art Schultz.

34. *Daily Clarion,* Oshawa *Times,* 12 April 1937.

35. *Ibid.;* Interview with Charles Millard; Letter to the author from Hugh Thompson, 19 February 1968.

36. *Canadian Forum,* June 1937; *Daily Clarion,* Oshawa *Times,* 12 April 1937; Interviews with Charles Millard, George Burt.

37. New York *Times,* 11 April 1937.

38. Toronto *Daily Star,* 12 April 1937; Interviews with Eamon Park, Joseph Salsberg.

39. Toronto *Globe and Mail,* 12 April 1937; Hepburn to Mackenzie King, 13 April 1937, Hepburn Papers.

40. King Diary, 13 April 1937.

41. Mackenzie King to Hepburn, 13 April 1937, Hepburn Papers.

42. Hepburn to Lapointe, 13 April 1937, Hepburn Papers; Toronto *Daily Star,* 13 April 1937.

43. Toronto *Daily Star,* 13 April 1937; OPP Constable Wilson to Hepburn, 9, 10, 11, 12, 13 April 1937, Hepburn Papers.

44. King Diary, 13 April 1937.

45. *Ibid.,* 14 April 1937; Lapointe to Hepburn, 14 April 1937, Hepburn Papers.

46. New York *Times,* 15 April 1937.

47. Toronto *Daily Star,* 15 April 1937; Toronto *Globe and Mail,* 16 April 1937.

48. Toronto *Globe and Mail,* 17 April 1937.

49. Interviews with David Croll, Arthur Roebuck and a Hepburn aide, Roy Elmhirst.

50. Hepburn to Croll; Hepburn to Roebuck, 14 April 1937, Hepburn Papers.

51. Croll to Hepburn; Roebuck to Hepburn, 14 April 1937, Hepburn Papers.

52. Toronto *Globe and Mail,* Toronto *Daily Star,* 15 April 1937; *New Commonwealth,* 24 April 1937.

53. Toronto *Globe and Mail,* 16 April 1937; Interview with Charles Millard.

54. Oshawa *Times,* 17 April 1937.

55. Minutes of meeting, 17 April 1937, Hepburn Papers.

56. Toronto *Daily Star,* 19 April 1937; Interviews with Roy Elmhirst, Charles Millard, Louis Fine.

57. Secret report from OPP Constable Wilson to Hepburn, 17 April 1937, Hepburn Papers.

58. Secret reports from OPP Constable Hitch, Timmins, Ontario, to Hepburn, 13, 14, 16 April 1937; OPP Inspector Creasy, Haileybury, Ontario, to Hepburn, 14 April 1937; H. Knox to Hepburn, 16 April 1937, Hepburn Papers. Also see New York *Times,* 19 April 1937; *Union News* (Mine-Mill newspaper), May 1937.

59. Toronto *Daily Star,* 19 April 1937; Oshawa *Times,* 20 April 1937; Interviews with Charles Millard, Alex Hall.

60. Interviews with Charles Millard, George Burt; Letter from Hugh Thompson to the author, 19 February 1968; Oshawa *Times,* 20 April 1937.

61. Minutes of the executive meeting, 19 April 1937; Martin to Thompson, 20 April 1937, Thompson Papers; both in UAW Labor Archives, Wayne State University, Detroit, Michigan.

62. McIntyre to Hepburn, 21 April 1937; Hepburn to McLaughlin, 20 April 1937, Hepburn Papers.

63. Minutes of meetings, 21-22 April 1937; McIntyre to Hepburn, 22 April 1937, Hepburn Papers.

64. Toronto *Daily Star,* 23 April 1937.

65. Toronto *Globe and Mail,* 26 April 1937.

66. *Daily Clarion,* 27 April 1937; Toronto *Daily Star,* 26 April 1937.

67. *Financial Post,* 8 May 1937; Interview with Charles Millard; Letter from Hugh Thompson to the author, 19 February 1968.

68. Toronto *Daily Star,* 1 May 1937.

69. Mrs. Bruce's Diary, May 1937, Bruce Papers, Archives of Ontario. I am grateful to Professor J.L. Granatstein, who generously allowed me to see his notes from the Bruce Papers.

70. Interview with Earl Rowe. In addition, Mr. Rowe kindly sent me a long memorandum on his recollections of these events.

71. *Ibid.;* D.M. Hogarth to Rowe, 5 July 1937, Bruce Papers. (Hogarth was the leading Conservative strategist at the time.) See also Neil McKenty, *Mitch Hepburn,* pp. 119-125.

72. Toronto *Globe and Mail,* 5 June 1937.

73. Interviews with Roy Elmhirst, Earl Rowe, David Croll.

74. *New Commonwealth,* 15 May 1937; Dennis Wrong, "Ontario Provincial Elections 1934-55," *Canadian Journal of Economics and Political Science* 23 (August 1957): 395-403.

75. See Gerald L. Caplan, *The Dilemma of Canadian Socialism: The* CCF *in Ontario* (Toronto: McClelland & Stewart, 1973).

5 Ford Windsor 1945

by David Moulton

One of the most important strikes in Canadian working-class history was that of the Ford workers of Windsor in 1945. For this story to wait so long to be told indicates the extent to which Canadian historians have neglected the research and writing of the history of labour in this country. It is not sufficient to say that this is unfortunate, or that such neglect has somehow been "benign." The perpetuation of a particular version of Canadian history, the myth of the "peaceable kingdom," depends upon ignorance of the bitter struggles that Canadian working people have fought in order to obtain some rights on the job.[1] The right to organize a union of their choice, the right to a collective agreement, the right to strike, all were rights never willingly given to workers. Rather, they were conceded to them after a tremendous amount of hardship, pain and blood. Furthermore, those rights have never been guaranteed to all Canadian workers, as some present-day strikes in Ontario clearly illustrate.

The Ford workers in Windsor were not guaranteed those rights in 1945, and their successful fight to win them makes their strike all the more important to remember today. They faced the combined forces of the company, the federal and provincial governments, the Ontario Provincial Police and the RCMP, yet they won most of their demands. Their victory did not come from the bargaining table but from the solidarity of their ranks and the support of the Windsor community and other brothers and sisters in the union movement in Windsor and across Canada. Although this unity faltered somewhat towards the end of the strike, it was still made very clear to all parties concerned that unless the Ford strikers obtained their demands there would be no peace in Windsor. "Union shop and checkoff" was their rallying cry, and the arbitrated settlement that followed the conclusion of the walk-out gave them in large part what they wanted. This agreement, now known as the Rand Formula, has since become a cornerstone of Canadian labour relations.

Very few working-class fights have been carried on solely around the question of the immediate demands of the workers. The question of the political direction of the trade-union movement is oftentimes on the agenda and the Ford strike of 1945 was no exception. At this time an intense struggle was taking place between the Communist and CCF political forces within the Canadian union movement and this naturally had a great impact on the events in Windsor. This political struggle did little to further the workers' cause and did nothing to assist them in fighting their principal foes—the industrialists and the federal and provincial governments of the country. That such debate will always be an integral part of trade-union politics cannot be denied, but certainly the primary focus of working people must be the forces that attempt to deny or take away the rights for which they are struggling. The lesson for the future is not to let such political disagreements distract the workers' movement in Canada from vigorously fighting the same forces that the Ford workers faced in 1945.

On Wednesday, September 12, 1945, at ten A.M., plant workers walked off their jobs quickly and quietly to form the picket lines that ushered in the Ford Windsor strike of 1945. The central issue of the dispute was the union demand for union shop and checkoff[2] and the strike was called when it became clear that neither the company, nor the government through its conciliation board, were willing to accede to the workers' demand. An agreement signed by the Ford Motor Company with the American UAW in August 1941 had given the Ford workers in the United States both union shop and checkoff. However, the Canadian company's reluctance to do so crystallized the relationship between the company and the union that had existed since the Canadian UAW first appeared in full force at Windsor in 1941.

The Ford Motor Company had established itself in Canada in 1904[3] and, with a handful of automotive manufacturers including General Motors and Chrysler, it had survived and grown during the hectic twenties and hungry thirties. By the forties Ford of Canada had attained a major position in the car industry, which in turn made it a substantial force in the general industrial sector of the nation. As such, it was considered to be a leader in many areas by Canadian manufacturing interests; one of the most important had become labour relations.[4]

Ford of Canada had never been known as the best company to work for but the oppressive working conditions in the plants were alleviated somewhat by relatively good wages.[5] Although men could be and were dismissed for any number of reasons, the most important was always involvement in union organizing or any related activity. There were purges of suspected union men in 1934 and 1937, for example, but neither the company service department nor the foremen could find them all. Even though the conditions in the plant were ripe for union organizing, particularly during the thirties, the impetus for such a development was lacking.[6]

The UAW-CIO had made some progress in organizing plants in Canada, most notably with the Oshawa strike and settlement of 1937.[7] However, in the following five years Ford of Canada had remained an open shop with no contractual agreement with its workers. The Canadian UAW leadership recognized that unless Ford was organized, any attempts to further their gains with the other auto companies would almost certainly be met with failure. The opportunity to make a major effort at Ford Windsor came when the Ford concern in Dearborn, Michigan, signed a contract with the American UAW-CIO in August 1941. Interest in the establishment of a union at Ford Windsor immediately intensified and resulted in what has been termed a "whirlwind campaign."[8] After two overflow meetings, and with large numbers of workers signing up, the new UAW Local 200 formally requested recognition from the company on October 23, 1941. Wallace Campbell, the company president, refused the demand, stating his belief that the UAW did not represent the majority of plant employees at Ford. Instead, Campbell proposed the formation of a company union that would reach an agreement for the workers with the company. George Burt, Canadian regional director of the Auto Workers, denounced Campbell's proposition, claiming that it disregarded Dominion Order-in-Council 2685. The order provided that employees should bargain with genuine unions chosen by the workers.[9]

After some vigorous behind-the-scenes action,[10] the matter was finally resolved by the federal government, which obtained agreement from both sides to hold a recognition ballot. A vote was to be taken with the ballot offering the following alternatives: "Acceptance of the company's offer of negotiations through employee representation elected by secret ballot, or, representation by the UAW of America, CIO.[11] Roy England, president of Local 200, was allowed free access to the plants in the campaign preceding the vote. Campbell spoke to the workers in the plants and in the parking lots; the company used the radio and press as well. Selective Service personnel were used as DROS (the government was still not equipped to carry out such votes) and both sides had scrutineers. The balloting took place on November 13 and the results gave the union just over sixty per cent of the vote.[12]

On November 24 negotiations over the first contract between the union and the company began, and on January 15, 1942, an agreement was signed. Although the contract did not give the Canadian workers the same concessions won by their American counterparts, it was an improvement over the contract that had been signed earlier with General Motors.[13]

Apart from the success of the UAW across the river with Ford, a major reason for the victory of the organizing campaign at the Windsor plants was Canada's involvement in the Second World War. The resulting labour shortage and the necessity of war production had made governments, both federal and provincial, considerably more amenable to labour's demands. Not only was it extremely difficult for any employer to fire a worker[14]; any interruption of war supplies became the interest of the federal government. The fact that Ford workers played a major role in the Canadian war effort meant that Ottawa always had its finger on the pulse of Windsor.

The contract may have been signed, and the union established with stewards and committee men in the plants, but the company continued to make decisions as it had in the past, without regard to the men or the union. This attitude led to a number of work stoppages during the war period over various issues. The walkouts in November 1942,[15] April 1943[16] and April-May 1944[17] were just preliminary skirmishes leading directly to September 1945. These strikes were to occur in spite of the Canadian UAW-CIO's strong desire to aid the war effort to the greatest degree possible. The American CIO under Philip Murray, which included the international UAW, had gone so far as to accept a "no-strike" pledge, although George Burt had obtained an exemption for the Canadian region. He maintained that acceptance of the blanket pledge would jeopardize UAW organizing efforts in Canada because of the lack of labour legislation comparable to that which existed in the United States.[18]

At times sudden work stoppages seemed to be the only course of action for the men in their attempts to deal with the company. The hostility and the overbearing attitude of the "Model T" foremen and the pressures and push of production resulted in men simply laying down their tools, a tactic that was used very often by union stewards in order to meet with the workers under their jurisdiction.[19] The Windsor plants suffered from a number of these incidents, although the situation there was mild compared to the Ford River Rouge complex in Dearborn.[20] The root of the problem lay in the assumption of foremen and management that, once the war had ended, a return to prewar procedures would be forthcoming. This attitude only intensified the workers' desire for a union shop to protect them on the job.

During the 1944 shutdown, a lack of unity within the UAW leadership brought to the surface the political struggle being waged within the union. Both Burt and England called on the workers to return to work and disavowed their "wildcat" action, while Tom MacLean, the assistant Canadian director of the UAW, called for more militant strike action. The Labour Progressive (Communist) party supported the position taken by Burt and England, but for different reasons than theirs. Following the invasion of Russia by Germany in June 1941, the LPP had been calling for the "no-strike" pledge in the Canadian labour movement as part of an all-out effort to win the war and defeat fascism. This policy was a reversal of the party's pre-1941 "anti-war" position, for which the Communist party in Canada had been declared illegal after the declaration of war in September 1939. It was this "alliance" between Burt, England and the LPP during the 1944 strike which led many critics of their leadership to claim that Burt and England were working hand-in-glove with the Communists.[21]

The settlement of the 1944 walkout included the appointment of Louis Fine[22] as an umpire to settle any day-to-day grievances. Negotiations commenced for a new contract but antagonism mounted when the company refused to implement the government-approved plan of a week's vacation with pay. After the union had failed to win a week's paid vacation in the 1943 contract, it petitioned the Regional (Ontario) War Labour Board. Approved at that level, the proposal was forwarded to the National War Labour Board which also approved the measure. However, Ford of Canada stalled and refused to implement the board's decision; not until the union threatened legal action did the company finally back down.

The negotiations for a new contract continued until January 22, 1945, when the Ontario Labour Relations Board requested that the Ontario minister of Labour appoint a conciliation officer. Such a request was normally made when one of the disputants advised the board that no agreement had been reached and that negotiations had been in progress for over thirty days. The minister appointed Louis Fine on January 29 and Fine met with both sides. On March 28 he reported back, stating "that in his opinion an agreement was impossible and the situation was very complicated and difficult."[23]

Following Fine's report, Ford of Canada requested an interpretation from the National War Labour Board of the termination clause in the existing contract. The union took the action to mean that the company had "declared its intention of terminating our present union contract . . . the clause on which the company bases its attempt to terminate the contract states that all union contracts may be terminated after one year, on two months' notice, by either party to the agreement."[24] The termination action was never carried through.

Mr. Justice S.E. Richards of Winnipeg was appointed on April 18 by federal Labour Minister Humphrey Mitchell to investigate the dispute. His efforts with the union and company broke down in June, although he did not submit his report to Mitchell until August 3.[25] Two weeks later Mitchell released the report to each side. Richards commented on the intransigence of the two parties. He recommended that the old agreement be maintained until the end of the year, which would allow for a "cooling-off period"; negotiations could then be resumed on October 15 with both sides presumably more willing to settle.

Local 200 rejected the report, which prompted Richards to advise Mitchell to appoint a conciliation board. Mitchell established such a board on August 30; the following day the union announced Bora Laskin as its nominee while S.L. Springsteen became the company representative. Without a joint nomination from the two board members, Mitchell proceeded to name Mr. Justice G.B. O'Connor as chairman.[26]

Meanwhile, the union held a mass meeting on Sunday, August 26, where authorization was given for a strike ballot. On the previous Thursday, Local 200 had sent a telegram to the federal government outlining the seven "contentious" issues involved in the dispute. They were: union shop, checkoff, two weeks' vacation with pay, added compensation for work on Sundays and statutory holidays, veterans' seniority, layoff pay and non-reduction in take-home pay.[27] The strike ballot was held from August 30 to September 1 and although ninety per cent of the votes favoured strike action, the date was not set pending the results of the conciliation board.[28]

The conciliation board convened and both sides presented their cases. However, it became evident that the board would be unsuccessful no matter how it reported. Neither side would move on the essential issue of union shop and checkoff and, even with this difference set aside, the problems of layoffs at Ford had now become serious. On August 31, the union had been informed that eight hundred men would lose their jobs, including 250 veterans not previously employed at Ford. Then, on September 4, the company announced a further layoff of 1656 men to take place through to September 14. "Hopes for a settlement of the dispute . . . decreased . . . after a company layoff announcement was described by a union official as a 'provocative act' which 'destroys the basis for any conciliation.' "[29]

It was, therefore, in an atmosphere of mistrust and hostility, fear and frustration that the conciliation board was to make its report. The Ford Motor Company in Dearborn had conceded union shop and checkoff four years earlier, yet the Canadian company refused to establish it with its employees in Windsor. The endless struggle in the plants and the drawn-out fight for vacation pay made the rank and file all the more bitter. The job security and prosperity that had existed during the war now appeared to be vanishing as thousands were laid off with no guarantee of a return to work. The assumption of the "Model T" foremen that prewar working conditions would return only gave the men further resolve not to capitulate. Endless months of negotiations had not brought either side any closer. The issues at stake were not simply monetary; the confrontation was nothing less than a fight to maintain the existence and strength of the union. As far as the men were concerned, no compromise was possible until that point had been settled. One cannot understate the militant mood of the Ford workers. They were determined that if union security could not be gained from deliberations at the negotiating table, it was necessary that the issue be won on the picket line.

The conciliation report was handed down September 11. It addressed itself to only two issues. It refused to recommend a union shop, although Laskin and O'Connor proposed a voluntary checkoff irrevocable during the life of the contract. Alone, Laskin further recommended a "maintenance-of-membership" clause. At once the stewards and joint policy committee of Local 200 gave unanimous approval for strike action and, on September 12, the men walked out.[30]

Roy England, in the union statement, made it clear that the strike "was provoked by [the] persistent chiselling down of collective-bargaining mechanics by the company, and an obvious effort to destroy the union which signed its first contract in 1942." The decision to strike was taken "after calm deliberation following 18 months of failure to reach an agreement. The contract signed under war conditions was a sub-standard one. Now the workers are determined that they will not return until they have signed a contract providing union shop and checkoff and decent wages and working conditions."[31]

The battle lines were now drawn and the most important strike in Canada's postwar labour history had begun.

Following the walkout and the organization of the picket line, a union meeting was held on the night of September 12 at the Market Hall, where Windsor Mayor Art Reaume addressed the gathering. Giving his full support to the workers and their strike, he praised the eight thousand men in attendance for their war work and asked that they remain cool. Reaume further stated that "Every member of my city council stands prepared to see that no man or woman is starved in this land of plenty. Heads have been smashed in other places by imported police, but let me pledge to you that it will not happen here.'' Roy England also spoke at the meeting. After reading out the conciliation report to the assembled strikers, he dramatically ripped it in two and the audience responded with cheers. ''Ford workers decided that is what should be done with this report when they walked out 100 per cent today . . . We will not go back to work until we get a contract that is satisfactory to all our members and the agreement will be written while you are on the picket line.''[32]

The next day the picket line refused entry to a number of company officials who attempted to drive through the plant gates. Approximately one thousand office workers showed up for work at eight A.M. and they were denied entrance as well. Although the office staff were organized under UAW Local 240, they did not participate in any strike vote. However, they remained off the job for the duration of the strike.[33]

There were further attempts by President Campbell and other executives to cross the lines, but to no avail. Appeals to the Windsor Police Commission by Ford of Canada were dismissed; instead, the WPC instructed the police on duty to use their discretion. In the meantime, the company set up temporary offices at the Prince Edward Hotel and the police left permission to enter the plant up to the union. The powerhouse workers and the service department remained on the job but no one else was allowed to enter.[34]

On Friday the union announced that the powerhouse employees would sit down with the joint policy committee[35] to discuss strike action. As members of Local 200, the fifty-odd workers could legally strike and the proposed discussion was seen by one observer as further illustrating ''the sharpness of the conflict.''[36]

A pledge of support came immediately from C.S. Jackson, the director of District 5 of the United Electrical Workers (UE) and, on September 19, the Ontario Federation of Labour (OFL) strongly endorsed the actions of Local 200. However, at a special meeting of the Canadian Congress of Labour executive, the attitude towards the union and its strike action was not very favourable. Except for Jackson, the rest of the executive was upset that they had not been consulted about the timing of the strike and the issues involved. Both Aaron Mosher, president of the CCL, and Charles Millard, director of the Steelworkers, expressed reluctance to support the strike. Consequently, ''a motion to support the strike was withdrawn. Instead the council voted simply to endorse the demands of the Ford strikers, to urge all affiliated unions to give moral and financial support to the

UAW and to set up a 'National Ford Strike Committee' of council members to aid in these efforts."[37]

On the picket lines the strike became a community affair as people from Windsor, including priests and servicemen, joined the Ford workers in their twenty-four-hour-a-day vigil of the plant. The union had its own marshal system and the Windsor police simply directed traffic.

Strike benefits to the men and their families were minimal, with the maximum family benefit being fifteen dollars per week.[38] Milk and bread tokens as well as free medical care were available through the union. Even though some of the hardships were alleviated by outside sources,[39] the whole issue of strike relief became an important concern of the Windsor city council. Acting on his promise to insure minimal hardship for the Ford strikers, Mayor Reaume asked his council to approve city relief for those in need. Although it was approved for a two-week period, when the measure came up for renewal a motion to continue the program was defeated 8-5; the council by then had decided to abandon this radical innovation for fear of bankrupting its coffers. Further endeavours by Reaume to obtain provincial or federal aid proved fruitless. Despite this, it would seem that some leniency was shown by city welfare services throughout the dispute. This was especially true for Ford workers who were not members of the union and thus not even entitled to union benefits.[40]

It was not long before both the federal and provincial governments were being called upon to involve themselves in the dispute. Union officials and Mayor Reaume made initial statements asking for the governments to intervene in order to settle the strike. But it was not until September 26 that federal Labour Minister Humphrey Mitchell disclosed that both his department and the Ontario Department of Labour had joined forces in their efforts to seek a settlement in Windsor. Mitchell, although a trade unionist himself, had union experience within the Trades and Labour Congress, the Canadian labour body closely affiliated with the American Federation of Labour.[41] He was therefore suspicious of the CCL-CIO wing of the Canadian labour movement and their methods of organizing. "The UAW was more modern, which he didn't understand... whose leadership, their flamboyancy he didn't appreciate... He was interested in industrial peace... he reflected, in a sense, the age gap."[42] Earlier, when Mitchell had been appointed Labour minister, there had been some negative reaction in the Canadian CIO, and later the CCL sought his dismissal because of his "hostile attitude towards labour."[43]

Mitchell proposed a meeting for Monday, October 1, to be held in Toronto with company, union, Ontario and federal labour officials in attendance. The union accepted but Campbell refused, stating that company officials would not attend until the "mass unlawful picketing" at the Ford works was discontinued. The meeting was therefore cancelled and Alex Parent, president of UAW Local 195 in Windsor, warned that unless the government took some speedy action his amalgamated local would walk out in sympathy.[44]

The impasse caused debate in the House of Commons, with the Conservatives criticizing the union for its picket tactics and the company for refusing to attend the meeting. David Croll (Liberal, Toronto-Spadina), who had previously been mayor of Windsor and a former Ontario minister of Labour under Mitchell Hepburn, expressed the fear that the Ford dispute might lead to a national general strike. He suggested that under the War Measures Act, both sides could be compelled to meet in Ottawa.[45]

The Liberal MP for the area, Paul Martin, defended the actions of the Labour minister, claiming that he could not publicize all his actions for fear of ruining any chances of settlement.[46] For the CCF, Clairie Gillis of Cape Breton South demanded that the government appoint a controller for the Ford plants. He reiterated an earlier union request for such action but Mitchell dismissed the suggestion, accusing the CCF of attempting to achieve socialism with the instrument of trade unionism. He claimed further that the government did not have the power to implement such a measure.[47]

In the meantime, on the union level, Percy Bengough, the president of the Canadian Trades and Labour Congress, wired a message of support to the Ford workers. This was the first time the head of the TLC had supported a union affiliated with the CIO in Canada since the expulsion of the industrial unions from the congress in early 1939.[48] The following day a motorcade left Windsor for a mass "worker-soldier" rally to be held in Maple Leaf Gardens that night. The keynote speaker was George Burt, who called on the government to take over the Ford plants if the company continued in its refusal to negotiate. The ten thousand people in attendance heard other labour leaders, including Local 200 President Roy England, who commented on "the political partisanship on the part of the other speakers." England maintained he "had the sinking feeling [that the gathering] had been turned into a political meeting." He called on all political factions within the labour movement to unite so that they could "win labour's place in the postwar period."[49]

On Sunday night, October 7, the union took the first step that would eventually lead to the most dramatic events of the strike. The joint policy committee decided to withdraw the powerhouse workers. The action was legal and the crew on duty shut down the powerhouse completely; by three A.M. Monday the last worker had left. No smoke emanated from the huge Ford stack and all the light, heat and water systems of the vast complex were at a standstill as the union moved more forcefully to bring the company to the bargaining table. It appeared to be the men's only weapon in their attempts to reach a satisfactory settlement. Cold weather was fast approaching and Ford of Canada now faced the prospect of having their plants freeze up.[50]

That Saturday Mitchell announced that both sides would be meeting in Toronto with federal and Ontario government representatives. The union had agreed earlier to allow company officials into the plant. Monday, October 15, was the day of the long-awaited meeting and the two-hour session indicated no real signs of progress. Two more meetings were held on the Tuesday and Wednesday but they proved to be fruitless as neither side was prepared to compromise its position on the question of union shop and checkoff.

Mitchell returned to Ottawa and made his statement in the Commons the next day. His outlook reflected the dim hopes of settlement earlier expressed by both Burt and England. Mitchell's proposal of a revocable checkoff was rejected by both parties and he commented on the antagonisms that existed as reported to him by Justice Richards. He refused to comment on the report that Wallace Campbell had said during the meetings: "If the government felt that union shop and checkoff was good for the people of Canada, then they should pass legislation and if such legislation were passed, the company would go along with it."[51] On November 12, Stanley Knowles (CCF, Winnipeg) again raised the question of a government controller at Ford, maintaining that such action would be similar to the cabinet's action in the packinghouse industry. Mitchell again dismissed the idea.[52]

The demand for government control of the operations of the Ford complex remained a UAW proposal throughout the strike. The CCF was to continue pressing for it in the House of Commons and many labour leaders called for this specific government action. Even though the federal cabinet was continually left with this option as a method to end the strike, it was never given any real consideration. "The appointment of a controller, the cabinet felt in this situation was not desirable . . . It would give argument to those who were calling for the nationalization of the industry . . . it was not seriously pursued."[53]

With the failure of the Toronto negotiations the strike continued. By now the temporary relief period granted by the Windsor council had ended, but Art Reaume continued his attempts to obtain aid from other levels of government. Unsuccessful, he understated the situation by commenting: "The positions taken by the federal and provincial governments is most confusing [*sic*], each disclaiming responsibility and placing the onus upon the other."[54] The union, meanwhile, was carrying on an extensive campaign both in Canada and the United States for financial assistance.[55] The drive not only brought funds, but it also made the strike an event of national importance to working men and women across Canada. In the end it was estimated that between three hundred thousand and half a million dollars had been donated to the strike fund.[56]

Back in Ottawa, Humphrey Mitchell announced in the House on October 29 the details of a government plan to settle the strike. An "umpire" would be chosen by the cabinet and each side would agree to his decisions as "final and binding." The union would remove the pickets and the powerhouse would reopen within forty-eight hours. The company was to call back the employees on a seniority basis without discrimination. Four days later the union turned down the offer, requesting that negotiations begin immediately, and maintained that the strike would only terminate once a written agreement had been worked out.[57]

The calm atmosphere surrounding the strike came to an abrupt end on Friday, November 2. In a morning session, the Windsor Police Commission ordered the city police to enter the Ford gates to allow the opening up of the power plant. That order was given on a split vote, as Mayor Reaume opposed the action of the other two members of the commission. This order followed a number of statements by the Ford management that such action was necessary to save plant property from being ruined.[58] Ironically, on Saturday, October 27, the powerhouse employees had sent a letter to Mitchell requesting his immediate involvement in the strike and warning that delay might cause serious damage to the physical plant.[59] Two days prior to the commission's decision, the union limited entry into the plant to five watchmen per shift, charging that watchmen were doing the work of millwrights.[60]

The earlier signs of sympathy that the Windsor police force had shown towards the Ford workers was again evident when they made a lacklustre attempt to enter the plant gates on November 2. A pushing match between the two groups lasted about five minutes and resulted in the police being forced back across the road to the opposite sidewalk. No weapons were used. What in the end became the only picket-line confrontation of the strike reported one black eye to a policeman as the only injury.[61]

However small it may now appear, the picket-line incident produced immediate and decisive action from the Windsor Police Commission. They wired Ontario Attorney-General Leslie Blackwell, requesting police reinforcements to aid in maintaining law and order.

Mayor Reaume again opposed the decision. Blackwell was quick to respond; he not only authorized the transfer of 125 OPP officers to Windsor but obtained equal numbers of RCMP personnel from the federal Government.[62] Blackwell's actions were a complete about-face after earlier promises both he and Premier George Drew had made to Reaume that no police would be sent to Windsor.[63]

With the police reinforcements arriving all during the weekend, the union leadership moved quickly to deal with this threat to the strike. Roy England declared the actions of the WPC to be an "attempt at strikebreaking." On Sunday, November 4, a mass meeting of Amalgamated Local 195 voted to walk out from some twenty-five different plants, and another eight thousand men joined the Ford picket line. The Windsor Trades and Labour Council and various other unions and labour organizations across Ontario voiced their opposition to the actions taken by the authorities.[64]

The erection of a massive automobile barricade, however, was the key to the union's successful attempt to preserve the picket line and prevent a violent confrontation between police and picketers at the plant gates. Using a tactic that had been successfully deployed by the Ford UAW-CIO organizers in Dearborn,[65] the decision to build the barricade was made Sunday night.[66] Quickly and quietly union members were notified. At six A.M. Monday morning, Tommy MacLean arrived at the Ford complex, parking his car directly in front of the main gates. Building the barricade along Doulliard and Sandwich Streets in a T formation, union men used not their own vehicles but trapped those of commuters. Buses and trucks dotted the barricade which, at its height, totalled some 1500 to 2000 vehicles. Traffic was eventually re-routed and, although there was some angry reaction, most people caught on the barricade took the disruption amiably.[67]

Although the barricade cost the workers some public support, it was effective in achieving their objectives. The 250 police remained in Windsor for the duration of the strike, but the picket line was never dispersed and the Ford complex remained closed down.

News of the event travelled quickly and Mitchell and Blackwell headed directly for Windsor. Upon arrival, the federal minister travelled to Dearborn and had a three-hour parley with Henry Ford II. The *Globe and Mail* reported: "Ford Motor Company is understood to have effective control over Ford of Canada, whose president, Wallace Campbell, has been reported ill after suffering a stroke two weeks ago."[68]

Monday evening the Windsor city council issued an ultimatum, "calling for the Ford strikers to remove the motor-car barricade outside the Ford plant or troops may be called in to remove the vehicles."

Roy England defended the actions of the union; he "regretted that private citizens' cars had been used, but any attempt to free them would be contingent with allowing strikers' cars to remain." George Burt also expressed regrets but claimed: "The original union plan was only to use their own members' cars but traffic was fairly heavy . . . and the scheme got out of hand."[69]

Mitchell met with union representatives the next day for three hours but nothing substantial was accomplished. In Ottawa, Pat Conroy, secretary-treasurer of the CCL, indicated that, "while there is hope of a settlement . . . a call for a national sympathy walkout by CCL unions will not go out but otherwise it is still within the realm of possibility." Conroy urged all members of the congress to donate one day of their wages to support the strike in Windsor.[70]

On Wednesday, Mitchell again found himself engaged in stalled talks. The obstacle in earlier deliberations reappeared when "Company officials refused to grant security. It is understood that although the company agreed to a number of union demands . . . it refused to budge over the issue of union security."[71]

Also by late Wednesday the streets had been cleared of vehicles, although "there was strong reluctance on the part of strikers to remove the barricade."[72]

Mitchell again met with Henry Ford II on Thursday morning in the company of Attorney-General Blackwell. After a three-hour session it was agreed that Ford would sit down with Canadian company officials in an attempt to formulate a basis for a settlement. Upon his return from Dearborn, Blackwell met with George Burt for three more hours. It was reported that the acting Ontario Labour minister told Burt that "the picketing was not illegal in terms of the power plant and the offices as long as company officials and maintenance men are allowed to pass."[73]

Some indication of union support across Canada for the Ford workers comes from the *Globe and Mail* of November 9: "It seems that nationally union officials are having a difficult time in keeping their men at work for a number of them wish to strike in sympathy with the Ford workers." The day before, members of Local 50 of the United Electrical Workers at Westinghouse in Hamilton had walked out in solidarity with the Ford strike.[74]

Friday's activity centred around a new offer from the company which the union rejected. The proposal was similar to the one presented earlier by the federal Labour minister. It appeared as a break in the dispute: "Henry Ford II apparently had been able to move the Canadian company"[75] because the offer would have placed all points of difference under arbitration. This meant that the management had abandoned its rigid position vis-à-vis union shop and checkoff. They were now willing to have an arbitrator make a final and binding decision on the matter.

It was on exactly this point that the union refused acceptance. Arguing that there was no assurance of union security for the Ford strikers, George Burt commented that the union was no farther ahead in the strike than it had been at the beginning. It was mentioned that some felt the company offer might prove embarrassing to Mitchell because of the similarity in offers that he and the company had proposed.[76]

The joint policy committee of locals 195 and 200 simultaneously called on all CCL unions to walk out in sympathy with the Ford workers for one day. The verbal declaration was followed by scores of telegrams that were sent to local unions across Canada asking them to support a one-day sympathy strike on Monday, November 12. The telegrams, with the attached signatures of Alex Parent and Roy England, were an unexpected development in the strike. Pat Conroy of the CCL left Ottawa quickly for Windsor, declaring that the action was unauthorized. His presence in the city was expected "to give the moderate group in the union some support and to prevent the occurrence of a one-day national strike in support of the Ford strike."[77] George Burt was opposed to the tactic, stating that he "knew the history of general strikes, [and] none of them had been won whether in Britain, Canada or any other place."[78] Although the majority of the CCL's National Ford Strike Committee also opposed the mass walkout, one member was not deterred in expressing his enthusiasm for such action. C.S. Jackson of the UE predicted a spontaneous show of support across the country for the Ford workers at a Market Hall meeting of Local 200 on Sunday.

The next day the union wires were shown to have had little effect without the official sanction of the CCL. There were reported walkouts in Kitchener and Sarnia involving some 3200 workers at four plants, but that was the extent of it. Despite this, "the possibility of a nationwide sympathy strike loomed larger on the horizon again . . ."[79] when Ford of Canada issued a refusal to a new union offer. On Monday the union had proposed to reopen the powerhouse provided that the company renewed negotiations. Company officials maintained that "the union proposal did not provide for the discontinuance of the strike while negotiations proceeded, that it did not provide for discontinuance of picketing at the Ford offices and admission by union pickets of company protection men."[80]

Meantime, Mitchell was presenting a statement to the House of Commons. He maintained that "neither [Henry] Ford nor the US company had control over the Canadian concern'' and ''the company's . . . stand for reopening the powerhouse and office building was reasonable.'' Both he and Blackwell had been given assurances that the company was willing to bargain in good faith.[81]

Aside from the apparent mellowing of the company's position, people close to the union became increasingly aware of the possibility of the union losing the strike. Although the barricade had prevented certain bloodshed, it had caused a deterioration in public support. Furthermore, the unauthorized call for a national general strike had done damage to the strikers' efforts even within the ranks of Canadian labour. It appears that about this time, Paul Martin, by his own account, became involved. Working with Pat Conroy he made phone calls to the US in hopes of getting someone to help and eventually obtained the services of George Addes, international secretary-treasurer of the UAW-CIO. On Tuesday, November 13, Addes, along with Conroy, Burt and England, travelled to Ottawa to confer with government officials. Once in the capital, Martin played an intermediary role.[82]

The next day the union officials returned to Windsor amid speculation about a compromise. At a general meeting of Local 200 on Thursday night, the union decided to allow the reopening of the power plant and admit executives to their offices. The government felt that such moves would give the company an opportunity to show its good faith by agreeing to negotiate. Inexplicably, the company stated that they had not issued instructions to the powerhouse employees to return to work, even though union sound trucks had asked the men to return. The next day, Thursday, November 15, Ford of Canada made it clear that they were not satisfied with the union's offer. Although ''the company statement made no specific request for the discontinuance of the strike . . . it did ask for removal of all pickets from the plant as one of the conditions for negotiations. The last paragraph . . . indicates that the company wants to get back into production before it sits down to negotiate . . .'' They also suggested a ten-day period of negotiations to be followed immediately by arbitration.[83]

The union's reply was short. ''There appears to be little change or concession on the part of the company. The workers are not going to throw away the only economic power they have after seventeen months of what the company statement chooses to describe as 'debate.' '' The light, heat and water systems at Ford remained shut down as the company refused to call back the necessary staff.

During the weekend of November 17-18, speculation mounted that arrangements were being made to bring both sides back to the negotiating table. On Monday they did meet for two hours and declared their intention to meet again. The discussions on Tuesday ended with a joint declaration that stated simply: "The parleys were held with a view to laying the basis for settlement of the dispute." Any hopes of an agreement were quickly shattered at Wednesday's meeting. Union security continued to be the major stumbling block, but the breakdown was also caused by the company's assumption that the two sides were there only to negotiate a strike settlement, and that a collective agreement would be worked out when the union returned to work.[84]

The following day the union reiterated its offer to reopen the powerhouse and declared the company to be responsible for the fate of the Ford complex. Ford officials must have soon realized the awkward position they had put themselves in. The union's offer was eight days old, the company had done nothing, and yet most of the controversy of the strike had arisen from management's demand that the power plant be reopened. On Friday, November 23, the company recalled the necessary staff to rekindle the fires.[85]

In Toronto, Attorney-General Leslie Blackwell stepped into the limelight of the dispute with a radio broadcast in which he reviewed the events of the strike. He stated that the "actions of the Ford Company strikers at Windsor in recent weeks constituted open insurrection against the Crown" and he attacked the "radical elements of organized labour." The federal government was criticized for inaction in formulating a clear wage and price policy, and he warned that "the motor industry [must] get off a seasonal basis for it throws thousands out of work." However, not unexpectedly, his main attack was directed at the union.[86]

Local 200 quickly replied, charging Blackwell with "complete misrepresentation of the union's position." His speech, they said, indicated "a planned attempt to bolster the position of the Ford Motor Company against the union."[87]

Indications of a settlement were in the air again on Monday, November 26, when Mitchell and Charles Daley, the Ontario minister of Labour who had just returned from Europe, met with company and union officials separately in Ottawa. At the conclusion of the talks the next day, Mitchell announced in the Commons that "a formula has been developed that we feel will be acceptable to both sides." The formula was outlined in detail on Wednesday. A government-appointed arbitrator would sit in on company-union negotiations and matters not settled there would be the arbitrator's responsibility. An "umpire" was to be appointed as well to oversee a smooth return to work. All decisions by either official were to be final and binding. With the certainty that the company would force the union shop and checkoff to arbitration, it appeared on the surface that the union's agreement to these terms was a major compromise on their part.[88]

The union leadership, however, had been discussing the possibility of placing union security before an arbitrator. Paul Martin and Pat Conroy had discussed the idea and Conroy had then proposed it to the UAW leadership when he went to Windsor over the unauthorized telegrams.[89] It was after this confidential meeting that the National Ford Strike Committee, with the exception of Conroy, was banished from Windsor. Conflicting statements about the proposals from Charles Millard of the Steelworkers and C.S. Jackson and George Harris of the UE had created a critical situation. According to Burt, "England and I then dismissed the NFSC with the exception of Conroy and told them never to appear in Windsor again because they were just wrecking our chances by playing politics with the strike."[90]

Whatever their difficulties with the NFSC, the union leadership eventually accepted the negotiation-arbitration proposal. From Burt's account, "Conroy came up and gave us to understand that the government would pick a strictly impartial person sympathetic enough . . . they almost told us they would give us some kind of union security . . . we couldn't tell the workers that . . ."[91] Paul Martin, even though he promised to work for the appointment of Justice Ivan Rand ("someone who I believed reflected progressive ideas"), maintains that no prior understanding or deal was assumed to have been made at the government level.[92]

The new proposal met stiff opposition when presented to the union in Windsor. Although the negotiating and joint policy committees accepted the formula, agreement was not unanimous. It was at a marathon four-hour meeting of the plant stewards that the first real signs of trouble appeared. Acceptance of the proposal was defeated 71-67. Even with this setback, the recommendation for settlement went forward to the general membership at a meeting Thursday afternoon in the Market Hall. Although disappointment ran deep, the leadership believed the rank and file would accept the compromise.[93]

An air of anxious excitement pervaded the hall as the meeting was called to order. Roy England, George Burt and George Addes addressed the men and spoke in favour of the proposal. They were met with catcalls and boos. Harry Ford of the negotiating committee and Tom MacLean led the opposition. The latter "blasted the hell out of the settlement at the membership meeting, saying you can't depend on the arbitrators . . . Tommy thought we could win the whole thing on the picket line . . ."[94] MacLean insisted that unless the government were willing to put the agreement in writing, any verbal agreement was totally unsatisfactory.[95] When the vote was tallied the proposal was turned down by a plurality of some 350 votes. The union later made a short statement. "The membership has spoken. The officials and leaders of the UAW-CIO have exerted every effort to bring about a harmonious settlement. Now that the decision has been made we will continue to find some avenue of solution that will achieve the objective of the union."[96]

The decision of Local 200 to continue the picket line did not deter all the units of Local 195 from beginning to return to work, and within a week the various smaller plants in the Windsor area were back into production.

With the company lined up behind the government's negotiation-arbitration procedure, the union had very little room to manoeuvre. A counter-proposal was made by the union[97] even though George Burt opposed it; it was rejected by both the company and the government. The failure of the counter-proposal forced the anti-settlement people to call for a re-balloting. With a united leadership, a meeting was held Sunday, December 16, and a re-vote was approved.[98] With the balloting held on the following Tuesday and Wednesday, it was announced at ten P.M. Wednesday, December 19, that the membership had approved the original proposal by a margin of three to one.[99]

The end of the strike allowed the company to proceed with the retooling necessary for domestic production, and callbacks were made at the end of December and throughout January 1946.

The OPP and RCMP officers stationed in Windsor since November 3 were finally withdrawn the day after the strike vote was announced. In Ottawa, Humphrey Mitchell announced the appointment of Ivan C. Rand of the Supreme Court of Canada as arbitrator. H.R. Pettigrove of Fredericton, N.B., was appointed umpire.[100]

The selection of Rand as arbitrator appears to have been satisfactory to both parties. Paul Martin claims that there was opposition within the federal cabinet to Rand's appointment. However, having agreed to allow the minister of Justice to make the final decision, the cabinet bowed to Mr. St. Laurent and his choice. Martin, who knew Rand personally, recalls, "I talked with him about these problems . . . I knew his views . . . he was a man who knew the evolution that was taking place in social thinking . . . he had been thinking about these questions for a long time . . . and it just happened I was in a position to help bring about his appointment."[101]

As arbitrator, Rand held hearings and also toured the Ford works. The hearings and submissions which make up the arbitration proceedings are on the public record and need not be dealt with here.[102] What is of concern, though, is the binding decisions Rand made a month later.

Justice Ivan Rand handed down his final decisions regarding the Ford dispute on January 29, 1946. Before detailing his awards, the judge outlined some of the more notable occurrences of the strike. He also gave a general overview of labour-capital relations in Canada and their future as he saw them. "That we cannot draw back and try to reverse the whole progress of the last one hundred years in labour-employer relations, that we must go through to a higher evolution of them, must, I think, be accepted as axiomatic . . . The question is whether the remaining controversies are to be settled in the mode of war or reason."[103] Not only did Rand see both labour and capital as necessary partners in economic development; he also realized that his decisions in the Ford dispute would greatly determine whether Canada's postwar industrial disputes were to be settled by "war or reason." In such a situation, he compromised.

He refused to grant a union shop. "It would deny the individual Canadian the right to seek work and to work independently of persons associated with any organized group." However, Rand did award the union a blanket checkoff. "I consider it entirely equitable then that all employees should be required to shoulder their employment, the union contract; that they must take the burden along with the benefit." The Supreme Court judge believed that by giving the union a firm financial basis on which to grow, it would mature and become a responsible entity. To encourage such a development Rand outlined a scheme of penalties to be used in the case of "illegal" or "wildcat" strikes. The union would be liable to lose the checkoff for a specified amount of time according to the seriousness of the violation. There were also penalties on the individual level. "Any employee participating in an unauthorized strike or other concerted cessation of work not called by the union shall be liable to a fine of three dollars per day for every day's absence from work and to a loss of one year's seniority for every continuous absence of a calendar week or part thereof."[104]

Provisions were made for returning veterans and a more detailed grievance procedure was outlined by Rand. Aside from the checkoff, the other important outcome concerned a group medical, hospital and life-insurance plan for the Ford workers.[105]

Reaction to the "Rand Formula" was, for the most part, favourable. In his statement, Rand mentioned that "Mr. Aylesworth [the company attorney] conceded that the scheme [concerning union shop and checkoff] . . . went 'quite' a way to meeting his objections to a union shop."[106] Local 200 President Roy England declared: "The provision that everyone covered by the agreement must pay dues for the benefits he received is in effect a modified union shop . . . It is true that under the present agreement everyone does not have to belong to the union, as in a union shop, but it is a condition of employment that everyone must pay his dues." England called the insurance-plan proposal an "outstanding feature" of the new contract and commented, "There are many other improvements . . . better grievance-procedure and seniority provisions; more liberal leave-of-absence clause; extra time for committee men and plant chairmen for the settlement of grievances; . . . the union to be the sole bargaining agent; three hours call-in pay; payment of wages on company time and a more liberal injury allowance."[107]

The only reported objections to the Rand decisions came from C.S. Jackson, Canadian director of the UE. He emphasized that "it must be recognized that the judgement contains a cleverly devised formula which, if not fully understood and properly dealt with by the union, could mean a setback for genuine union security and a major obstacle in the way of achieving wage demands." However, it appears that David Croll, in a statement made the same day as Jackson's, expressed the general attitude of the organized trade-union movement to the Rand settlement. "The decision of Mr. Justice Rand is of tremendous social and economic significance. Stripped of its nonessentials, it grants to the Ford workers the union shop and checkoff. The award . . . is a resounding blow for the advancement of labour's rights in our economy. It is a great milestone in the development of labour-management relations as was the initial recognition of collective bargaining."[108]

Further on in his remarks Croll commented, "What Mr. Justice Rand has done is obvious. He has taken management-labour disputes out of the brick-and-tear-gas stage. His decision has delivered potential members to the union and given it union security. And to the company he has given a measure of security as well, protection from wildcat strikes."[109] This latter declaration would seem to have been quickly appreciated by the Ford management. Company stockholders were advised in their report of April 1946 that "Word comes from all our plants that the men seem anxious to produce. Since the strike, which began on September 12, 1945, and ended on December 19, 1945, grievances, which to some extent are a barometer of labour relations, have been at a minimum. Infractions of company rules are also at a minimum."[110]

The results of the Ford Windsor Strike of 1945 were to be felt throughout the whole industrial sector of Canada during the postwar period. The Rand Formula became and still remains an integral part of Canadian labour relations. Various labour leaders and other persons involved may have disagreed on the timing, the conduct and the initial settlement of the dispute. However, with regard to the "Rand remedy," there is nothing but unanimity in declaring that the outcome of the Ford walkout of 1945 made it the most important postwar strike in Canada.

It should be noted that almost thirty years of experience with the Rand Formula has qualified the initial enthusiasm of labour leaders somewhat. The concession of union shop and checkoff, for instance, although initially a tremendous victory for workers in Canada, has produced some problems. The contact between union officials and the men they represent has diminished, because it is no longer necessary to approach the men monthly on an individual basis to collect union dues. Art Schultz, a founding member of UAW Local 222 in Oshawa, was opposed to the checkoff from the beginning because he felt that it would weaken the close links the union leadership had developed with its rank and file when the plants were first organized. "When the company starts doing things for the union, like collecting union dues, then you know the union is in for some trouble . . ."[111]

The heavy penalties set down by Rand for wildcat strikes, which led to reliance on the grievance procedure to settle disputes, has also created problems. Stoppages of work over complaints that workers had about working conditions usually brought an immediate response from the company; management would want to settle the dispute quickly in order to get production rolling again. The grievance procedure, however, has a tendency to be carried out much more slowly, sometimes taking weeks or months before the problem is resolved. The grievance is usually handled by union officials rather than by the men themselves and this decreases substantially the number of workers who become involved in settling controversies. These problems can, of course, be overcome, but they do give a critical perspective to the remarks made by David Croll.

Throughout the Windsor strike of 1945, the UAW not only struggled with the Ford Motor Company; it also had to contend with a serious dispute within its own ranks and those of the Canadian Congress of Labour. Before, during and after the Local 200 walkout, a battle to determine the political direction of both the UAW and the CCL was carried on between the forces of the CCF and the Labour Progressive party. The rivalry between the CCF faction, led by Steelworker Director Charles Millard, and that of the Communist LPP, directed mainly by C.S. Jackson of the United Electrical Workers, became particularly acute in Windsor as a result of provincial and federal elections held earlier in 1945.

Since its emergence in 1933, the Co-operative Commonwealth Federation had become the rising star of Canadian "third" parties during the war period. It reached its zenith in Ontario in the election of 1943 and on the national level with its reported Gallup-poll lead over the Liberals in 1944. Then, both the Ontario provincial and the federal elections of 1945 saw attempts by the CCF to replace either the Liberal or Conservative party fatally thwarted. One of the key areas of this reversal was Windsor. In both elections, a strong coalition of the Liberals and the LPP had been effective in denying the CCF any members from the Windsor ridings. Federally, two Liberals—Paul Martin and Ed Brown—were elected. Of more serious consequence to the CCF, however, were the results of the provincial election of June 1945. Before the contest the CCF held all three Windsor seats, yet they came away from the polls with nothing. The combination of a Liberal-Labour-LPP coalition running against CCF and Conservative candidates produced two Tory victories and one for the Liberal group.[112] Because the UAW leadership had been actively involved with the anti-CCF forces, they came under attack as LPP sympathizers from federation supporters within and without the Canadian labour movement.[113]

With the conclusion of the war and the calling of the UAW strike at Ford of Canada, a change of LPP tactics once again occurred. From the declaration of war by Canada in September 1939 to the German invasion of Russia in June 1941, the Communists had been engaged in opposing Canada's war efforts. However, during the rest of the war the Canadian Communist party reverted to what Gad Horowitz calls their "right-wing deviationism" and "class collaborationism."[114] Concerned with strenuously urging Canadians to win the war against fascism and actively supporting the "no-strike" pledge, the LPP supported the political group that they felt best reflected their demands. In most cases, the Liberal party reaped the benefits. The end of the war then brought the Communists full circle as they "advocated an unrelenting battle to the death with Ford."[115] The approach of the Labour Progressive party to the strike was certainly closer to the militant mood of the Ford workers than that taken by the CCF,[116] although charges made during and after the strike that the walkout was led and directed by the Communists cannot be substantiated.[117]

There can be no doubt, however, that the Communists were active in all stages of the development of the UAW in Windsor up until that time. "Many Ford workers who tried to organize during the thirties were fired and blacklisted . . . many of these were Communists . . . because Communists always played an initiative role in organizing, particularly at Ford where there was a large plant . . ."[118] Oscar Kogan, the Windsor leader of the LPP throughout this period, claims that the Communists had little to do with the actual decision-making process of the union at any time, even during the strike. When he arrived in Windsor in late 1941, the LPP was strongly pushing the "no-strike" policy. Even so, "over the years throughout the war the workers were . . . restrained by the UAW leadership, not by the LPP, but by the UAW leadership . . . from fighting for their full and just demands because of the 'no strike' policy . . ."[119] This was not true in all cases. Before June 1941, George Burt maintains that he was criticized by the LPP for not calling strikes of his union "to resist [the] capitalist war that was going on in Europe." Then, following the German invasion of the USSR, he "pulled out people against LPP wishes."[120]

Burt does not deny the fact that he was willing to accept the help of the LPP although he was a member of the CCF[121] and usually voted for the federation. He also worked with the Communists within the union. "It wasn't official . . . generally I got along pretty good with the leadership of the Communist party . . . I didn't give in to them . . . neither did I oppose them . . . I believed the CCF people were trying to defeat me . . . I faced opposition wherever I went . . . so I reacted . . . I accepted the support of the LPP if they had anybody to support me with . . . Anybody who wasn't with the CCF at this time was called a Communist . . . in our union Thomas and Addes were accused of being Communists."[122]

The case of George Addes, the UAW international secretary-treasurer, proves to be an interesting example of the misconceptions and red-baiting that were rife within and without the auto workers. In a letter dated March 9, 1944, David Lewis relates a conversation he had with Walter Reuther about George Burt. "Walter told me that George still is completely in the camp of Addes and Frankensteen. He always votes with the Communist gang on the international board."[123] Paul Martin says that, during the 1945 walkout, on the advice of Pat Conroy, he contacted Addes in efforts to develop a settlement. "He had the reputation of being a Communist . . . it was thought that with Communist backing for the UAW directorate in Windsor, he would be an appropriate person to intervene." It was only after Martin had met with Addes in Ottawa that he became convinced Addes was not a Communist at all.[124]

Alex Parent, the president of Amalgamated Local 195, was another man who was tagged a Communist and was thereby defeated in his efforts to retain his position in 1946. Again, in his case the claim would appear to have been unfounded.[125] "He was pretty close to the LPP . . . [but] neither Parent nor England were members of the LPP."[126] Oscar Kogan states that although "Parent, England and I were good friends . . . they were not members of the LPP.''[127]

Both Kogan and Joseph Salsberg[128] claim that they and the party had nothing to do with the important tactical decisions that were made by the union during the strike. The massive picketing, the withdrawal of power-plant workers, the building of the auto barricade, the sending of the one-day-strike telegrams and even the initial rejection of the negotiation-arbitration settlement plan were all decisions made by the union itself with little Communist influence.[129] Thus it was without realizing the militancy of the union leadership and their rank and file that people like Charles Millard charged that the union and the strike were Communist-dominated.

The dismissal of the National Ford Strike Committee of the CCL during the strike[130] did not deter Millard, the head of the Canadian Steelworkers, from continued attempts to impose himself on Burt and the UAW. Millard, in a letter dated December 31, 1945, confides to Burt that, ''As a result of my personal and union interest in the UAW and . . . as a member of the Congress NFSC, I am quite concerned about the present situation and outlook in Windsor.'' Going on to allude to membership dissatisfaction with the present leadership at the local level and asking Burt what he feels should be done, Millard then offers his assistance.[131]

Although Burt made it clear that he did not need his help, Millard did actively involve himself. After the conclusion of the strike, ''The CCFers in Windsor, guided by their friends in Steel and the Ontario CCF-TUC, were organizing to overthrow the Communist leaders of Locals 195 and 200.''[132] Within a very short time, the CCF groups within the two locals were to be successful in replacing most of the ''Communists'' within their executives.[133]

The Ford Windsor strike of 1945 proved to be the major turning point for Communist involvement and participation in the Canadian UAW. The successful drive to push the Communists out of the union began with the settlement of the dispute. Certainly the Canadian Communist party made mistakes in its involvement with the Canadian labour movement. However, it is ironic that, on an occasion when the LPP actively supported the cause of the Ford workers and in a genuine sense effectively reflected the mood and militancy of the union rank and file, it was that same occasion that was to be misread by the CCF and other ''anti-Communists'' within the labour movement as a sign of LPP ascendancy, and that was to set off the movement to remove the LPP from the UAW.

Notes

1. "Canada during this century has been a country having a record of labour unrest and industrial conflict, with illegal and violent overtones, second only to the United States, and far greater than that of most European countries." Stuart Marshall Jamieson, *Times of Trouble: Labour Unrest and Industrial Conflict in Canada, 1900-66,* Privy Council Task Force on Labour Relations, study no. 22 (Ottawa, 1968), p. 9.

2. No wage dispute was involved because the wage-policy legislation established during the war was still in effect. There was no real purpose in going on strike for higher wages because the increases were subject to approval from the war labour boards.

3. The Ford Motor Company of Canada Limited was incorporated at a value of $125,000, of which the parent company controlled $63,750 (from an advertisement placed by the Montreal Joint Ford Strike Committee in the Montreal *Star,* 4 December 1945). From its genesis the Canadian company was effectively controlled by Ford Dearborn. The issue of foreign control of Ford becomes important later in the strike when company officials argue that Ford of Canada was independent of the parent company in the United States.

4. Apart from strong anti-union beliefs, Wallace Campbell, the president of Ford of Canada during the 1945 walkout, maintained that his position in Canadian industrial circles prevented him from granting the union shop and checkoff. Interviews with George Burt and Paul Martin.

5. However, good wages meant very little if you were employed on a seasonal basis. Arthur Reaume, mayor of Windsor during the strike, recalled the situation: "We [the municipality] kept in pretty fair health a ready know-how number of people who knew how to make automobiles. So the industry would employ them when they needed them and then when things got a little slow, they'd say, 'You feed them and then back they'd come on top of you . . .' " Interview with Arthur Reaume.

6. Interviews with Charles MacDonald and Pat Lauzon. Macdonald tells of one instance when a group of assemblymen who had had enough started to walk off the job. When they reached the plant gates they were told that if they returned to work, they would get helpers; but at quitting time they were fired, having trained their own replacements. Men were dragged from the line to plant windows and forced to look at the unemployed lined up at the company gates. They would then be told that unless they hurried up, someone outside the fence would have their job. Swearing and minor physical abuse was not uncommon and fights occurred regularly between workers

rushing to complete their task in the line. "Every foreman had favourites; chore boys who would cut his lawn and paint his home . . . a foreman would mark on his pink slip that he turned into the Industrial Relations Department whether he wanted a man back to work or not and there was no respect for seniority, years of service or age." Raymond Houlahan, *A History of Collective Bargaining in Local 200 UAW* (M.A. thesis, University of Windsor, 1963), p. 2.

7. See Irving M. Abella, *Nationalism, Communism and Canadian Labour* (Toronto: University of Toronto Press, 1973), pp. 7-22. Although the contract did not recognize the UAW-CIO, the union had effectively organized the plant.

8. Interview with George Burt.

9. Houlahan, *A History of Local 200,* pp. 5, 6.

10. According to George Burt, Campbell initially proposed a ballot that simply read, "Are you in agreement with the company's offer?" No mention of the UAW was of major concern because by this time a majority in the Ford plants had been signed up. Burt went to R.J. Thomas, the international president of the UAW, and R.T. Leonard, Ford UAW director in the US, and told them of his problem in Windsor. Unless the Canadian plant was closed down, Burt believed that the union could lose the whole thing by not being on the ballot. Apparently Harry Bennett, the labour-relations head at Ford in Dearborn, heard about this and invited Burt, Thomas and Leonard to dinner. During the occasion at the Rotunda building, Bennett asked Burt what he wanted. Informing him of the problem, Bennett replied, "I never did like that Campbell. He's too proud a man for me. But what do you want Thomas to do? Surely you're not going to ask Thomas to close down the River Rouge to satisfy your demands against the company in Windsor are you? That little tin-can place over there?" Burt said all he wanted was the material going to the Canadian plant from the States to be stopped. This would strangle production in Windsor and force government involvement because Ford Windsor was a war plant. Bennett then stated, "This is the answer isn't it? We'll show that guy over there, Mr. Burt." He then proceeded to phone the Ford transportation department and ordered the supervisor to stop all shipments destined for Windsor. With Bennett's action, production began to fall off and the government stepped in. It is at this point that the UAW-CIO was included in the ballot. Interview with George Burt. Mr. Burt informed the author that he has written confirmation from R.T. Leonard concerning the above incident with Harry Bennett.

11. Houlahan, *A History of Local 200,* p. 6.

12. Interviews with George Burt, Thomas MacLean, Pat Lauzon, Charles MacDonald; Houlahan, *A History of Local 200,* pp. 6,7. The final figures of the vote were 4455 in favour of the company offer, 6833 in favour of the UAW-CIO.

13. Interview with George Burt; Houlahan, *A History of Local 200,* pp. 7-15. Burt remarked at the time, "It is the best agreement we have signed with a major Canadian auto plant." The contract recognized the union (UAW-CIO), whereas the GM contract read "an agreement between General Motors of Canada and its employees." Burt believes they obtained what they did, ironically enough, because of the bargaining inexperience of the Ford management.

14. "When the widest measure of government control was in effect, a change of employment of any person between the ages of 16 and 65 could be made only with the permission of the Selective Service officer." Stephen Cako, "Labour's Struggle for Union Security: The Ford of Canada Strike, Windsor 1945" (M.A. thesis, University of Guelph, 1971), p. 34.

15. The strike of November 1942 concerned a company attempt to hire women at

two-thirds the rate of men and the union demand of "equal pay for equal work." The union won the issue but no women were ever hired to work in the plant.

16. Troubles with a foreman and a speed-up charge precipitated the April 1943 shut-down.

17. A speed-up charge led to a dispute and then a number of stewards were suspended by the company. The men then walked out and the company attempted to cancel the agreement on grounds of "breach of contract." Work was finally resumed when an umpire was appointed to settle all disputes until the parties agreed to a new contract.

18. Interviews with George Burt, Oscar Kogan, Charles MacDonald.

19. Interviews with George Burt, Pat Lauzon.

20. In an advertisement that appeared in the Windsor *Star*, 24 November 1945, Ford cited their experience in the United States as a reason for objecting to union security and checkoff. They maintained that the company had encountered 773 work stoppages since the American contract had been signed in 1941.

21. Interviews with George Burt, Thomas MacLean; *Backstage at Windsor*, pp. 1, 2. *Backstage* was a pamphlet "published by a group of United Automobile Workers, members of Local 195 and 200." There is no doubt that the pamphlet was written by people in the CCF faction within the union.

22. Louis Fine at this time was chief conciliation officer for the Ontario Department of Labour.

23. Quoted from a *Short Chronological History of the Dispute* (p. 2), given by the conciliation board, which reported on 11 September 1945.

24. *Ford Facts*, 29 March 1945; Conciliation Board, *Short Chronological History*, p. 2.

25. Conciliation Board, *Short Chronological History*, p. 2; Toronto *Globe and Mail*, 20 December 1945.

26. Conciliation Board, *Short Chronological History*, pp. 2, 3; Toronto *Globe and Mail*, 4,5 September 1945.

27. Toronto *Globe and Mail*, 4 September 1945. See *Ford Facts*, 30 August 1945, for union rationale of demands made to the company.

28. Toronto *Globe and Mail*, 4 September 1945.

29. Toronto *Globe and Mail*, 5 September 1945; *Ford Facts*, 30 August 1945.

30. Toronto *Globe and Mail*, 12,13 September 1945; Windsor *Star*, 12 September 1945.

31. Toronto *Globe and Mail*, 13 September 1945.

32. Windsor *Star*, 13 September 1945.

33. Interviews with George Burt, Pat Lauzon. The office workers were paid their salaries for the duration of the strike by the company.

34. Windsor *Star*, 15 September 1945.

35. The joint policy committee was made up of union officials from both UAW Locals 200 and 195.

36. Toronto *Globe and Mail*, 15 September 1945.

37. Toronto *Globe and Mail*, 13, 20 September 1945; I.M. Abella, "The Struggle for Industrial Unionism in Canada" (Ph.D. thesis, University of Toronto, 1969), pp. 223-224. Millard expressed fears of a reappearance of Communist elements and Mosher felt the strike should not become a "national issue."

38. A married couple was entitled to five dollars per week, one dollar for each child under three, $1.50 for a child three to six years of age, and two dollars for any child older than six. Single workers received three dollars per week.

39. Local merchants extended credit, outlying farming districts contributed produce (a number of farmers moonlighted at Ford of Canada) and large and small donations came from numerous unions and locals.

40. Toronto *Globe and Mail,* 23 November 1945; Interview with Arthur Reaume; Cako, "Labour's Struggle for Union Security," p. 70. When arguing his case, Reaume mentioned a man with a family of nine whose outlay for food and rent alone amounted to $164 a month. With a paycheck of $187.70 from Ford, he only had $23.70 left for other essentials such as clothing and medical care when he was working.

41. *Labour Leader,* 26 December 1941. Mitchell was a member of the Electrical Division of the International Union of Steam and Operating Engineers—he was an electrical operating engineer by trade.

42. Interview with Paul Martin.

43. Abella, "The Struggle for Industrial Unionism," pp. 109-110.

44. Toronto *Globe and Mail,* 29 September, 1 October 1945.

45. Toronto *Globe and Mail,* 10, 11 October 1945.

46. Toronto *Globe and Mail,* 10 October 1945. Martin argued that "These industries will have to learn that they cannot treat their workers as bits of steel on the cement floors of their plants. There could be no greater mistake than to attempt to break the union as some people connected with the plant have suggested."

47. Toronto *Globe and Mail,* 10 October 1945.

48. See Abella, "The Struggle for Industrial Unionism," pp. 48-50.

49. Both Charles Millard (USA) and C.S. Jackson (UE) were speakers. Toronto *Daily Star, Globe and Mail,* 9 October 1945.

50. Interview with George Burt; Toronto *Globe and Mail,* 16, 17, 18 October 1945.

51. Quote is taken from *Special Ford Strike Bulletin* signed by George Burt (n.d.), p. 3. Mitchell's "compromise" was less than what the conciliation board had recommended the union accept.

52. On October 12, Burns Meats had been placed under a government controller through an order-in-council. Walkouts by packinghouse workers, organized under the CIO-CCL union, forced the government's hand as Ottawa attempted to deal with the problem of wartime meat shortages and civilian rationing. On October 16 Swifts and Canada Packers were also placed under government supervision. The actions made Mitchell's earlier statements about such actions not being within the realm of federal or provincial power look ludicrous.

53. Interview with Paul Martin.

54. Windsor *Star,* 19 October 1945.

55. George Burt made missionary trips to Flint, Pontiac, Detroit, Toledo, and in one instance Local 200 received eleven thousand dollars (Canadian) from the Willow Run bomber plant in Michigan. Windsor *Star,* 30 October 1945; Letter from George Burt to all UAW-CIO locals in the US, 9 December 1945.

56. In a statement published 20 July 1946, Local 200 listed the union contributions in Canada, which totalled $159,961.54. Interview with George Burt.

57. Toronto *Globe and Mail,* 30 October, 2 November 1945; Windsor *Star,* 30 October 1945.

58. Windsor *Star,* 2 November 1945. See also Abella, "The Struggle for Industrial Unionism," p. 225, where mention is made of a letter from the Association of Insurance Underwriters of Ontario supporting the company's statements.

59. Letter from Local 200 powerhouse employees to the federal minister of Labour, Humphrey Mitchell, 27 October 1945, UAW Labor Archives, Wayne State University, Detroit, Michigan.

60. Windsor *Star,* 2 November 1945. Normally a contingent of between twenty-five and forty men were allowed into the plant for each shift.

61. Interview with Arthur Reaume; Toronto *Globe and Mail,* 3 November 1945.

62. The decision to send the RCMP was made by acting Prime Minister Ilsley without any discussion with the cabinet. Interview with Paul Martin.

63. Windsor *Star,* 14 September 1945.

64. Toronto *Globe and Mail,* 5 November 1945.

65. Known as the Millar Road barricade, it was formed around Ford River Rouge when the UAW-CIO struck the Ford Motor Company in April 1941. See Irving Bernstein, *Turbulent Years: A History of the American Worker, 1933-1941* (Boston: Houghton Mifflin, 1969), p. 744. Interviews with George Burt, George Addes.

66. Interview with George Burt.

67. Toronto *Globe and Mail,* 6 November 1945; Interviews with Thomas MacLean, Pat Lauzon. Insurance companies were quick to notify car owners whose vehicles were in the barricade that "The policy provisions exclude loss of car, or damage done to car, in riots or civil commotion." Windsor *Star,* 6 November 1945.

68. Toronto *Globe and Mail,* 6 November 1945. George Addes maintains that Campbell's illness was a major factor in the company's attitude and believes that Henry Ford II probably did all he could, given the situation. Interview with George Addes.

69. Toronto *Globe and Mail,* 6 November 1945.

70. Toronto *Globe and Mail,* 7 November 1945.

71. Toronto *Globe and Mail,* 8 November 1945.

72. Cako, "Labour's Struggle for Union Security," p. 85.

73. Toronto *Globe and Mail,* 9 November 1945.

74. Toronto *Globe and Mail,* 8 November 1945.

75. Cako, "Labour's Struggle for Union Security," p. 86.

76. Toronto *Globe and Mail,* 8, 10 November 1945.

77. Toronto *Globe and Mail,* 12 November 1945.

78. Cako, "Labour's Struggle for Union Security," p. 87.

79. Toronto *Globe and Mail,* 13 November 1945.

80. Toronto *Globe and Mail,* 13 November 1945.

81. Toronto *Globe and Mail,* 13 November 1945.

82. Interviews with Paul Martin, George Addes. Martin first phoned Phillip Murray, president of the CIO, and then R.J. Thomas, international president of the UAW-CIO.

83. Toronto *Globe and Mail,* 16, 17 November 1945.

84. Toronto *Globe and Mail,* 21, 22 November 1945.

85. Toronto *Globe and Mail,* 23, 24 November 1945.

86. Toronto *Globe and Mail,* 24 November 1945.

87. Toronto *Globe and Mail,* 24 November 1945.

88. Toronto *Globe and Mail,* 27, 28, 29 November 1945.

89. Interviews with Paul Martin, George Burt; Toronto *Globe and Mail,* 12 November 1945.

90. Interview with George Burt.

91. Interview with George Burt.

92. Interview with Paul Martin.

93. Toronto *Globe and Mail,* 29 November 1945.

94. Interview with George Burt.

95. Interview with Thomas MacLean.

96. Toronto *Globe and Mail,* 30 November 1945.

97. Toronto *Globe and Mail,* 8 December 1945.

98. Toronto *Globe and Mail,* 17 December 1945.

99. Toronto *Globe and Mail,* 20 December 1945.

100. Toronto *Globe and Mail,* 21 December 1945.

101. Interview with Paul Martin.

102. The minutes of the Rand arbitration hearings are available at the UAW Labor Archives, Wayne State University, Detroit, Michigan.

103. From the written text of the Rand decision, p. 1251, UAW Labor Archives.

104. *Ibid.,* pp. 1255-1257.

105. The insurance plan was worked out later.

106. Rand decision, p. 1257.

107. *Ford Facts,* 11 February 1946.

108. Toronto *Globe and Mail,* 31 January 1946.

109. Toronto *Globe and Mail,* 31 January 1946.

110. Stephen Cako, "Labour's Struggle for Union Security," p. 141.

111. Interview with Art Schultz.

112. In the provincial election, George Burt, Alex Parent and Arthur Reaume all ran against Conservative and CCF candidates initially as UAW nominees. "All three were then nominated as official Liberal candidates by the Liberal constituency associations. They ran as 'UAW-Liberal-Labour' candidates endorsed by the LPP. Paul Martin . . . not only placed the whole Liberal organization at work for the UAW . . . candidates, but personally spoke on many mutual platforms." Gad Horowitz, *Canadian Labour in Politics* (Toronto: University of Toronto Press, 1968), p. 113.

113. George Burt explained the election as follows: "We were trying to get rid of Colonel Drew [the Ontario Conservative premier] . . . I ran in Windsor-Walkerville with Liberal support . . . The CCF ran a candidate against me even though they made deals elsewhere with the Liberals . . . we would have won the riding with CCF support . . ." Interview with George Burt. Also see Horowitz, *Canadian Labour,* pp. 108-113.

114. Horowitz, *Canadian Labour,* p. 89.

115. Horowitz, *Canadian Labour,* p. 114.

116. "Communist trade unionists and laymen in contrast to the CCL-CCFers, came out one hundred per cent behind the Ford strike. C.S. Jackson . . . George Harris . . . Joe Salsberg MPP-St. Andrews, Tim Buck, national LPP leader, and Leslie Morris, Ontario LPP leader, spent much of their time in Windsor speaking at meetings of unionists and conferring with strike leaders. The Communists devoted hours to walking the Ford picket line and to distributing copies of the LPP newspaper, the *Canadian Tribune*..." Cako, "Labour's Struggle for Union Security," p. 115.

117. See Horowitz, *Canadian Labour,* pp. 113-115. "Unfortunately the direction of affairs in the Windsor auto union had fallen under the influence of members and supporters of the Labour Progressive (Communist) party and the needs of the LPP . . . From what was left [of the strike] they might pick up some choice pieces and while the Ford workers might starve this winter the Communist party would, if the stragegy worked, end up with domination of the Canadian Congress of Labour." From *Backstage at Windsor.*

118. Interview with Oscar Kogan.

119. *Ibid.*

120. Interview with George Burt. One such incident was a strike called at McKinnon Industries of St. Catharines, a subsidiary of General Motors.

121. Contrary to Horowitz, Burt claims he became a member of the CCF in 1938. See Horowitz, *Canadian Labour,* p. 109. Interview with George Burt.

122. Interview with George Burt. The Canadian director of the UAW claims that the problem arose after he defeated Charles Millard for the directorship of the union in 1939. Because of the struggle within the union between the LPP and the CCF, and since Millard was a staunch CCF supporter, Burt was then considered to be in the Communist camp. However, he states that his desire was to remain apolitical. "I didn't want to get involved in it . . . I was interested only in organizing the autoworkers . . ."

123. Lewis to Jollife, 9 March 1944, in Horowitz, *Canadian Labour,* p. 109.

124. Interview with Paul Martin. Martin recounts that when he saw Addes kneel beside his bed in prayer at the Lord Elgin, his belief that Addes was a Communist was completely disspelled.

125. See Horowitz, *Canadian Labour,* p. 113. "Alex Parent [and other members of the Local 195 executive] . . . All were members of the LPP." Cako, "Labour's Struggle for Union Security," p. 110.

126. Interview with George Burt.

127. Interview with Oscar Kogan. Kogan, however, does not deny that he attempted to win over Parent to become a member of the party. Further evidence that Parent was not a member of the LPP comes from Norman Penner, a member of the party at this time.

128. Besides being the LPP member of the legislature from Toronto-St. Andrews, Salsberg was the party's expert in the labour movement.

129. Interviews with Oscar Kogan, Joseph Salsberg.

130. Oscar Kogan described the dispute as he saw it between the union and the NFSC as follows: "The dispute with the NFSC was one [in which] the local people who were directly involved in the strike felt that one thing should be done and the people in Ottawa leading the NFSC felt another thing should be done . . . I think the people on the spot certainly knew what was best for them, more so than Millard or Conroy."

131. Letter from Charles Millard to George Burt, 31 December 1945, UAW Labor

Archives. Part of Millard's letter reads as follows: "I am writing this letter to ask for your opinion as to what you think ought to be done to meet the situation in the Windsor UAW . . . in the matter of personal leadership for those members who feel that much, if not most, of the present local union leadership should be replaced." Millard also sent a letter to Pat Conroy the same day, informing him of his letter to Burt and explaining his position.

132. Horowitz, *Canadian Labour,* p. 115.

133. See Cako, "Labour's Struggle for Union Security," p. 131. Although Parent was defeated as president of Local 195, Roy England was able to hold on to the top position in Local 200. Cako relates CCF success to the Gouzenko spy disclosure case just prior to the elections and the Communist scare that developed immediately afterwards.

6 Asbestos 1949

by Fraser Isbester

A frequent comment on Quebec's not-so-quiet revolution is that the first encounter, or at least that which galvanized the province and began the deterioration of the Duplessis era, was the Asbestos workers' strike of 1949. Writing at or close to the time of the strike, Father Jacques Cousineau predicted that it would live as "... one of the most important events in the social history of French Canada."[1] Jean C. Falardeau saw the strike as a "quasi-revolution."[2] In the view of both Frank R. Scott[3] and of Stuart Jamieson,[4] the strike was the turning point in the postwar social history of Quebec. It was the key that unlocked the door to the quiet revolution.

Viewed through spectacles one-quarter century thick, it seems less probable that the strike was an initiator of social change so much as part of a process of change already well begun. Pierre Elliott Trudeau observed five years after the strike:

> It was the date that was the determinant and not the place, nor the particular industry; chance could well have dictated that the strike break out in another location than Asbestos.[5]

Not only chance, but simple logic would seem to dictate that the strike break out elsewhere than in the sparsely populated asbestos fields of the Eastern Townships. By mid-twentieth century Quebec had become Canada's most urban province, statistically speaking, with more than one-half of its population living in metropolitan Montreal. The urban population had been increasing at an annual rate in excess of fifteen per cent since the turn of the century, and while there remained a discrete resources economy and an agricultural or traditional economy, the provincial industrial economy had become the real "new Quebec." The descendants of the agriculturally oriented, rural parishioners of a century past had come to man the mines and mills of Quebec, concentrating their numbers where industry concentrated.[6]

Cut loose from its parochial bonds, strangers among strangers, this new industrial working class was only the most obvious manifestation of the changed character of Quebec. The Church, because of its slow adaptation to the changing circumstances of the province and because, too, of its great reluctance to challenge the political authority of the government of Maurice Duplessis, was becoming increasingly ineffectual in its traditional leadership role. Duplessis' well-entrenched National Union government cared as little for the problems of the urban workers as it did for their votes, and continued to address itself primarily to the rural minority and the traditionalists of the province.

Nature abhors a vacuum and, in the absence of traditional leaders for the industrial working class, the vacuum was easily filled by the unions. This is not to suggest that Quebec's labour unions are of recent date, but rather that their role as leaders and their powerful status are recent. In particular, this is the case for the Catholic unions, including the asbestos workers' unions.

Beginning in 1937 and 1938 with the Sorel shipbuilding and Dominion Textile strikes, the militancy of the Canadian and Catholic Confederation of Labour (CCCL) was comparable to that of its rivals in the Trades and Labour Congress (TLC) and the Canadian Congress of Labour (CCL). During the forties each of the three national union centrals grew dramatically as Quebec expanded its secondary manufacturing sector. In 1940 the CCCL comprised 239 "syndicates" or locals, 11 trade or industry federations, 7 regional federations and 8 city centrals.[7] Its membership was 46, 341. By 1948 the confederation included 428 locals, 16 industry or trade federations, 7 regional federations and 15 city centrals. There were 93,370 members.[8]

The change was by no means exclusively physical. With expansion had come a new leadership—one very much attuned to the bread-and-butter issues of modern industrial unionism. Additionally, the cultural homogeneity of the unions had been somewhat diluted by an infusion of new workers, neither "Canadien" nor "anglais," and by an increase in the female participation rate. The clergy, too, had changed. Most of the younger clerics had come of age in an urban, industrial Quebec and, as early as the Sorel strike, individual clerics (such as Monseigneur Desranleau in Sorel) were adapting to the predominant North American norm—business unionism—by assuming the role of counsel and, sometimes, leaders of the unions.

Somewhat insular, the unions in the asbestos fields tended to have been washed into a prosperous but little disturbed backwater of Quebec's economy. During the late thirties and the war years, the demand for asbestos had grown at an unprecedented rate. By 1948, only one other area (the Belgian Congo) in the non-communist world could produce the quantity and quality of the mineral found in the Eastern Townships. Thus, both companies and employees prospered.

Asbestos, the mineral, has great commercial value because it is fibrous and non-combustible, and may be woven or molded into fireproof fabrics or objects. First discovered in Quebec in 1862 by a farmer named Webb, it was for several years regarded as no more than an annoying impediment to farming. Within fifteen years, however, the first asbestos mine was opened at Thetford and, in spite of extreme fluctuation in demand and consequent great price instability, by 1892 there were nineteen producers with a combined annual output of about ten thousand tons.[9]

By 1949 the number of producers in the Eastern Townships had been reduced to six: the Asbestos Corporation, the Johnson Company, Bell Asbestos, Canadian Johns-Manville (CJM), Nicolet Asbestos and Flintkote Mines.[10] Together, they accounted for the total consumption of asbestos in the United States and Canada and they were developing new markets in Europe and Asia.

The largest of the producers was and is CJM. Located on the site of farmer Webb's "ledge," the company's mine is the biggest open pit in the world. Nearby, in the town of Asbestos, a virtual company town with a population in 1948 of 8650[11] (eighty-nine per cent of whom were dependent on CJM), is the company mill and factory. At the time of the strike the company employed 2100 persons in its mine, mill and factory.

The changes in the central administration of the CCCL which most intrigued the asbestos workers were a decision, taken in 1947, to commission a study of asbestosis, a respiratory disease caused by inhaling asbestos dust, and, in the same year, the decision to introduce a standard contract for all mines. The individual unions authorized the Federation of Mining Employees, with which they were associated, to negotiate this contract in their name. The first contract was negotiated speedily and without incident. It expired on January 1, 1949.

The second contract negotiations were to lead to one of the most dramatic strikes in Canadian history.

On December 10, 1948, in Thetford Mines, the negotiations for a new labour contract for the coming year were begun between representatives of the Asbestos Corporation and CJM on industry's side, and representatives of the Federation of Mining Employees and the CCCL on labour's side. The management negotiating committee was made up of Mr. G.K. Foster, general manager of CJM in Asbestos, Mr. C.M. McGaw, for twelve years industrial-relations manager of CJM, and Mr. Soutar of Thetford Mines. Labour's negotiating committee consisted of Mr. Jean Marchand, secretary of the CCCL, Mr. Randolph Hamel, president of the Federation of Mining Employees, and Mr. Armand Larivée, president of the Asbestos Workers' Union.

Negotiations continued on the 11th, 20th and 21st of December, by which time it had become fairly obvious to all concerned that a resolution of the conflicting points of view would not be reached easily.[12]

The union demands were as follows:

1. Elimination of asbestos dust inside and outside of the mills.
2. A fifteen-cent-an-hour general increase.
3. An eighteen per cent increase for employees on incentive-pay system.
4. An increase of five cents an hour for night work.
5. Placing by the company of an amount equal to three per cent of gross salaries into a social-security fund to be administered by the union.
6. The Rand Formula.
7. Double-time payment for work on Sundays and holidays.
8. Nine paid holidays a year.
9. An increase in vacation benefits.
10. The right to consultation in all cases of promotion, transfer or discharge.
11. The right for employees to accept or refuse production standards.
12. An inquiry by the union into Sunday labour.
13. A change in the contract date for the local at Asbestos from February 1 to January 1.

According to the company, the union demands could be broken down into five categories. Management considered the fifth, "to take over management rights," to be the most significant. The company version of union demands was as follows:

1. *Wages and working conditions:*
   An increase of fifteen cents per hour.
   For night work an extra five cents an hour.
   An eighteen per cent increase to all people on incentives.
   Nine paid holidays—no work but full pay.
   Two weeks vacation with pay.
   Double pay for Sundays and holidays.
2. *Elimination of dust:*
   A provision in the contract to guarantee elimination of all asbestos dust inside and outside the mills.

3. *Welfare fund:*
   An amount of dollars equal to three per cent of gross earnings to be turned over to the federation for a welfare fund.
   Disabled employees to be retained on company payrolls.
4. *The Rand Formula:*
   The company must deduct from each employee's pay all syndicate dues, whether the employee agrees or not and whether the employee is a member or not.
5. *To take over management rights:*
   Promotions to be approved by syndicate.
   Disciplinary action by management to be approved by syndicate.
   No incentive installed on any job unless approved by syndicate.
   No changes in job method or rates unless approved by syndicate.[13]

The companies did not counter with a specific offer but, instead, chose the alternative course of trying to reduce the demands of the union.

Throughout the early negotiations CJM followed a process of publishing periodic "progress reports" on the negotiations. These reports, which were made available to all the workers, were a source of considerable friction. Nevertheless, on December 24, CJM established direct contact with the local in Asbestos. Negotiations at this level occurred on the 4th, 5th and 10th of January. The negotiating committees of the federation and the companies met only once more, on January 7. It appeared that further meetings would be useless and, on January 24, the union appealed to the provincial Labour Relations Board for the appointment of a conciliator.

On February 1, 1949, the Quebec Department of Labour sent Mr. Leopold Rogers to Asbestos to act as conciliator. Within a short time he realized that he would be unable to effect a conciliation. On Sunday, February 13, with the agreement of both labour and management negotiators, he wrote to the minister of Labour, Antonio Barrette, suggesting arbitration. In Asbestos a meeting of the workers was called by the union leaders for that same evening to announce this latest development. About 1800 workers were present.[14]

> Discussion centred on the tactics to be adopted to force the company to revise its policy. Mr. Jean Marchand explained that only two alternatives were open: recourse to arbitration as the law provides, or opting immediately for an illegal strike. The secretary-general recognized, for his part, that the institution of arbitration had been seriously compromised locally. The unionists of Asbestos had only used arbitration on one occasion and the president of the board then would have been willing to endorse management's position without giving any consideration to the union's arguments.[15]

At the conclusion of Mr. Marchand's speech, the miners indicated that they chose to strike. Mr. Marchand then suggested a twenty-four-hour delay during which time he could communicate their decision to the minister of Labour. His suggestion was drowned by shouts of "No, no" and "On with the strike." There could be no turning back now and, accordingly, representatives were sent off to intercept the night shift which was due to begin work at midnight. The secretary of the Asbestos syndicate was delegated the task of preparing and issuing special passes to maintenance crews and other essential workers who would be obliged to enter the plant. Plans for picketing were made, and the first pickets were hastily dispatched to all of the entrances of the CJM property. As Gilles Beausoleil points out in his history of the strike, these pickets were soon forced to seek shelter from the cold and took up their positions within the heated confines of the factory and mill.[16] Spirits were high as the meeting broke up; there was general expectation of a quick capitulation by the company and an early return to work.

All accounts would indicate that the strike came as a considerable surprise to CJM and provincial government officials. Certainly, the press in the province was caught off guard for it gave no indication of the possibility of a strike in the days before the event; on the morning the strike broke out, newspaper coverage was very general and all accounts tended to duplicate the first one filed. The tone of these stories would indicate that they were probably released by the union. For example, the Sherbrooke *Daily Record,* which remained quite aloof throughout the strike, first mentioned it as follows:

> Approximately 2100 employees of Canadian Johns-Manville are idle today as a result of a strike for higher wages. Syndicate officials said the decision to call the strike was taken at a meeting in the church hall last night at which some 1800 persons were present . . . seeking a general wage increase from 85 cents to $1.00 per hour. An increase of 18 per cent for jobbers is sought as well as an increase for night workers to give them $1.05 per hour. Double time on Sundays and holidays is included in the demands as well as two weeks holidays after two years in service instead of the present two weeks after five years, . . . nine paid holidays a year and a social security plan to which the company would contribute three per cent of the workers' salaries. The syndicate wants administration of this plan.[17]

The company did not issue a statement until the afternoon of February 14, when it was announced that an illegal strike was in progress and that, for the company's part, there could be no further negotiations until the strikers returned to work. That night the Thetford syndicates voted unanimously to join the striking Asbestos workers. Only two producing mines were not affected, the Bell Mines in Thetford, whose workers were members of another union, and the Quebec Asbestos mines in East Broughton. Even so, the workers at the Bell Mines left their work temporarily rather than create bad feelings between their union and the federation.

By the second day of the strike a holiday atmosphere had taken hold in the town of Asbestos. "People strolled about in happy groups exchanging optimistic ideas, all of which stressed the point that the miners had chosen the most effective method..."[18] "Fiddlers, accordion players and their associates provide almost continuous music for the jig dancers, impromptu quartets and other artists who are entertaining the strikers. So far, the strikers are in the best of humour. [However] union officials say that the men are united in their intentions to stay away from the pits until their sweeping demands are granted completely... The 'man in the street' is not so sure... To every employee the prospect of a long walkout is none too pleasant and a certain degree of discontent is apparent."[19] Widespread rumours of stockpiling and other company preparations for a long siege, worry over meagre personal resources with little prospect of extended assistance from the union, and rank-and-file discontent over the "excessive demands" of the union which had created the situation were also reported.

As for the company, comment from that quarter was positively laconic. "Company spokesmen," reported the Sherbrooke *Tribune*, "are non-committal. They hint at the possibility of the illegality of the strike affecting proceedings at a later date but as the strike is now a *fait accompli* they say the matter of its illegality is purely a theoretical consideration."[20]

Theoretical or not, it was on this ground that the government chose to take its stand. On February 15, Mr. Barrette, the minister of Labour, sent telegrams to Mr. Hamel and Mr. Marchand outlining the government's position. The following Canadian Press dispatch, datelined Quebec, February 16, tells the story:

> Labour Minister Antonio Barrette said today that the strike is illegal because the workers involved, members of the National Federation of Mining Industry Employees, have refused to submit their case to arbitration. Mr. Barrette recalled that he had intervened personally in a dispute in the asbestos industry in late 1947. He said he thought that the settlement of the dispute, with the increases totalling 27 cents an hour by January of last year, had settled the case. If they continue to refuse arbitration the labour department will be forced to recommend cancellation of the bargaining certificate of the union to

the QLRB. Mr. Barrette said he had sent a telegram to Randolph Hamel, president of the employees' federation, advising him that the strike must be condemned as long as there is no recourse to arbitration. The companies concerned are Canadian Johns-Manville, Asbestos Corporation, Johnson Co., Flintkote Mines Ltd., and Bell Asbestos Mines Ltd.[21]

The following day the company issued a statement describing union claims that dust conditions were a primary cause of the strike as "merely diversion designed to bid for public sympathy and to conceal the real aim which is to tie up the entire asbestos industry in Canada with industry-wide bargaining."[22]

Friday, February 18, 1949, marks an important day in the history of the strike. First, it was to be the last payday for the strikers for a period of some four and a half months. Second, it marked the first overt use of force by either side; and third, events of the day led to the appearance of the Quebec Provincial Police in unusually large numbers. Briefly, events took place as follows: During the morning, Mr. Foster and CJM's company counsel, Mr. Yvan Sabourin, appeared before Mr. Justice Césaire Gervais in Sherbrooke to demand an injunction against picketing. This was granted. They also filed suit for half a million dollars against the union and requested additional police protection for company property, claiming that strikers were preventing company officials and maintenance personnel from maintaining essential services. This was strong medicine indeed, and indicated management's determination. It was met by an equally strong, if unco-ordinated reply from the strikers.[23]

By noon on that Friday the pay cheques were finished and awaiting distribution, and the office staff were to spend the rest of the day bringing the pay accounts up to date. Some time after the pay had been distributed a parade of workers, organized at the strike headquarters which were located in the town hall, descended on the company offices led by a pair of drummers. The office staff was forced to leave. The union's control of CJM property was now complete, and what followed provided the basis for the full-scale intervention of the provincial police. According to company spokesmen, "The company was informed that, if the union's demands were not met before Saturday night, no maintenance employees would be allowed to enter or to remain in the plant, the water pipes would freeze, the boilers would be flooded, the fire prevention and protection systems would be paralyzed . . ."[24]

The following day, a Saturday, was one of rumour and counter-rumour. The police had been sent; the police had not been sent. Negotiations were to be resumed; negotiations were not to be resumed. In general, hopes remained high for an early settlement of the strike. At noon hour, the rumours ceased as the entire community focused its attention on the arrival of about one hundred provincial police under the command of Inspector-General Norbert Labbé. The plant was soon cleared of strikers, and the police organized themselves for the task of guarding the company property. They established their headquarters at the company-owned Hotel Iroquois.[25] The presence of the police was to become the central issue in the weeks that lay ahead.

The immediate reaction was one of outraged surprise. Citizens, both strikers and non-strikers, appealed to the town council for action, and on the following Monday the council sent an appeal for the removal of the police to Mr. Hilaire Beauregard, director of the provincial police. This document suggested that until the arrival of the police the strike had been conducted in a peaceful manner and that the 150 police officers who had been introduced allegedly to protect the CJM property were, in reality, more likely to provoke incidents.

> Be advised that on their arrival a great many of the police were under the influence of alcohol.
>
> Be advised that a certain number of these policemen are guilty of committing indecent acts in the streets and of creating disturbances in public places.
>
> Be advised that these acts [of violence] were committed without warning and evidently with the aim of provoking troubles.[26]

This statement was given to the various news media and received widespread circulation. The mayor of the town, Mr. Albert Goudreau, who had been absent at the time, publicly dissociated himself from the council's action.

For a few days all attention and activity focused on the police issue. The union arranged a meeting between its representatives and Mr. Duplessis to demand the withdrawal of the police. This failed to materialize because the union delegation included Mr. Jean Marchand. The premier said that he would see representatives of the National Federation of Mining Industry Employees and the Asbestos Workers' Union. He refused to meet with any representative of the confederation. Mr. Marchand refused to withdraw.[27]

On the same day, February 24, the minister of Labour, in offering his services to mediate the strike, restated the government's position, emphasizing again the government's contention that it was an illegal strike and that the strikers must return to work before any further action could be taken. The police remained.[28]

On February 25, Mr. G.K. Foster, general manager of CJM, issued a fifteen-point statement outlining his terms for negotiation. Briefly,

Mr. Foster's statement deplored the resolution of the town council asking for the withdrawal of the QPP. He stated the company belief that the police were necessary for the protection of company property. He stated his belief that the workers were not informed or were ill-informed regarding the breakdown of negotiations before the strike, and that if they had been properly informed there would have been no strike. Finally, he stated categorically that there could be no negotiations before the workers returned to their jobs.

The next week passed without serious incident. The issue of the strike was introduced into debate in the legislature on several occasions, and Mr. Duplessis made clear his personal feelings when he described the strike leaders as a group of saboteurs. "It is not the workers who are unsatisfied," he said, "but certain labour leaders who place their personal interests before that of the workers and who seek to cause trouble."[29] On February 28 workers at the Bell Mines ended their token strike, and on March 2 CJM re-established direct contact with its workers in a letter urging them to return to work so that negotiations might be resumed.[30] The following day the offices of the strike-bound companies at Thetford Mines were closed after strikers threatened to enter the buildings.[31] Most of the earlier optimism had gone out of the workers by this time and there was little hope for an early settlement. With this change in attitude, the conflict gradually became more intense.

In an attempt to prevent the prolongation of the strike, Mayor T. Labbé of Thetford Mines led a delegation to Quebec City on March 8 to discuss the possibility of renewed negotiations with Mr. Barrette. The minister replied on the following day that, "if the workers conform with the law in returning to work . . . I will be pleased to recommend the renewal of the certification of their syndicates and, moreover, I am ready to act as mediator . . ."[32] On March 10 CJM again appealed to the workers by letter and in full-page newspaper advertisements. It invited *anyone* who chose to work for the company to do so, simultaneously offering a ten-cent increase in the base rate and four paid holidays a year. With this action the company introduced a new factor into the struggle—strikebreakers.[33]

About this time the provincial police in Asbestos became quite active. They carried out a systematic patrolling of the streets in the little town and, it is alleged, resorted to various threats to force the miners to return to work. For example, Gérard Pelletier reported in *Le Devoir* that, on the one hand, the police were making it extremely difficult for miners to renew their automobile licences and, on the other, they were enforcing the "cutoff" date for 1949 licences very rigidly.[34] These allegations were hotly denied by the police both then and after the strike in a booklet entitled *La Police Provinciale à Asbestos*. It is difficult to determine the veracity of the claims even today; however, it is certainly true that the very presence of a large force of police officers in the area was an invitation to violence, and that the extra police called in did not limit their activities to the protection of the CJM property. For these reasons the police became the focus of hostility during this period of the strike.

On March 14 a dynamite explosion destroyed part of the railroad track leading into the CJM property. It was the first act of violence of real significance and it marked the true beginning of the long drawn-out hostilities that were to follow.[35]

On March 16 a company jeep containing a driver and two company engineers was stopped by a group of strikers. They attempted to overturn the vehicle and, in the attempt, a man was struck by the side of the vehicle and injured in both legs. As a result of this action the municipal police force was augmented by six men.[36]

Two days later a group of men abducted a company official, Mr. Lionel Prize, from his home, severely beat him and left him badly injured on a country road.[37] On March 21 the police made nine arrests. Four of those arrested were charged with intimidation.

The police action stirred up a tempest of newspaper criticism led, as usual, by the fiery Mr. Pelletier. The arrests were described as the "worst examples of police brutality."[38] Three days later a "high official" in the QPP replied to the criticism in a statement released in Quebec City. He claimed that members of the force had been subjected to brutality and had been criminally assaulted. He further stated that the strikers were defying the law and he cited several examples as evidence.[39]

The "defiance" continued, and yet another attempt at settlement initiated by the Chamber of Commerce of Asbestos failed. A dynamite charge was exploded in the yard of the home of Albert Johnson, president of Johnson Mines, on March 27. The same day, a non-striker and two more CJM company officials were beaten. In the legislature, Mr. Duplessis reiterated his government's stand and denounced the anarchy and violence that the government considered to have grown out of the union's illegal act.

By April 1 the strike had assumed definite characteristics. The workers, though acting in defiance of the statutory law, had succeeded in mobilizing the not inconsiderable force of public opinion in their favour. Their point of view was explained to the public by their chaplain, Father Louis Phillippe Camirand, in the following manner: "They are not depriving themselves and their children of their wages for the sake of pleasure; they have been forced to do so because of the unqualifiedly provocative attacks." Nevertheless, in the face of this hostility, "the miners of Asbestos . . . have been and are patient and docile in the extreme."[40] But editorial support makes poor food for hungry children, and by this time food supplies were at their lowest since the strike had begun. To insure the miners' ability to prolong their strike the federation was busy securing food and financial assistance from other CCCL unions and federations and, in spite of the hardship imposed by the lack of income, the strikers gave every indication of being ready and willing to outwait the company.[41]

If it was to be a war of attrition, however, the company also had weapons at its disposal. Secure in the knowledge of the illegality of the strike, CJM had proceeded to hire strikebreakers since its first newspaper ad on March 10.[42] By the end of March, 122 men were at work. Some were old employees and some were new, having been attracted from the outlying towns and villages. The company was thus able to continue producing, according to a "revised production schedule" it is true, but in sufficient quantity to prolong its resistance to the strikers indefinitely.

The strike dragged on. The strikers' food supplies were replenished by truckloads of goods donated by other syndicates, and the federation voted additional sums to augment the depleted syndicate treasury and the relief money paid to needy families.[43] On the company's side the shortage of asbestos was beginning to make itself felt. The new workers were inept and slow to produce, and the labour force did not grow quickly. By the end of April, 252 men were at work but the company was faced with mounting public opposition to this use of strikebreakers. Encouraged by journalistic support, the strikers shifted their attention from the police to the "scabs." Stones were hurled through windows of the homes of strikebreakers, and mysterious phone calls and "threats" were directed at the non-striking workers. The result was the reinforcement of the provincial police in the town of Asbestos, and the wholesale introduction of outside workers who were escorted to and from the company premises by the police.[44]

In a Report to the Stockholders on April 20, the president of CJM pointed out that if the strike continued for many more weeks, stockpiles of asbestos would be exhausted and factories in the United States, Europe, Canada and South America would be forced to close their doors. He calculated that as many as one hundred thousand people could be put out of work. This report was published verbatim in full-page newspaper ads.[45] Mr. Brown also implied that the leadership of the union had passed into the hands of communists. He reiterated CJM's willingness to negotiate but only after the workers had returned to their jobs.

The following day the company announced that it might have to evict some 250 families from company-owned homes. The union, and particularly its chaplain, Father Camirand ("Evictions will take place over my dead body"), were quick to protest, and the minister of Labour advised Mr. Foster "that the government was of the opinion that these threats must be withdrawn."[46] Mr. Foster pointed out in his reply to the minister that the eviction notices had not been sent and that the company's statement was in the nature of a warning because, "sooner or later, it will be necessary for us to find accommodation for the employees who are now working."[47] The workers, for their part, replied to the company's threat and to the importation of "foreign" labour by organizing a long parade on April 22. Early in the morning, two by two, they walked in silent procession through the quiet streets of the town. In Gérard Pelletier's words they were "like soldiers coming out of the mines."[48] For taking part in the organization of this demonstration, Mr. Pelletier, in company with Pierre Elliott Trudeau and Georges Charpentier, was given thirty minutes to get out of town. When he refused Mr. Pelletier was allegedly interrogated in an arrogant manner by the police and then forced to leave Asbestos.[49]

Acts of violence and vandalism directed, in particular, against the strikebreakers continued to increase; in view of this burgeoning atmosphere of hostility, Mr. Barrette made yet another attempt at settlement on April 23. Five days previously, in a much-publicized radio broadcast, Mr. Barrette had declared that, in the government's view, the syndicate was openly challenging the whole of society by calling a strike that was illegal. The government did not say that the workers' claims were unreasonable, but it did say that the workers must submit their claim to arbitration. Union reaction had been instantaneous and strongly critical. At Asbestos and Thetford Mines, meetings of the striking workers had been called to listen to the broadcast. In Asbestos Mr. Picard, president of the CCCL, addressed the workers immediately after the radio speech was concluded. In Thetford Mines Mr. Marchand did the same. Mr. Picard declared that the Labour minister had delivered a "coup de grace" to the hopes of all the workers. In Mr. Marchand's view the minister represented "not labour, but capital." He claimed that the government must be trying to prevent the settlement of the strike, and that it must be acting for the companies in this regard. In the name of the workers, a telegram was sent to Quebec demanding the resignation of Mr. Barrette.[50]

On April 23, at a meeting in Quebec City, Mr. Picard made a more reasoned reply to the remarks of the minister of Labour. Following a description of the asbestos union, its history and its aspirations, and an account of negotiations in the present strike to date,[51] Mr. Picard attempted to fit the strike into its context as a manifestation of a greater economic and social malaise within the province of Quebec. He contended that "it is useless to integrate collective problems into legislation of the past which is meant for the individual."[52] Thus challenged on his own ground, Mr. Barrette announced the next day that an arbitration board was being established to study the points at issue. Workers and company were each to choose a representative, and the representatives together with the Labour Relations Board were to choose a chairman and a third member. The union had agreed that it would order its men back to work as soon as a chairman was selected according to the minister's announcement.[53]

> Once this arbitration board has been constituted, the leaders of the syndicates will recommend a return to work of the strikers; the employers will take them back without discriminating against them on account of the strike, and will not oppose the syndicates being certified anew.
>
> Immediately after the return to work, the arbitration board will study all clauses of a labour agreement . . . the award will not bind the parties unless they decide otherwise . . .
>
> This proposal has already been accepted and the names of the two representatives will be made known in the course of the day . . .[54]

Mr. Marchand denied that such an agreement had been reached. To clarify the union's position, he issued a statement to the press stressing the following points:

1. There has been no contact between the minister of Labour and the representatives of the workers for the past month.
2. *A third person made us a proposition concerning the formation of an arbitration board.* We accepted its principle because the representatives of the workers never oppose the formation of such a board. The union representative, in any event, has been named since February 12, 1949.
3. We note that the proposition of the minister does not necessarily lead to a solution since it is quite possible that the representatives will not agree on the choice of a president or chairman, and no procedure has been set up for the appointment of the latter.
4. We regret that the government objected to the designation of a certain judge when the proposal was made to it by an intermediary of the highest authority.
5. There never was any question of a board whose decision would not bind the parties.
6. We hope that the declaration of the minister has not had as its effect, the misleading of public opinion as to the real situation of the negotiations with respect to the asbestos strike.[55]

Mr. Picard had even stronger doubts. Speaking in Montreal on April 24 he said that the "choice of a chairman will be effective only if the choice guarantees the integrity of the tribunal." He went on to say that the workers had "lost confidence in the arbitration machinery" and that they had gone on strike this time because they had been cheated in the past every time they had gone to arbitration.[56]

With Mr. Sabourin representing the companies and Mr. Théodore Lespérance, the chief legal advisor to the Catholic syndicates, representing the union, four meetings were held between the 26th and 30th of April. Their ostensible purpose was the selection of a chairman; however, representatives of both sides were in reality seeking some common ground as a basis for negotiation. The union insisted that:

1. The company should not oppose re-certification of the federation.
2. The company should exercise no discrimination against any of the workers and all of the former workers should be taken back within five days of the return to work.
3. The company should dismiss all civil suits for damages.
4. The Crown should drop all criminal suits against the strikers.

Canadian Johns-Manville offered the following:

1. The union's certification would be restored but not until after the men had returned to work, and only on the recommendation of the minister of Labour.
2. There would be no discrimination against the strikers, and re-employment of former employees would take place as they were required for production.
3. The minister would take all useful steps in the service of the company to reach friendly settlement of civil proceedings pending before the courts.[57]

On April 30 negotiations broke down. Mr. Barrette, in making the announcement, indicated that there had been agreement on re-certification and return to work, but that the companies had been unwilling to drop all civil damage suits. The disposition of pending criminal suits was a matter for the Crown to decide. The minister declared "that he was not able to salvage any basis for an agreement or the establishment of an arbitration board."[58]

No agreement at all had been reached on the selection of a chairman and third member. Mr. Picard blamed "the intolerable attitude of the Johns-Manville Company"[59] and Mr. Lespérance elaborated on these remarks, explaining that the company wished to keep "certain forms of reprisal."[60] Mr. Sabourin, expressing "great surprise" and regret at the withdrawal of the union negotiating committee from the discussions, said that the company was of the opinion that the wages and conditions of work were equal to those anywhere in the province.[61] Thus the status quo was restored. The company withdrew the concessions proffered during the abortive negotiations, and the union resumed its demand for a written guarantee against reprisals before the return to work.

The breakdown in negotiations had two effects. Public opinion in favour of the strikers was greatly broadened and intensified, and the Catholic Church was officially shaken loose from its fence-straddling position. As one editorialist expressed it, "The strike . . . has entered a tragic phase. People had begun to hope that a settlement would be reached. The work stoppage has lasted more than two months. Families starve. The commercial life of the areas affected by the strike is paralyzed. The workers have made an enormous sacrifice."[62] The writer was clearly indicating what he considered to be a job for the Church. His article proved to be prophetic for, with the breakdown of negotiations, the Church at last took a stand.

This does not mean that individuals within the clergy had not long since spoken out one way or the other. The formidable Father Camirand had been actively supporting his union since the strike vote of February 13. Newspaper interviews with him left little doubt as to where he stood and may, conceivably, have had some influence on public opinion. His point of view was simply that he knew the people of Asbestos and their problems, and were he a miner, he too would be on strike. In Montreal, the students at the University of Montreal held pro-strike demonstrations early in April. Led by Father Jacques Cousineau, S.J., of the faculty of Social Sciences, they visited the strike-bound town to give aid to the strikers. Father Cousineau, who contributed two very pro-labour articles to *Relations* while the strike was still in progress, saw the strike as a manifestation of profound social changes that the "new generation" of French Canadians were making. Of the strike itself, he said that social justice must be placed above legality. Within the Church there were many who agreed with him, although another expedition to Asbestos, this time by students at Laval, was prevented by the rector of that university "because of possible repercussions . . . for the students."[63] Nevertheless, clerical support of the strike was so strong that on April 18 *Le Devoir* drew attention to the "numerous statements of sympathy and encouragement which the strikers have received from religious authorities and from diverse social groups," drawing the editorial conclusion that "there can be no doubt that this strike is lawful from a moral point of view."[64]

On April 19, the well-known and respected nationalist historian,

Canon Lionel Groulx, made a public appeal to end the strike "... which brings dishonour to the province of Quebec. I pray for a national collection and a crusade of prayers."[65] Following the break-down in negotiations on April 30, the Priests' Committee on Social Questions followed Canon Groulx's lead. "The committee," its spokesman declared, "has done everything it could to hasten the end of the strike." The prolongation of the strike was bringing misery into thousands of homes and under these circumstances, "charity now becomes the duty of everyone ... This is why we are issuing a pressing appeal to all organizations and ask their collaboration with the religious authorities in organizing a collection for the starving families."[66]

The following day Archbishop Charbonneau of Montreal declared that "it is the duty of the Church to intervene." He therefore called for collections in aid of the strikers to be taken at the door of every church in his diocese every Sunday until the strike ended.[67] Archbishop Roy of Quebec, who had just returned from Rome, made a similar announcement in his diocese.

In the face of this new pressure CJM issued a statement urging the striking employees to return to work. On May 2 Mr. Foster reported that one full shift was now in operation, and that more than two hundred men were now at work. He declared that the company was ready to start a second shift but that as production and employment gained momentum, it was becoming increasingly difficult to hold positions open and maintain seniority for old employees who, for "various reasons," did not report back. "We are making a serious effort to get back to work and at the same time to protect the status of our old employees," he said.[68] The striking workers were impressed by the gravity of his remarks. Two days later, on the day that has become known as Bloody Thursday, they attempted to interrupt production by intercepting the strikebreakers on their way to work and by renewing picketing of the company property in spite of the injunction against such action.

It is these climactic days of the strike which have attracted the great interest of sociologists and historians. The period has been chronicled several times in far greater detail than will be attempted here. It is worth noting at the outset that different accounts of the events that took place on the night of May 4-5 vary as night from day, and it is unlikely that a truly accurate description will ever be possible. No one, it seems, who was in Asbestos at the time can be considered impartial. Even the question of motivation, for example, gives rise to fierce debate. Extreme labour spokesmen claim that the intention of the strikers was only to stop the strikebreakers and reason with them. On the management side, there are some who seriously contend that the events of May 4-5 were the culmination of a communist plot having profound political implications. Somewhere between these extremes is the point of view expressed by Randolph Hamel and, in view of his position as president of the Federation of Mining Employees, it would seem reasonable to accept his description as accurate. The aim of the strikers, he claimed, was to put an end to "the campaign of lies launched by the company in the newspapers of the country," by taking matters into their own hands and preventing "scabs" from coming into town from outside to work.[69] "The strikers had learned that the strikebreakers had been engaged by the Canadian Johns-Manville Company on a permanent basis and were afraid of losing their jobs to others," he explained.[70] Therefore, on the evening of May 4 at a general assembly of the strikers, it was proposed that a demonstration much the same as that of April 22 be organized. The object of such a parade of strikers would be to "influence the strikebreakers."[71] Just when this planned orderly demonstration turned into a resumption of picketing is not clear. Gilles Beausoleil suggests that it was a spontaneous decision. "During this time [the early hours of May 5] the strikers had formed themselves in parade ranks when, from several groups, the cry flashed out, 'Let's get on the roads.' In a short time all had left that place to find themselves again, by groups, on various roads and at the entrance to the company property."[72]

The probability of this explanation is open to serious doubt. Aside from the obvious unlikelihood of a spontaneous outburst leading to such a well-organized and immediate response, there seems to be good evidence that the strikers' action was the result of a conscious, willful decision taken by a general vote.

The meeting of May 4 in the church hall of St. Aimé's parish was attended by over 1500 people. It lasted late into the night and resulted in the decision that was to put Asbestos into the headlines of newspapers around the world. In a telephone interview given on May 5, Mr. Hamel himself admitted that the decision had been taken by the men during the night, although he stressed that the picketing was organized by the men themselves and not by the syndicate.[73] Nevertheless, nine days after the riot, the police arrested Hamel, Daniel Lesage, the secretary of the federation, Armand Larivée, the president of the Asbestos Workers' Union and Réné Roque, a union organizer. They were charged with inciting to riot and inciting to gather in an illegal fashion.[74] Ultimately, all were released except for Mr. Roque, who was found guilty of "having conspired between the 1st and 6th day of May, 1949, in the aim of preventing, by acts of violence, certain people from doing that which they had a right to do.''[75]

Gérard Pelletier described the night's preparations as follows:

> Picket lines were set up at strategic points at the mine and the factory and the five main entrances to the town of Asbestos were guarded to prevent strikebreakers from coming into town. All was ready at five in the morning. The strikebreakers were transported by trucks and cars to the different posts. Different groups of strikers sang on their way. By seven all the entrances were covered.
>
> The provincial police had posted groups of men at all gateways to the factory; the police had received reinforcements yesterday. As from the beginning of the strike, the strikers scrupulously obeyed the strict orders to steer clear of the company property.[76]

At the mill the police hastily gathered themselves to break the picket lines. They attacked the strikers with tear gas but quickly realized that their numbers were too few to disperse the ranks of the workers, and, having withdrawn to their headquarters, they called for assistance from outside. Meanwhile, at the roadblocks, one of the first cars stopped was found to contain four provincial police officers in plain clothes. After identifying themselves they were allowed to pass through the wedge of cars that barricaded the road, only to find their further passage blocked by a second barricade of trucks. Thus trapped, one of the policemen fired two revolver shots out the window of the car to warn off the menacing crowd of men that had begun to press in on them. It was a vain attempt, and the four officers were unceremoniously taken from the car, kicked and beaten into unconsciousness and left at the side of the road. Later in the morning eleven other police officers tried to pass the barricade. All met with similar treatment. By the end of the day twelve policemen were injured and in the custody of the strikers in the basement of St. Aimé's church. One of their cars had been overturned in the ditch, a second had been burned and a third stolen.[77]

Needless to say, none of the strikebreakers were at work that morning. The strikers had complete control of the town and they were anything but gentle in the exercise of that control. Only emergency or essential traffic was allowed past the barricades, and several reporters were subjected to much the same treatment as the police on their arrival.

> Our car was blocked by a solid phalanx of bodies. The doors were ripped open. A hefty arm yanked me out into the mob, nearly all of whom were armed with sticks and a dozen varieties of weapons.
>
> The mob was milling about, shouting, waving its cudgels. It

> seemed to have no head man. Nobody seemed to know what to do with me. Finally a few of them quieted down enough to let me prove I was a newsman. They gave me a rough frisking for weapons and let me go.[78]

Another group of reporters was not so lucky. Caught between the two roadblocks, it was ordered to turn around.

> While they were doing so rocks were thrown at them. One man then came up and broke the window of the car. He reached inside and tore off Kaufman's glasses. Another man pushed a crowbar through another window in an attempt to strike Allan but Allan dodged.
>
> The man with Kaufman's glasses then broke them in two, hurling one half back into the car.
>
> As Kaufman and Allan managed to drive away they were told: "Don't come back and don't speak English. This is a French country."[79]

Meanwhile, at the church hall, harassment of the unfortunate police officers who had been captured was continuing. Police Chief Albert Bell of Asbestos appealed in vain for their release. Several of the policemen were bleeding profusely and in need of medical attention. One of the constables, Detective Léopold Quévillon, later reported that he asked the Abbé Camirand (who was present in the hall) for assistance but was told, " 'I can do nothing for you, see him, he is in charge,' and pointed to one of the strike leaders who continued to stand idly by while the torture went on."[80]

Finally, all of the police were allowed to leave the hall to seek medical attention with the exception of Detective Quévillon, who was marched to the town jail and lodged there for two hours until the arrival of the company doctor to treat his wounds.[81] In the meantime Lieutenant Timlin, the officer in charge of the Asbestos detachment of the provincial police, had divided his men into two groups. One remained to guard the company property. The other gathered the families of the company officials at the Iroquois Hotel and stayed there to protect them. Throughout the day the police received phone calls from non-striking workers who had been threatened or molested. Lieutenant Timlin was not able to offer any assistance.

Gradually, the excitement generated in the early hours of the day died down, giving place to a quiet determination on the part of the strikers. Union leaders were powerless to stop the striking workers and when, at last, they were informed by telephone that a large body of provincial police had been assembled in Sherbrooke and would enter the town by force if necessary, they had to admit their impotence.

About eleven o'clock at night the chief of provincial police, Mr.

> Hilaire Beauregard, telephoned to the strike leaders to tell them that the Riot Act would be read the next day; members of the mob would receive very severe sanctions. About eleven thirty, Mr. Beauregard telephoned Abbé Camirand and advised him very strongly to ask the strikers to return home so as to avoid the exemplary sanctions that might be imposed after the reading of the Riot Act.[82]

The priest took this advice; the men dispersed, and at two thirty in the morning of May 6 the police entered the town unmolested. Their entry was described as follows:

> Heavily armed, carrying shotguns, sten guns, revolvers, tear gas and billies, the blue-and-brown-clad gendarmes, traffic-squad officers and provincial detectives moved into town with dramatic suddenness at 2:30 A.M. today. They were prepared to blast their way, if necessary, through the roadblocks . . .[83]

After hasty consultation with Lieutenant Timlin, the leader of the police reinforcements (once again Inspector-General Labbé) directed his men to search the town for troublemakers. Several arrests were made and, at six in the morning, with the discovery of some forty Thetford Mines strikers in the basement of St. Aimé's Church, violence once again broke out. This time the roles of the strikers and the police were reversed. Probably with the idea of "getting even," "setting an example" or some like motive, the police subjected their captives to all sorts of contumelious behaviour.

> Under the eyes of a battery of journalists and photographers a policeman hit one of the young strikers in the face with a club until he fell to the floor. Then the policeman proceeded to kick him many times.[84]

> Newspaper reporters who watched police work over the men said police struck with fists and feet and left the men bruised and bleeding. "It made me sick to watch it," said Mike Rouget, photographer for *Time* and *Life* magazines.[85]

At six forty-five in the morning the Riot Act was read from the steps of the church by the justice of the peace, Mr. Hertel O'Brady. In addition to the forty men taken in the town hall, another 125 had been arrested during the night. By the end of the day the number of arrested strikers had reached two hundred.[86] Gradually peace returned to the town, but great bitterness remained. It was directed almost exclusively against the provincial police.

> And so ended what will long be recalled as one of the most infamous episodes in the labour-relations history of the province of Quebec. Anything so ill-advised and ill-manoeuvred could not in

justice be branded otherwise. Instead of crushing both the hated provincial police and the "scabs," it succeeded only in increasing their numbers, and in prolonging an already burdensome, incomeless period.[87]

During the weekend of May 7-8 the Riot Act was lifted and all but sixty of the arrested strikers were released. The question was, had the strike been broken? On May 9, in Asbestos, Mr. Hamel claimed that the strikers could hold out for another five months at least. He said that if the federation were unable to continue supporting the strikers, assistance could be obtained from the CIO. He made it clear, however, that the strikers had no idea of ending their affiliation with the CCCL, and that he was simply looking into the future.[88] The same day, in Montreal, Mr. Marchand released a signed statement to the press in which he directed abuse at the provincial police for their behaviour during the riot, comparing them to "Hitler's élite troops." Mr. Picard declared that "the strike continues until victory" and *Le Devoir* reported on the same day that the resistance of the strikers remained strong in spite of "three days of reprisals by the police."[89] Meanwhile, the strikers continued to receive aid from their relatives, friends, other unions and the Church. Fourteen parishes in Quebec diocese contributed on May 8, and other bishops were said to be considering following the lead of Bishops Charbonneau and Roy.[90]

On May 10 the lawyers for the arrested strikers, Mr. Lespérance and Mr. Drapeau, protested that they were not being allowed to see their clients. Mr. Drapeau published details of a letter he had sent to Mr. Duplessis, who was also the attorney-general of the province.[91] The following day three men found guilty of intimidating a strikebreaker were sentenced to three months hard labour by a Sherbrooke court. Demonstrations of protest took place before the courthouse. In Asbestos, fifty of the extra police were returned to their normal duty.

Owing to the continued attacks of the newspapers, especially *Le Devoir,* and the union leaders, the alleged police brutality was now becoming the dominant issue in the strike. On May 16 the Federation of Mining Employees demanded a federal government inquiry into the police behaviour.[92] It was not the first time that federal government intervention in the strike had been mentioned. By coincidence, on the day preceding the riot of May 5, Mr. Clarence Gillis, Mr. W.R. Thatcher and Mr. Angus MacInnis, all CCF members of Parliament, had raised the issue of the strike. They had suggested that it was a disgrace to the entire country and, therefore, worthy of federal intervention on the side of the strikers. The minister of Labour, the Honourable Mr. Humphrey Mitchell, while sympathetic to their point of view, had expressed the belief that he could do absolutely nothing. "Let it be clearly understood that I am taking no sides in the present dispute. There is an old saying: stay in your own back yard . . . I believe in the rule of law and without equivocation I can say that this present dispute is completely within the jurisdiction of the provincial government."[93]

On May 14 the arrest of the four strike leaders previously mentioned took place. The following day saw the resumption of attempts to settle the strike. Mr. Barrette met almost every day with Mr. Picard and Mr. Sabourin until June 2, when once again the minister was forced to announce that all possible means of affecting a settlement had been tried in vain and that negotiations had once more been broken off.[94] Progress had apparently been made towards settlement; however, the negotiations had again foundered on the issue of a president for the arbitration board. Mr. Picard had refused to accept any of the proposed provincial judges, and had countered with the proposal that the chief justice of the Court of Appeals be named. This was, of course, unacceptable to the government since it cast doubt on the impartiality of provincial jurists. The company, for its part, was still refusing to discharge all strikebreakers or to take back all of the strikers, regardless of their role in the strike. This the union leaders were adamant in demanding.

As reports of excesses by the strikers were gradually revealed in the court cases arising out of the events of May 5, public opinion began to turn against the strikers. However, other dioceses had taken the lead of Montreal and Quebec in instituting church-door collections. The Bishop of Sherbrooke, Monseigneur Desranleau, who was in Rome throughout the strike, published a message of sympathy for the strikers in the diocesan newspaper.[95] On May 26 seven tons of foodstuffs collected by the Canadian Brotherhood of Railway Employees arrived for the strikers.[96] Talk of a province-wide general strike of the CCCL in support of the asbestos workers was widespread. Meanwhile, the labour force of strikebreakers had risen to 648 by the end of June, and production by CJM was just over one-third of normal three-shift capacity.[97] The CJM management, with good cause, could feel satisfied with the results of its firm stand, and this was reflected in its unhurried and unyielding approach to bargaining. Thus the two sides appeared to be as strong as ever on the surface, and settlement remained a faint hope.

However, beneath the surface, certain forces were at work to effect a settlement. Not the least of these was the general discontent of the workers, a discontent which could as easily be turned against high union officials as it had been against the strikebreakers and the police a few weeks previously. Messrs. Picard and Marchand were not unaware of this danger. The subsequent history of the negotiations and the wording of the final settlement would tend to indicate that they were at pains to save face.

At a closed meeting on June 12 the confederation turned down the suggested general strike, and instead voted for a monthly collection from all syndicates to aid the asbestos workers until the end of the strike.[98]

The following day Archbishop Roy entered the scene personally when he met with Mr. Lewis H. Brown, chairman of the board of Johns-Manville. The purpose of the meeting was to establish some basis for mediation. Also present was the company counsel, Mr. Sabourin.

> From this moment, Monseigneur Roy became the principal mediator in the asbestos conflict. On several occasions he contacted Mr. Barrette and Mr. Duplessis to discuss conditions of return to work for the men and also the judicial proceedings occasioned by the strike. He also met with Mr. Gérard Picard to discuss the various compromise formulas put forward.[99]

On June 17, CJM approached its workers directly with another offer which was rejected the next day in a general vote by a majority of over eight hundred. Through the offices of Monseigneur Roy, negotiations involving Mr. Barrette, Mr. Sabourin, Mr. Picard and Mr. Lespérance were resumed on the same day as the vote. On June 24 all of the companies at Thetford Mines (Abestos Corporation, Flintkote and Johnson Mines) reached agreement with the union and work was resumed. Terms of the settlement included:

1. Return to work on Monday, June 27.
2. Re-certification of the union.
3. Companies not obligated to re-engage men convicted of disorders.
4. Arbitration of issues that could not be settled by direct negotiation within ten days.

This left only the 2100 men at Asbestos still out on strike.[100] The points at issue were the company's insistence on its right not to rehire certain workers, and to give priority of work to the strikebreakers. At last, with the help of Archbishop Roy, a settlement was reached on July 1. Terms of the settlement included:

1. A ten-cent-an-hour pay increase.
2. Respect for the seniority rights of striking workers.
3. Re-employment of all strikers without discrimination.
4. Four paid holidays a year.
5. The remaining five cents an hour to be negotiated.

6. The company to retain the right to discriminate against strikers who were convicted in court.[101]

A happy ending to a sad story? Not quite. When the terms of the settlement were announced by the strike leaders to the workers of Asbestos, there was literally dancing in the streets. They could not, or perhaps did not wish to see that the terms of the settlement spelled out unconditional surrender, and that the vague wording of the agreement left it open to the widest possible range of interpretation. For many of the men, realization of the unfavourable terms came within the next few days as they waited in vain for some word from the company. Specifically, the strikebreakers stayed, and in consequence, all of the strikers were not rehired. The settlement stated that the company would re-engage "as many men as possible under efficient working conditions," but when, at last, full production was resumed, seventy-five to one hundred men remained idle.[102]

Isolated acts of revenge began to take place. Some cattle were slaughtered, a barn was burned and rocks were hurled through the windows of the homes of strikebreakers who remained with the company. The company felt bound to take a firm stand against these acts; after informing Archbishop Roy of his intentions, the CJM board chairman, Lewis Brown, published a letter on June 18 addressed to all of the former strikers and the company employees. Its purpose was to outline the terms of the settlement and the company's interpretation of the terms. Mr. Brown left no doubt as to the permanence of the strikebreakers on the company payroll. To the men who remained unemployed, men who had so recently won the admiration of the whole country for their determination and courage, there remained no alternative but removal to another town and another job, or relief.

On July 23, in a strongly worded editorial, *Le Devoir* took exception to Mr. Brown's letter. The company, it said, was misinterpreting the terms of the settlement to the disadvantage of the workers; the editorial noted that the company was claiming concessions that had never been part of the original settlement. Mr. Picard was quoted at length on the subject of the perfidy of CJM, although he steadfastly maintained that, in spite of subsequent developments, the settlement had been a great victory for the workers.[103] In any case, as a result of the agreement of June 24, the government had announced the formation of an arbitration board on July 13. Judge Thomas Tremblay, a chief justice of the Quebec Superior Court, was named as president, with the full agreement of both interested parties.[104]

The arbitration award in the asbestos strike[105] was rendered on December 19, 1949. It confirmed for the workers the union security already existing before the strike, under the form of an irrevocable checkoff of union dues.

The arbitration award granted a wage increase of $0.10 to the miners and this was made retroactive to January 1, 1949. The award also suggested the formation of an employer-employee committee to study the problems of social security. The arbitration award, finally, granted the workers two more paid holidays. The arbitration board recommended that the 1949 collective labour agreement, in view of the fact that it was on the point of terminating anyway, be continued into 1950.[106]

This judgement was received very badly by the union. In Mr. Picard's opinion,

> The Tremblay majority report (Mr. Lespérance, the union representative on the board, dissented from the findings of the other two members) seems to want to put the cause of the asbestos miners in a straightjacket bearing a false label of legality. Justice and law do not seem to have inspired it. It is not an arbitration award, but is, in reality, a vengeance.
>
> Consequently, nothing has been settled in the asbestos industry, and the arbitration institution has once more been shaken.[107]

The federation appealed its case to the Quebec Labour Relations Board on December 26 and the premier took personal charge of the negotiations to give effect to the arbitration award. Owing to his intervention, the companies agreed to a "cost-of-living" clause in the new labour agreement. It called for an increase of from twenty-five to forty cents a week for each increase of one point in the cost-of-living index.

On December 29 the collective labour agreements were signed. They were retroactive to January 1, 1949, and were to extend to December 31, 1950. The problem of the still-unemployed workers was not brought up at this time since immediately after the return to work the minister of Labour had assigned a government conciliator, Mr. Bérubé, the task of settling the numerous grievances resulting from the return to work.

If the strike resulted in no material gains for the workers in Asbestos, it was at least a psychological victory and it underscored the effect of Quebec's rapidly changing society and economy. Catholic labour not only laid to rest forever its reputation for equivocation and appeasement, but also unified the rest of organized labour in its support. It mobilized the French-Canadian intellectual community to its side; it put the Church in a position that demanded it support the strike; and it exposed the dark underside of the Duplessis government to international attention. In retrospect, it seems that only English Canadians were unaffected and remained aloof from the strike, with the exception, of course, of the TLC- and CCL-affiliated unionists, who were directly involved in providing support.

Among English-language journalists, only Blair Fraser[108] felt the wind of change and wrote about it. For most Canadians, both English and French, it was inconceivable that a handful of workers, employed by a great multinational corporation and with only the most meagre physical support, should undertake an attenuated strike, a challenge not just to capital but to the existing social, political and economic systems. That the strike was in Asbestos made it more incredible.

For the Church, the decision to support the strikers was a Rubicon. The strike was undeniably contrary to the law of Quebec and had been declared illegal by the minister of Labour and by the premier. Furthermore, it had been called at a union meeting, in spite of an agreement between the parties to await arbitration. In addition, its long duration and the lack of an adequate union strike fund caused great hardship to the families of the striking workers and virtually paralyzed the commercial life of the surrounding area. All of this evidence should have led the archbishops and bishops of Quebec to call for an end to the strike. That they did not was mainly due to the attitude of the lower clergy.

The chaplain of the Asbestos local, Father Louis Phillippe Camirand, seemed to be speaking for all of the lower clergy when he made his famous pronouncement: "If I were a miner I too would be on strike."[109] Father Jacques Cousineau, the Jesuit activist from Montreal, also helped through his lucid writings in which he depicted the strike not as a revolution but as a symptom. It was, he said, a manifestation of the profound social changes that the new generation of French Canadians were making. Within the clergy there had been deep division at the outset. Many agreed with Cousineau, but it required the intervention of Archbishop Charbonneau to release the senior clergy from the spell of conservatism.[110]

The Church had become committed to a new approach in industrial relations and, after the strike, this was clarified in a collective Pastoral Letter, published on February 1, 1950.[111] Unequivocally, the Pastoral Letter removed the clergy from its leadership role in the Catholic unions and laid down a broad general scheme for the relationship of labour, church, state and management. In addition, it clearly stipulated the responsibilities of chaplains of unions. In effect, it gave official recognition to what was already fact—that the chaplain in the union had lost his temporal power and authority, becoming no more than a religious figurehead maintained, like the Governor-General, for the sake of form.

In this it is possible that the Asbestos strike performed its greatest service to the CCCL—opening up thereby the possibility of the extensive internal reforms that Marchand and Picard were to make within the next decade. Was it deliberately planned as such—part of the grand strategy of the new leadership? In spite of Marchand's role in possibly initiating the strike by his speeches and by his influence on the federation leadership, this seems unlikely. There is no doubt, however, that Jean Marchand and Gérard Picard took advantage of the strike and its symbolism to advance their own plans for a centralized, non-confessional, apolitical confederation of national unions.

For the workers of Asbestos and Thetford Mines, however, the strike was no revolution. It was an industrial dispute—a hard-fought, bitter and unyielding attempt to improve wages, hours and working conditions within the confines of the existing industrial-relations system. That it has come to take on a deeper, symbolic meaning is hardly their affair; indeed, it has a touch of irony to it. For, after the polarization of the Confederation of National Trades Unions (formerly CCCL) during 1972, the Asbestos Workers' Federation was one of several unions that broke away to form a new confederation having conventional trade-union objectives.

Notes

1. Jacques Cousineau, S.J., "La grève de l'Amiante," *Relations* no. 103 (June 1949): 146.

2. Jean C. Falardeau, *Bulletin des Relations Industrielles* 4, no. 7 (March 1949): 68.

3. In *La grève de l'Amiante,* ed. Pierre Elliott Trudeau (Montreal: Cité Libre, 1956), p. ix; (Toronto: James Lewis & Samuel).

4. Stuart Jamieson, "Labour Unity in Quebec," in *Canadian Dualism,* ed. Mason Wade (Toronto: Universities of Toronto and Laval, 1960), p. 299.

5. Pierre Elliott Trudeau, "La Province de Québec au moment de la grève," in *La grève de l'Amiante,* p. 81.

6. See Nathan Keyfitz, "Population Problems," in *Essais sur le Québec Contemporain,* ed. Jean C. Falardeau (Montreal: Université de Montréal, 1953), and Yves de Jocas and Guy Rocher, "Intergeneration Occupation Mobility in the Province of Quebec," in *Canadian Soçiety,* ed. Bernard L. Blishen *et al.* (Toronto: Macmillan, 1961).

7. Canada Department of Labour, *Labour Organizations in Canada 1940* (Ottawa, 1941).

8. Canada Department of Labour, *Labour Organizations in Canada 1948* (Ottawa, 1949).

9. F. Cirkel, *Chrysolite-Asbestos* (Ottawa: Department of Mines, 1910), as quoted by Jean Gérin-Lajoie, "Histoire Financière de l'Amiante," in Trudeau, *La grève de l'Amiante,* p. 97.

10. *Ibid.,* p. 114.

11. *Bottin de la Ville d'Asbestos* (Asbestos: Junior Chamber of Commerce, 1949), p.5.

12. "Histoire des Négotiations," in Trudeau, *La grève de l'Amiante,* p. 214.

13. *The Asbestos Strike,* a Canadian Johns-Manville pamphlet signed by Lewis H. Brown, 1949.

14. Sherbrooke *Daily Record,* 14 February 1949.

15. Gilles Beausoleil, "Histoire de la grève à Asbestos," in Trudeau, *La grève de l'Amiante,* p. 168. This refers specifically to a grievance concerning adjustments in pay for workers remaining at a certain job after automation had reduced their numbers. It

was the union's first experience with arbitration; the decision *was* in favour of management; and it *was* still fresh in their minds, having taken place in October 1948. The strike, nevertheless, appears in this light as a premeditated illegal act, taken on the advice of (but not on the orders of) the leaders of the union. This aspect of the strike action is justified as follows by Professor Fernand Dumont. "In particular, one is very shocked that, throughout the strike of 1949, the workers did not have recourse to the accepted judicial processes; one does not see that, in part, this is explained by the superficial manner in which the National Labour Council, during the war years just past, considered and judged their demands. The syndicates' loathing of recourse to official bodies is explained also, and perhaps entirely, by certain facts which would make one believe that collusion exists between the companies and the judicial or political bodies. In the course of an arbitration (made in accordance with the law of the province) on a grievance which was lost by the syndicate in Asbestos in 1948, the president of the tribunal stayed, in the hotel, in the suite of the president of the Johns-Manville Company . . . " ("Histoire du syndicalisme dans l'industrie de l'amiante," in Trudeau, *La grève de l'Amiante*, pp. 162-163.) At a later date the union leaders were to deny all foreknowledge of the decision to strike.

16. Beausoleil, "Histoire de la grève," p. 169.

17. 14 February 1949.

18. Beausoleil, "Histoire de la grève," p. 170.

19. Sherbrooke *Daily Record*, 15 February 1949.

20. Sherbrooke *Tribune*, 15 February 1949.

21. Mr. Barrette was referring in this instance to the previously negotiated contract in which the unions relinquished their bargaining powers to the federation. The Labour minister's services were needed to hasten the legal process of certification of the federation since negotiations, though satisfactorily finished for all practical purposes, were hung up on this point.

22. Sherbrooke *Daily Record*, 17 February 1949.

23. It is perhaps worthwhile to examine two points of view on management's motivation at this juncture. Beausoleil, in his account of the strike, mentions the fact that on the night of February 13-14, picketers penetrated the company property in search of warmth and shelter from the weather. He further mentions the establishment of a gate-pass system for essential maintenance personnel, and he implies that this was done with the co-operation of management. ("Histoire de la grève," p. 169.) He also points out that Mr. Morrison, the factory manager, when attempting to visit the factory, was intercepted and sent home by a group of strikers. Beausoleil concludes that management grew frightened at the strength and determination of the union and acted in panic. "Nevertheless, the strike caused strong anxiety among the directors of the company . . . The militant character of unionism during recent years, the profound discontent of the miners, the doctrinal and radical allure of their claims could not help but lead, in the minds of the Johns-Manville management, to excesses. The syndicate leaders would quickly lose control of the situation because the democratic structure of syndicalism lent itself so easily to anarchy . . . Because of the rapidity of events, and the dramatic character of the declaration of the strike, fear and even the beginning of panic were substituted for a lucid, objective analysis of events." (*Ibid.*, p. 173.) The company's version of the same period is given as follows: "On the morning of February 14, a Monday, Messrs. Armand Larivée and R. Pellerin, president and secretary, respectively, of the Asbestos syndicate, presented themselves at the office of the mine manager, G.K. Foster. The company officers asked those of the syndicate to get the pickets

to allow the members of the maintenance crews to pass through the picket lines. This legitimate and normal request was refused by the syndicate. The company, furthermore, also needed coal with which to heat its plant and thus to prevent incalculable and irreparable damage from being caused by the prevailing cold weather. This was why the company asked the syndicate to let through the picket lines the railway coal cars waiting at Danville and the coal load which was needed to heat the plant. The syndicate also refused this just and logical request. Late this same Monday morning, a group of strikers entered the offices of the company and, by the use of force, obliged the general foreman, Mr. Bruce Mills, to leave. These strikers were getting ready to take Mr. Mills to the general strike headquarters when some employees who knew him removed him to safety and brought him to his home. The pickets, at eight o'clock on the morning of Monday, February 14, were in complete and full control of the plant and even refused the office personnel the right to enter it. Shortly before noon, on the same day, the plant manager, Mr. J.E. Morrison, was assaulted by a group of strikers, expelled by force from the plant and was escorted home with orders to stay there. This caused company officers to ask Mr. Larivée, the president of the syndicate, to provide that the plant manager could move about in safety . . . Mr. Larivée, the following day, informed the company that it was impossible to grant Mr. Morrison permission to enter his own office. The only permission the company actually got . . . was that allowing the office personnel comprising the payroll staff to enter the plant's offices . . . The officers of the company, from Wednesday on, weren't even able to communicate by telephone with the few maintenance men still left inside the plant. It was on that same day that the syndicate replaced the regular maintenance crew with men of their own choice." (From an unpublished report, *A Clarification of the Asbestos Industry Strike,* prepared by company and government legal advisers, pp. 4, 5.)

24. *A Clarification of the Asbestos Industry Strike,* p. 5.

25. Sherbrooke *Daily Record,* 21 February 1949.

26. *Le Devoir,* 21 February 1949.

27. *Le Devoir,* Sherbrooke *Daily Record,* 24 February 1949.

28. Sherbrooke *Daily Record,* 24 February 1949.

29. *Le Devoir,* 24 February 1949.

30. Sherbrooke *Daily Record,* 2 March 1949.

31. *Ibid.,* 3 March 1949.

32. *Le Devoir,* 10 March 1949.

33. Sherbrooke *Daily Record,* 10 March 1949.

34. *Le Devoir,* 11 March 1949.

35. Sherbrooke *Daily Record,* 15 March 1949.

36. *Ibid.,* 17 March 1949.

37. *Ibid.,* 19 March 1949.

38. *Le Devoir,* 21 and 22 March 1949. The examples cited include the arrest of two persons in their beds during the small hours of the morning and interrogation of prisoners for up to seven hours.

39. Sherbrooke *Daily Record,* 26 March 1949.

40. "Si j'étais mineur, je serais gréviste . . . L'Abbé Camirand," *La Presse,* reprinted in *Le Devoir,* 23 March 1949.

41. Sherbrooke *Daily Record,* 4 April 1949.

42. The mine at Thetford never followed CJM's lead in this activity, which accounts in large measure for the comparative peace that marked the entire strike period in that town.

43. Trucks carrying food to the strikers began arriving in the fifth week of the strike. The food was taken to a central distributing point where wives of the strikers were issued with their shares based on size of family. Most aid came from the Catholic syndicates but nearly all of organized labour in Quebec contributed in some measure. Relief and union funds gave families a small weekly allowance according to need and family size. In general, this aid was sufficient to sustain life but not at a very high level. In an interview with several veterans of the strike held in August 1961, the general concensus of opinion seemed to be: "I wouldn't go through it again unless we were affiliated with one of the big international unions and could count on them for help." These men recalled various examples of hardship such as going for several days without meat, eating canned goods that had been stored too long and had, therefore, been thrown out by the producers, and so on. They were all very short of money and accumulated large debts during the strike.

44. *Le Devoir,* 20 April 1949.

45. Sherbrooke *Daily Record,* 22 April 1949.

46. *Le Devoir,* 21 April 1949.

47. Beausoleil, "Histoire de la grève," p. 192.

48. *Le Devoir,* 22 April 1949.

49. *Ibid.*

50. Sherbrooke *Daily Record,* 19 April 1949.

51. These were given by Mr. Hamel and Mr. Marchand respectively.

52. Beausoleil, "Histoire de la grève," p. 192.

53. Sherbrooke *Daily Record,* 24 April 1949.

54. *Le Devoir,* 23 April 1949.

55. *Ibid.*

56. Sherbrooke *Daily Record,* 25 April 1949.

57. *A Clarification of the Asbestos Industry Strike,* p. 29ff.

58. *Le Devoir,* 30 April 1949.

59. *Ibid.*

60. *Ibid.*

61. *Ibid.*

62. *Notre Temps,* 23 April 1949, as quoted in *The Asbestos Strike* by Grace Mackenzie (M.A. thesis, University of Toronto, 1950).

63. Beausoleil, "Histoire de la grève," p. 193.

64. *Le Devoir,* 18 April 1949.

65. *Ibid.,* 20 April 1949.

66. *Ibid.,* 30 April 1949.

67. *Ibid.,* 2 May 1949.

68. Sherbrooke *Daily Record,* 2 May 1949.

69. Montreal *Gazette,* 6 May 1949.

70. Toronto *Globe and Mail,* 6 May 1949.

71. Beausoleil, "Histoire de la grève," p. 195.

72. *Ibid.*

73. Sherbrooke *Daily Record,* 5 May 1949.

74. *Ibid.*, 16 May 1949.

75. J.P. Geoffroy, "Le Procès Rocque," *Cité Libre* 1 (May 1951): 1.

76. *Le Devoir,* 5 May 1949.

77. Montreal *Gazette,* 6 May 1949.

78. Ronald Williams, *Financial Post,* 14 May 1949.

79. Montreal *Gazette,* 6 May 1949.

80. *Ibid.*

81. *Ibid.*

82. Beausoleil, "Histoire de la grève," p. 198.

83. Toronto *Globe and Mail,* 6 May 1949.

84. *Le Devoir,* 6 May 1949.

85. Toronto *Globe and Mail,* 7 May 1949.

86. Sherbrooke *Daily Record,* 7 May 1949.

87. Margaret E. Shay, *A Preliminary Review of the Asbestos Strike: A Study of the Dynamics of Social Change* (Ph.D. dissertation, Fordham University, New York, 1950), p. 89.

88. Sherbrooke *Daily Record,* 9 May 1949.

89. *Le Devoir,* 9 May 1949.

90. Sherbrooke *Daily Record,* 9 May 1949.

91. *Le Devoir,* Sherbrooke *Daily Record,* 10 May 1949.

92. *Le Devoir,* Toronto *Globe and Mail,* 16 May 1949.

93. Canada House of Commons, *Debates* 88, no. 49 (4 April 1949): 2292, 2293.

94. *Le Devoir,* 2 June 1949.

95. *Le Messager,* 22 May 1949.

96. Beausoleil, "Histoire de la grève," p. 203.

97. Shay, *Review of the Asbestos Strike,* p. 193.

98. Sherbrooke *Daily Record,* 13 June 1949.

99. Beausoleil, "Histoire de la grève," p. 204.

100. The employees of the Nicolet Mines at St. Remy de Tingwick returned to work on June 6. The terms of settlement were similar to those arranged at Thetford but included "temporary acceptance of a ten-cent-an-hour increase and four paid holidays a year." One hundred and fifty workers were involved.

101. Canadian Johns-Manville letter to employees, 19 July 1949.

102. Shay, *A Review of the Asbestos Strike,* p. 192.

103. *Le Devoir,* 23 July 1949.

104. Sherbrooke *Daily Record,* 14 July 1949.

105. On 23 August 1949, the arbitration board dealing with the dispute at the Quebec Asbestos Corporation of East Broughton, presided over by Chief Justice Bilodeau, rendered its decision. The East Broughton syndicate, though an affiliate of the federation, had decided in February to continue working and submit its demands to arbitration. The final judgement granted an increase of ten cents an hour retroactive to 1 January 1949, and four paid holidays a year.

106. *A Clarification of the Asbestos Industry Strike,* p. 44.

107. *Le Devoir,* 23 December 1949.

108. Blair Fraser, "Priests, Pickets and Politics," *Maclean's* 62, no. 13 (1 July 1949): 9, 50-52.

109. *Le Devoir,* 18 April 1949.

110. Archbishop Charbonneau was subsequently removed from office "for reasons of ill health." An investigation carried out at the request of the Vatican implied that the strike was inspired by Communists. It is generally believed that the investigation, its findings, submitted in the "Custos Report," and the removal of Charbonneau resulted from pressure by Quebec's conservative bishops on the Vatican. It seems unlikely, however, that these allegations will ever be established or disproved.

111. *Le problème ouvrière en regard de la doctrine social de l'église* (Montreal: Bellarmin, 1950).